CHERNOBYL:
LAW AND COMMUNICATION

Transboundary Nuclear Air Pollution—
The Legal Materials

edited, with an introduction, by

PHILIPPE SANDS, M.A., LL.M. (CANTAB)

Barrister of Law, Research Fellow of St. Catharine's College, Cambridge,
and Research Associate of the Research Centre for International Law,
University of Cambridge

A PUBLICATION OF
THE ANNENBERG WASHINGTON PROGRAM IN
COMMUNICATIONS POLICY STUDIES
OF NORTHWESTERN UNIVERSITY

and

THE RESEARCH CENTRE FOR INTERNATIONAL LAW,
UNIVERSITY OF CAMBRIDGE

CAMBRIDGE

GROTIUS PUBLICATIONS LIMITED
1988

SALES &   GROTIUS PUBLICATIONS LTD.
ADMINISTRATION   PO BOX 115, CAMBRIDGE, CB3 9BP, UK

British Library Cataloguing in Publication Data

Sands, Philippe Joseph, *1960—*
    Chernobyl: law and communication:
    transboundary nuclear air pollution—the legal materials.
    1. Nuclear power industries. Accidents.
    International legal aspects
    I. Title
    341.7'55

    ISBN 0-949009-22-9

Printed in Great Britain by
Gomer Press, Llandysul, Dyfed

to

MY PARENTS AND GRANDPARENTS

CONTENTS

PREFACE

In May 1986 The Annenberg Washington Program asked me to prepare a short paper on ''The Chernobyl Accident and Public International Law'' for a conference being organized on ''Global Disasters and International Information Flows''. It soon became apparent that the legal issues relating to nuclear accidents which have international effects are numerous, varied and complex. Research into these issues was complicated by the enormous amount of directly and indirectly relevant material produced by States, international organizations and writers. Some of this material is difficult to obtain. Accordingly, The Annenberg Program and I considered that it might be useful for international lawyers, and those interested in communications, environment and nuclear matters, to bring together in a single volume some of the more important materials needed to assess the issues and law arising out of the Chernobyl accident, as well as the likely developments.

It is with this purpose in mind that the materials have been chosen. The selection does not purport to be comprehensive. The chronological presentation of the texts selected indicates the way in which concern with the different issues has developed. Twelve of the twenty-four texts are treaties. Of these, nine are specifically related to nuclear matters: three concern the civil liability of operators of nuclear installations (Nos. 1, 2 and 3); two relate to the early notification of nuclear accidents (No. 14 is bilateral and No. 21 is multilateral); two establish rules concerning the provision of assistance following a nuclear accident (No. 4 is bilateral and No. 22 is multilateral); one regulates the siting of nuclear installations (No. 11); and one concerns general cooperation in the peaceful uses of nuclear energy (No. 17). The non-nuclear treaties include an example of a convention on inter-State liability (No. 5); a convention for the general protection of the environment which creates civil rights of action for, *inter alia*, damage to the environment (No. 7); and a convention on long-range transboundary air pollution (No. 10). The first of these last-mentioned is included as a model which might be used by States when drawing up an inter-State liability treaty to govern nuclear activities; the latter two provide rules applicable to nuclear pollution.

The twelve remaining texts include five guidelines and recommendations of international organizations, relating to nuclear accidents (Nos. 15 and 16), transfrontier pollution (Nos. 8 and 9), and the protection of the human environment (No. 6; this also includes two related UN General Assembly Resolutions); two restatements of international law by private associations of scholars (Nos. 12 and 23); the ILC Schematic Outline (No. 13); three post-

Chernobyl documents suggesting possible future developments in international nuclear law (Nos. 18, 19 and 20); and one example of national legislation on nuclear damage (Annex). It will be seen that these texts have been selected with a view to their usefulness not only in showing what the law is, but how it may develop.

Each text is introduced by a short Editorial Note summarizing its basic provisions and giving some background. Unless indicated otherwise, the complete texts are then presented. For treaties, a list of signatories and/or parties is included as effective on 1 September 1987. Reservations have only been included where they are relevant to the purposes of the book. Finally, the texts are accompanied by select bibliographies.

The Introduction seeks to identify the principal legal issues arising out of the Chernobyl accident, relate the texts and other materials to these issues, and draw some tentative conclusions as to the current state of the law.

A number of people have worked together to make this volume possible. I wish to thank The Annenberg Washington Program and its Director, Mr Newton Minow, for supporting the work as part of its project on disaster management. I am particularly grateful to Ms Yvonne Zecca, the Program's Associate Director, and to Mr Joel L. Swerdlow, for their trust and support, and to the latter for his very helpful editorial comments.

At the Research Centre for International Law at the University of Cambridge I wish to thank Eli Lauterpacht QC, for his advice and support, Miss Maureen MacGlashan, Assistant Director of the Centre, for her patience and editorial assistance, and Miss Christine Kay for her secretarial help. I also wish to thank Mr Robin Pirrie of Grotius Publications for putting the book so speedily through the press and Mrs Diane Ilott for her assistance in the publication of the book.

Ms Susan Marks and Mr Anil Varma deserve special appreciation for their research assistance and for the considerable amount of background work they carried out in the summer of 1987, gathering materials and contributing to the editorial work. Without their help delays would surely have occurred.

I am grateful to Ms Eliza Hedegaard for doing much of the early typing and to Ms Catherine Larré for preparing the maps. I would like to thank the Editors of the *IAEA Bulletin,* the *Nuclear Law Bulletin* of the OECD-NEA, and *International Legal Materials,* for granting me permission to reproduce materials originally appearing in their respective publications, as well as the numerous people who have kept me informed with up-to-date information, particularly those at the IAEA, the OECD, and the UK Ministry of Agriculture, Fisheries and Food.

Finally, I would like to thank three people who, in their various ways, have contributed to the development of this work: Ms Laurence Relin, Mr James Cameron and Ms Anya Hurlbert.

PHILIPPE SANDS

Research Centre for International Law
University of Cambridge
February 1988

INTRODUCTORY NOTE

No subject could be more suitable for a first essay by the Research Centre for International Law and The Annenberg Washington Program into the areas in which the fields of international law and communications overlap than that of transboundary nuclear pollution. The lawyer must take care not to approach this subject solely in terms of the allocation and discharge of responsibility once a catastrophe has occurred. He must apply his legal skills and techniques over a wide range of questions: the extent to which the construction of nuclear facilities requires prior international consultation; the degree to which proposals for construction require the preparation of environmental impact assessments; the precautions to be taken to prevent catastrophe and the measures to be taken to contain its consequences when it occurs.

The approach to the resolution of each of these questions necessarily involves the accumulation of information and its communication. Nothing can be satisfactorily done in this field unless people and States know what is going on: what is contemplated, why, where, how, when, in what dimensions, the existence, if any, of the alternatives, the character and likely effectiveness of precautions, the filing of performance reports, the admission of inspectors, the announcement of trouble, and so on through a variety of detailed arrangements. It takes but a moment's reflection to recall other spheres of international law, not least verification in relation to arms reduction (as exemplified in the Treaty between the USA and the Soviet Union on the elimination of intermediate-range and shorter-range missiles of December 1987) and economic activities in the oceans, in which the provision of suitable information lies at the root of acceptable solutions expressed in legal terms.

The Research Centre for International Law at Cambridge is glad to have been stimulated by The Annenberg Washington Program to provide the scientific support for the preparation by Mr Philippe Sands of the present collection of materials. This venture demonstrates how two organizations whose interests may at first sight appear to be rather disparate may share a substantial common core of concern. It is much to be hoped that the recognition, in the form of this study, of the place of information accumulation and presentation in relation to transboundary pollution will lead to further consideration of the relationship between communications and international law in other contexts.

E. LAUTERPACHT
Director

Research Centre for International Law
University of Cambridge
February 1988

FOREWORD

Chernobyl and the New Age of Communications

by Newton N. Minow*

In late April 1986, Central Intelligence Agency officials arrived on Capitol Hill to bring congressional leaders a frightening briefing. Satellite photographs confirmed radiological readings from Sweden: a nuclear reactor in the Soviet Union had exploded.[1]

The accident had occurred at reactor Number Four in Chernobyl, the lake-filled region famous for its flowers and its mushrooms. A 70-foot square chunk of graphite was pumping radioactivity into the atmosphere. A cloud of lethal cesium-137 and iodine-131 was already three miles high. Hundreds of millions of Europeans—and possibly residents of North America—faced exposure.

Seldom in recorded history had one event so directly threatened so many people so quickly.

The Soviet Government's public statements at that time were terse. Less than 250 words announced that an accident of manageable proportions had occurred.

Within days of the CIA briefing, the American Landsat and French Spot satellites provided news agencies with photographs showing details of Chernobyl. Farmers, geologists, and oil companies had been using such satellite photographs since the early 1970s, but only large objects had been discernible. By 1986, however, technological advances produced pictures that revealed details behind Russia's closed borders not just to the intelligence experts but also to the public. Pictures of destroyed vegetation and huge scorch marks began to fill television screens and newspaper front pages. Chernobyl was quickly dominating world news. An American intelligence officer was

---

*The author is Director of The Annenberg Washington Program and a Chicago lawyer and partner at Sidley & Austin. The Annenberg Washington Program's first purpose is to assess the role of communication and its technologies on foreign policy, education, medicine, law, politics and financial markets. The Annenberg Washington Program also provides a neutral center in Washington, D.C., for policymakers, scholars and men and women active in communications to examine whether current communications public policy serves the public interest. The author wishes to thank Joel L. Swerdlow for his contribution to this foreword.

[1] "Ukrainian Nuclear Fire Spreads Wide Tragedy With Radiation Cloud," *Wall Street Journal* (30 April 1986), pp. 1, 24.

astonished that such precise information was so rapidly available outside of highest government circles.

In 1955, President Dwight D. Eisenhower had proposed to the Soviet Union an ''open skies'' treaty guaranteeing the right to aerial reconnaissance. Soviet leaders dismissed this as ''nothing more than a bald espionage plot.'' Thirty years later, Chernobyl demonstrated that the skies are open no matter what political leaders want.

The human race had developed capacity for mass communications and mass destruction at roughly the same time in history, raising the ultimate question of whether we have the wisdom to use one to avoid the other. Satellite tracking of Chernobyl graphically added a dramatic reminder: as our ability to communicate has expanded, so too has our capacity to destroy.

•   •   •

In October 1986, The Annenberg Washington Program sponsored a major international forum on Global Disasters and International Information Flows. This forum was suggested by Ambassador Walter Annenberg and organized and convened by the Program's founding director Maurice Mitchell and his successor Dr Robert Pepper. The purpose of this conference was to examine the potential use of communications technologies during international emergencies.

The conference discussed a variety of disasters, with emphasis on Three Mile Island and Chernobyl. Conference participants included scholars, journalists and public officials from around the world. All welcomed *glasnost*, and sought to address problems transcending the Soviet actions at any particular time.

One of the many impressive and valuable papers presented** was ''The Chernobyl Accident and Public International Law'' by Philippe Sands, a Barrister, Research Fellow at St. Catharine's College, Cambridge, and Research Associate at the University of Cambridge Research Centre for International Law. Sands' paper analyzed whether international law requires States to prevent such accidents, and to minimize and repair damage when accidents do occur.

Sands noted that ''the last fifteen years have witnessed a dramatic increase in the amount of State activity devoted to the protection of the international environment,'' but that ''at the time of the Chernobyl accident there existed

---

**A complete listing of papers is available from The Annenberg Washington Program in Communications Policy Studies of Northwestern University at: Suite 200, 1455 Pennsylvania Avenue, NW, Washington, D.C. 20004. Copies of papers are available free of charge.

no multilateral treaty requiring the provision of prompt and detailed information, either for general air-carried pollution or specifically for radioactive materials.''

This changed on 26 September 1986, five months after the accident, when 52 States signed the Vienna Convention on Early Notification of a Nuclear Accident. Since then, 11 more have signed and the Convention has now entered into force with 10 Parties.

The Convention—negotiated under the auspices of the International Atomic Energy Agency which was founded in 1957 to regulate and promote peaceful uses of atomic energy—requires signatories to inform affected or potentially affected nations immediately about certain nuclear accidents. Signing for the United States, Energy Secretary John S. Herrington praised ''a cooperative framework in which all nations may participate in order to minimize dangers in the event of another nuclear accident.''[2]

In some ways, the Convention was not new. International treaties dating back at least a century included notification stipulations, covering situations which range from declaration of war to adoption of new trade policies. At the Hague Peace Conference of 1907, for example, nations promised to notify neutral powers of a state of war ''without delay.'' More recently, bilateral and multilateral treaties dealing with oil spillage, out-of-control satellites, and weather information—as well as nuclear accidents—contained an obligation to share information with other nations on a timely basis. Parties to these treaties realized that more and more issues—and emergencies—do not respect national borders.

In other ways, however, the Chernobyl notification stipulations are new. Their specificity, the broad ideological consensus that supported them, and the speed with which they were negotiated are unprecedented. Indeed, no other accident in recorded history has prompted such a response from the world community.

The Chernobyl agreement, therefore, can be a significant precursor to future treaties. For this reason, the Annenberg Washington Program encouraged Philippe Sands to enlarge his paper into *Chernobyl: Law and Communication* as part of its ongoing efforts to improve communication during international emergencies.

The New Age of Communications
The Vienna Convention on Early Notification can best be understood in historical context, which transcends the legal texts in this volume. A new

---

[2] Paul Lewis, ''Atomic Power Safety Steps approved,'' *The New York Times* (27 September 1986).

era—the New Age of Communications—was emerging when Chernobyl occurred.

When discussing the impact of any technology, we must remind ourselves that technology often promises more than it delivers. Communication will be no exception. At the same time, communication is unique. Other technological breakthroughs that changed life in the twentieth century—e.g. electricity and the automobile—have been easy to see, especially in retrospect. But the effects of communication are hard to see because you often do not "see" anything. Its impact is so pervasive we often fail to grasp its significance, in part because communication involves far more than one technology. It is not only television, but also microchips, computers, satellites, telephones, text facsimile, fiber optics, and cable. Often these technologies may be combined, as with the digitalization of sound, pictures and data into the Integrated Services Digital Network. We can now only begin to foresee the possibilities of such networks.

Communications technologies, moreover, have reached a critical mass in which the economic success of one augments utilization of others. The result is a re-mapping of our lives. Nothing is exempt: law, medicine, politics, business, government, and education are all affected. Distance has been eliminated as a significant variable. Most importantly, as satellite photographs of Chernobyl demonstrate so dramatically, government control over the flow of information is decreasing. Nowhere is this more evident than during time of international crisis.

To gain perspective, let us look back to a typical crisis occurring before the era of instantaneous intercontinental communication.

In late 1861, shortly after outbreak of the American Civil War, an American naval vessel fired upon, stopped, and searched a British Royal Mail packet sailing in international waters. On board, the Americans found the newly appointed Confederate commissioners to Great Britain and France, who were arrested and taken to Boston.

When news of this seizure reached England, public reaction was immediate: we want the diplomats or we want war. The threat was grave. Britain, the South's greatest trading partner and the world's mightiest naval power, could have brought victory to the Confederacy.

President Abraham Lincoln had not ordered the seizure and did not want another war. The British monarch Queen Victoria and her consort Prince Albert did not want to interfere in American affairs. But leaders of both countries found themselves pushed toward conflict.

As eight thousand British combat troops made ready to sail for Canada and war with the North, a note to Lincoln from Queen Victoria and Prince Albert demanded release of the diplomats. Lincoln confronted an American public eager to fight to keep the rebel officials in jail. As only one measure of the newly aroused patriotism, the naval captain who had stopped the British ship was given a hero's parade down Broadway.

War fever raged on both sides of the Atlantic. If communication had been instantaneous, would public opinion have sparked shooting? In 1861, for a message to cross the ocean and receive a reply required nearly a month. Time allowed passions to cool, and time allowed government officials to devise policies that were aimed beyond the day's headlines. Lincoln released the diplomats, and the affair was forgotten.[3]

An End to Government Control

Two fundamental changes have occurred since Lincoln's time. In the latter half of the nineteenth century, transoceanic telegraph cables revolutionized worldwide communications. The flow of information, however, remained largely under the control of central authorities, primarily governments.

The second change began to emerge only as communications technologies developed in the last decade. These technologies make it difficult for governments to control data flow, unleashing an unprecedented volume of news and information across national borders.

This loss of government control is irreversible, as demonstrated by two major trends:

(1) *The increased importance of public opinion in world affairs*

Political leaders in pre-modern times believed that they could control public opinion. Warned by advisers that he could not seize Vienna because it would shock world opinion, Frederick the Great responded that he would take the city and then "my professors at Heidelberg will explain the reasons why."

Modern democracies recognize that public opinion now has great force in international affairs. Even military leaders in a democracy acknowledge it. "Public opinion," Dwight D. Eisenhower told his staff during World War II, "wins wars."

In the late 1980s, extraordinary advances in communications technologies forced non-democracies to acknowledge public opinion. In the USSR a recent poll conducted via random telephone calls discovered that 53 percent of respondents wanted "total withdrawal of Soviet troops from Afghanistan."[4] While such findings had no immediate effect, they do indicate a significant long term change.

[3] Carl Sandburg, "Abraham Lincoln: the Prairie Years and the War Years," (New York; Harcourt, Brace and Company, 1954), pp. 267-70; Sir Winston Churchill, "History of the English Speaking Peoples," (London; B.P.C. Publishing, 1969).
[4] "Polling, Communist Style," *The New York Times* (13 November 1987).

The ability of technology to influence opinion has generated a new type of diplomacy, a direct personal appeal—via the mass media—to a worldwide public. Soviet leader Mikhail Gorbachev, for example, learned how to influence opinion in the West through appearances on television. He knew not to repeat his silent performance after Chernobyl. Indeed, after nearly 72 hours of silence, the Soviet Union switched to candor, providing up-to-date data. Other governments handling future emergencies will find it difficult not to emulate the Soviet candor, even if this involves disclosure of more information than required by treaty. The Soviets' two-day attempt to control the flow of news is a vestige of an ended era.

The growing role of public opinion also changed diplomatic negotiations. New communications technologies created a new reality. "The modern negotiator," former Israeli Foreign Minister Abba Eban wrote recently, "must transact business simultaneously with his negotiating partner and his own public opinion. This involve[s] a total modification of techniques. Whether this is a favorable development or not is irrelevant; it is certainly irreversible."[5]

This relationship between public official and public opinion can be seen in the Vienna Convention on Early Notification. Some governments were reluctant to sign this Convention, but the force of world opinion was too strong. No government with nuclear capability failed to sign. The power of public opinion—at least in democracies—can also be seen in public influence at the highest levels of foreign policymaking. Lloyd N. Cutler, a top adviser to President Carter at the time of the late 1970s Egypt-Israel negotiations, wrote an article that would have shocked previous generations of statesmen. "TV affects not only the timing of major policy decisions, but their substance as well," Cutler explained. "A TV news lead item hits viewers with the speed and force of a laser beam."

Cutler continued, "Because TV news accelerates public awareness, the time for response is now even briefer. If an ominous event [such as Chernobyl] is featured on TV news, the president and his advisers feel bound to make a response in time for the next evening newscast."[6]

The difference between this and how Abraham Lincoln was able to handle his 1861 diplomatic crisis is monumental.

---

[5] Abba Eban, "The New Diplomacy: International Affairs in the Modern Age," (New York; Random House, 1983), p. 345.

[6] Lloyd N. Cutler, "Foreign Policy on Deadline," Foreign Policy (Fall 1984), pp. 113-28.

(2)   *New impediments to keeping secrets*

Boundaries are now so porous that shutting off communication is impossible. Eastern Europe alone reportedly has over one million videocassette recorders. Tapes of Western newscasts work their way eastward to the Soviet Union. East and West Germans watch the same television channels. Satellite transmissions spill over into other nations, intentionally and unintentionally. Computers and telephones link hundreds of millions of businesses and private citizens. Perhaps most importantly, satellite photographs—of the type that brought Chernobyl home to the world—are now available to and from a variety of nations including the Soviet Union.

Such photographs make it increasingly difficult, if not impossible, to control contact with the outside world. It is believed, for example, that intelligence pictures from outer space can now show objects as small as one meter long; as Chernobyl demonstrated, pictures of objects ten meters long are already commercially available.[7]

United States Information Agency Director Charles Z. Wick points out that this could prove comparable in significance to development of moveable type because people will have the opportunity to get information once controlled by central authorities.[8]

Demonstrations recently occurred in the Baltic republics of the Soviet Union and in Tibet—about as remote from Western eyes as you can get. The Soviet and Chinese governments, respectively, were able to ban non-communist media. Stories about the demonstrations disappeared. But for how many more years will such control be possible? Nations like South Africa which use government decree to limit outside television coverage will find that cameras clicking overhead have made certain types of censorship impossible.

Perhaps the most compelling evidence that satellite photography is earthshaking is that governments—democracies and non-democracies—are trying to limit commercial access to satellite-generated photographs. But all governments will inevitably realize that the world has changed and that national boundaries are no longer inviolate.

•   •   •

[7] William J. Broad, "Private Cameras in Space Stir US Security Fears," *The New York Times* (25 August 1987); US Congress, Office of Technology Assessment, "Commercial Newsgathering from Space—a Technical Memorandum," OTA-TM-ISC-40 (Washington, D.C.; US Government Printing Office, May 1987).

[8] Irvin Molotsky, "Chernobyl and the 'Global Village'," *The New York Times* (8 May 1986).

The increased importance of public opinion and the new impediments to keeping secrets reinforce each other.

During the Chernobyl emergency, for example, the Soviet Union maintained a double standard—one level of disclosure to satisfy public opinion outside the country, another for domestic consumption. A Soviet journalist recently complained in an article—whose very existence is a sign of enormous change—that "answers [from government officials] are intended for foreigners, and not necessarily to open the eyes of our countrymen."[9] Porous borders, however, mean that this can no longer be an effective policy. Information leaks back too easily, as it did when residents of western Ukraine learned from Polish radio that they were in danger.

Democracies are not exempt from related problems. Less than ten days after Chernobyl, US Secretary of State George P. Schultz discussed "an inherent obligation that states have to provide information." In an emotional post-Chernobyl debate, members of the British Parliament accused government officials of failing to meet that obligation by misleading the public about radiation dangers. Critics charged that parents who could have taken precautions such as not giving fresh milk to their children were denied opportunity to make an informed judgment.[10]

The government strenuously denied these charges, but found itself debating on a new and unexpected terrain. Indeed, as the two year anniversary of Chernobyl approached in 1988, documents released under British secrecy statutes revealed that thirty years ago Great Britain had experienced its own Chernobyl. A plant manufacturing plutonium for military purposes had experienced a 16-hour fire, releasing deadly radioactive pollutants. The British government kept silent for two days and then downplayed the story. It has been reported that communities near this plant subsequently suffered a leukemia rate three times the national average.[11]

As the British government learned, rising expectations about being informed are simply new facts of life. Over two-thirds of everyone alive today was born after television became the dominant means of communication—at least in the developed world. Fewer and fewer people remember a world without easy-to-use long distance telephones. The new generation thinks of everything before home computers as ancient history. More and more people

[9]"Soviet Journalists Struggle Against Resistance to Glasnost," *The Washington Post* (20 December 1987), pp. A1, A34.
[10]David Webster, "How Ministers Misled Britain about Chernobyl," *New Scientist* (9 October 1986), pp. 45-6.
[11]"Britain Covered up 1957 Nuclear Accident," *The Washington Post* (31 December 1987).

take communications technology for granted, and with this comes belief that being informed is a basic human right.

A Trend Towards More Multilateral Agreements

The sharing of data was once something arranged by trade missions and intelligence agencies. As recently as 1970, international trade in data amounted to a few million dollars. Now it is into the billions. Data processing, electronic fund transfers, electronic mail, and information exchange systems move billions of bits of data every hour. "The amount of money that changes hands in the global financial market in one day exceeds $1 trillion," US Secretary of State, George P. Schultz, recently noted, "more than the entire budget of the US government for a year."[12] This is done via an infrastructure that instantaneously links the world's financial markets into a 24-hour-a-day operation whose center is the communications satellite.

Experts only guess what this new nervous system will mean to us, but they are confident its capacity will continue to expand. Satellites will bring communication to isolated areas, while fiber optics will increase capacity along heavily utilized routes. Copper wire which can carry dozens of simultaneous voice conversations is being replaced by much smaller fiber optics that carries over 8,000. The 1990s will bring fibers that can carry one million simultaneous voices.

Traditional units of economic analysis are being transformed in large part because distance between nations is no longer a major economic variable. US Coordinator and Director of International Communications and Information Policy Diana Lady Dougan in a recent speech cited examples of "a sweater factory in eastern Africa linked into computer-aided design in New York, or the overnight change orders for an architectural firm in Dallas done somewhere in southern India."[13]

"We're no longer living on the gold standard," former Citicorp/Citibank chairman Walter Wriston says, "we're living on an information standard."[14] Highlighting the importance of this new standard, a recent United Nations publication explains that "data should be treated as a resource indispensable to effective management of all other resources."[15]

[12] George P. Schultz, "A Time of Transformation," *The Washington Post* (30 December 1987).
[13] "Ambassador Diana Lady Dougan and an Open World Policy for Telecommunications," *Broadcasting* (19 October 1987), p. 38.
[14] Walter Wriston, "A New Kind of Free Speech," *Forbes* (14 December 1987), p. 264.
[15] "Transborder Data Flows and Poland: Polish Case Study. A Technical Paper" (A United Nations Publication, Sales No. E. 84.II.A.8, 1984).

Although Wriston's information standard does not threaten national sovereignty, communications capability has created an imperative toward internationalism. Closer bonds among nations mean more multilateral agreements such as those signed after Chernobyl. United Nations statistics show a steady increase in the number of multilateral treaties. This increase highlights the importance of *Chernobyl: Law and Communication* as a source for better understanding of where this imperative can—and should—take us.

•   •   •

International sharing of information, however, will not change some facts of life. More information does not mean less animosity or more justice in the world. The Iran-Iraq war, which now ranks fourth among twentieth century wars in human lives lost, remains unaffected by satellites zooming overhead taking pictures. Slavery, presumably a pre-technological phenomenon, is on the rise in parts of Africa.[16] These facts are reported via communications technology, but this changes nothing.

Disclosure, moreover, need not be equated with directness. To share information about an accident such as Chernobyl could be to admit fault and liability. Such an admission would be particularly unattractive when the long-term effects are scattered, scary and unknown. Chernobyl, for example, may have deposited more radiation in Lake Como than in Kiev; no one knows what the ultimate impact on northern Italy will be. The temptation under such circumstances will be to try to limit liability by minimizing release of meaningful information, and to hide behind public relations techniques. Thus, in the months following Chernobyl, Soviet officials argued that much of the economic loss in Europe came—not from radiation—but from media overreaction. Chernobyl, they said, had become a public relations rather than a nuclear issue.

New technology can also create problems. Speed of communication is a prime example. To be fast is a virtue when information can save lives or when it involves data that are quickly outdated. But speed is dangerous when news reported instantly is inaccurate or misleading. More up-to-date does not mean more accurate or more useful. Indeed, the new ethos of speed destroys opportunity for understanding, reflection and analysis.

Belief in the visual is another technologically based limitation. Television taps into the human instinct to assume that seeing is believing. Satellite photographs heighten faith in the visual, even though what may seem obvious

---

[16] "In Sudan, New Guns Mean Renewed Slavery," *The Washington Post* (29 November 1987).

in the delineations between light spectrum bands may not be real. A rushed, non-expert explanation of satellite photographs can be just plain wrong. This is particularly dangerous during an international crisis when time is limited and emotions are on edge. Satellite photographs were used as a source for a news flash that two reactors had melted down at Chernobyl. Specialists who examined the same photographs knew that only one reactor was involved.[17]

More communication will not make us all the same. There are, for example, different ways to define "being informed." Societies use notions like risk and newsworthiness differently. Each people and each political system has its own history and legends about what is important; what is irreplaceable to one may be an irrelevancy to another.

The world may be becoming a "global village," but problems in villages are sometimes caused by proximity. As communication increases international proximity, new problems—built upon fears and vulnerabilities—will appear.

Wisdom here lies, not in expecting communications media to solve all problems, but in using the technology to better understand each other. An instructive example can be found in what happened after Chernobyl. Many Westerners criticized Soviet leaders for downplaying news about the accident. Soviet scholar Jonathan Sanders noted in a recent paper, however, that "coverage of the Chernobyl disaster marked a turning point in the history of Soviet communications. For the first time television . . . began to meet people's demands for 'bad news,' to abandon the silence about domestic disasters . . ."

"Is a plane crash really news?," a Soviet official asked shortly after Chernobyl. "Does that crash have much bearing on people's lives in general? We don't think so. In our view news is something that is meaningful to people—that affects their lives." Another Soviet official explains: "Obviously we are applying different yardsticks. The Western press is overly active and commits blunders more often than not. We are striving for 100-percent truth and therefore sometimes suffer in speed."[18]

Conclusion

Reactor Number Four is now sealed in a sarcophagus. The power plant is running again, and has already had some minor—or at least manageable—

---

[17] Dino A. Brugioni, "Satellite Images on TV: the Camera Can Lie," *The Washington Post* (14 December 1986).

[18] Jonathan Sanders, "The Soviets' First Living Room War: Soviet National Television's Coverage of the Chernobyl Disaster," a paper prepared for a Program on Global Disasters and International Information Flows, The Annenberg Schools of Communications, Washington Program (8-10 October 1986).

safety problems. Work on two new reactors is underway. Agronomists have planted shallow-root crops whose yield they hope will be edible. Flowers bloom. People talk once again about eating the mushrooms.

"Chernobyl" has become a new word in every major language. It is a symbol for the unseeable effects of modern technology, a reminder that to avoid disaster we must do more than avoid war.

International response to Chernobyl—the influence of public opinion, the uncensored flow of information, and the quick signing of multilateral conventions—has shown the constructive influence of new communications technologies. They offer great power and opportunity for the sharing of insight and information, for averting disaster, and for promoting a humane response when disaster does strike.

Standing in the way are national rivalries, pride, lack of will or imagination and—at times—communications technology itself. Even in the midst of the increasing transborder data flow, limitations are clear. Decreasing government control does not guarantee accurate communication.

Faster and more visual sharing of data, for example, promotes a sense that what is newsworthy must be spectacular. Emotions of the moment define what we judge important. This is ironic because many things worthy of concern—radiation, ozone depletion, chemical contamination of water, the spread of AIDS—are slow moving and difficult to see.

Will communication continue after the drama has gone? One-half of the deadly material released by Chernobyl will still exist in thirty years. It will gather in human muscle tissues and continue to release radiation. Who, other than the victims and their families, will notice amid the noise of the day's events?

We cannot know for sure where the New Age of Communications will lead any more than we could know one hundred years ago what the impact of electricity would be, or where the automobile would take us. Many different futures are possible and we should try to shape—and prepare for—the one that is best for our children. The Vienna Convention on Early Notification is a new and major step in the right direction. When the next Chernobyl, in whatever form, occurs, that Convention will measure our capacity to choose mass communications over mass destruction.

ABBREVIATIONS

AFDI	*Annuaire Français de Droit International*
AIEA	See IAEA
AJIL	*American Journal of International Law*
Akron L Rev	*Akron Law Review*
All ER	*All England Law Reports*
Annals Air & Space L	*Annals Air and Space Law*
Annuaire IDI	*Annuaire de l'Institut de Droit International*
ANO	Association of Nuclear Operators
ASDI	*Annuaire Suisse de Droit International*
Assistance Convention	1986 Convention on Assistance in the Case of a Nuclear Accident or Radiological Emergency
Assistance Guidelines	1984 IAEA Guidelines for Mutual Emergency Assistance Arrangements in Connection with a Nuclear Accident or Radiological Emergency
Australian Ybk Int'l L	*Australian Yearbook of International Law*
AV	*Archiv des Völkerrechts*
BGBl.	*Bundesgesetzblatt*
Bos. Coll. Int'l & Comp. L Rev	*Boston College International and Comparative Law Review*
bq	becquerel
Brussels Supplementary Convention	1963 Brussels Supplementary Convention to the Paris Convention
BYIL	*British Yearbook of International Law*
Can. Ybk Int'l Law	*Canadian Yearbook of International Law*
Case W Res. J Int. L	*Case Western Reserve Journal of International Law*
CEGB	United Kingdom Central Electricity Generating Board
Cmnd.	Command Paper presented to Parliament by command of Her Majesty
Colum. J Transnat'l Law	*Columbia Journal of Transnational Law*
Cornell Int'l LJ	*Cornell International Law Journal*
DM	Deutschmark
Doc.	Document

DOM-TOM	Départements d'Outre-Mer et Territoires d'Outre-Mer
EC	European Community (ies)
ECE	United Nations Economic Commission for Europe
Ecology LQ	*Ecology Law Quarterly*
EEC	European Economic Community
EMEP	Co-operative Programme for the Monitoring and Evaluation of the Long-range Transmission of Air Pollutants in Europe
Env. Law	*Environmental Law*
Env. Policy & Law	*Environmental Policy and Law*
EURATOM	European Atomic Energy Community
FAO	United Nations Food and Agriculture Organization
Fordham L Rev	*Fordham Law Review*
Ga J Int'l & Comp. L	*Georgia Journal of International and Comparative Law*
Harv. Env. Law Review	*Harvard Environmental Law Review*
Harv. Int'l LJ	*Harvard International Law Journal*
IAEA	International Atomic Energy Agency
IAEA Leg. Ser.	IAEA *Legal Series*
ICJ	International Court of Justice
ICJ Rep.	International Court of Justice, *Reports of Judgments, Advisory Opinions and Orders*
ICLQ	*International and Comparative Law Quarterly*
ICRP	International Commission on Radiological Protection
IDI	Institut de Droit International
IDI Resolution	1987 IDI Resolution on Transboundary Air Pollution
ILA	International Law Association
ILC	International Law Commission
ILM	*International Legal Materials*
ILO	International Labour Organization
IMF	International Monetary Fund

Information Guidelines	1985 IAEA Guidelines on Reportable Events, Integrated Planning and Information Exchange in a Transboundary Release of Radioactive Materials
INSAG	International Nuclear Safety Advisory Group
Int. Affairs	*International Affairs*
Int. Law.	*The International Lawyer*
IPrax	*Praxis des Internationalen Privat- und Verfassungsrecht*
IRALF	Interim International Radionuclide Action Levels for Food
JDI	*Journal de Droit International*
J Mar. Law & Com.	*Journal of Maritime Law and Commerce*
J of Space Law	*Journal of Space Law*
J of World Trade Law	*Journal of World Trade Law*
JORF	*Journal Officiel de la République Française*
kg	kilogram
l	litre
LNTS	*League of Nations Treaty Series*
McGill LJ	*McGill Law Journal*
Misc.	*Miscellaneous Papers* (UK)
Montreal Rules	1982 ILA Montreal Rules of International Law Applicable to Transfrontier Pollution
Natural Resources J	*Natural Resources Journal*
NEA	Nuclear Energy Agency
NIL Rev	*Netherlands International Law Review*
NLB	*Nuclear Law Bulletin*
no.	number
Notification Convention	1986 Convention on Early Notification of a Nuclear Accident
NRPB	National Radiological Protection Board
NYIL	*Netherlands Yearbook of International Law*
NYU J Int'l L & Pol	*New York University Journal of International Law and Policy*
OCDE	See OECD

OECD	Organization for Economic Co-operation and Development
OEEC	Organization for European Economic Co-operation
OJ	*Official Journal* of the European Communities
OSART	Operational Safety Review Team
Paris Convention	1960 Paris Convention on Third Party Liability in the field of Nuclear Energy
PCIJ	Permanent Court of International Justice
Proc. ASIL	*Proceedings of the American Society of International Law*
RC	*Recueil des Cours*, Académie de droit international de La Haye
Rev. Roum. d'Et. Internat.	*Revue Roumaine d'Etudes Internationales*
RGDIP	*Revue générale de droit international public*
RIAA	United Nations *Reports of International Arbitral Awards*
Riv. dir. internaz.	*Rivista di diritto internazionale*
Rüster	Rüster & Simma, *International Protection of the Environment* (1975)
Schematic Outline	1983 ILC Special Rapporteur's Schematic Outline Annexed to Fourth Report on International Liability for Injurious Consequences Arising out of Acts not Prohibited by International Law
SDR	Special Drawing Rights
SI	Statutory Instrument
SK	Swedish Krona
Tex. Int'l LJ	*Texas International Law Journal*
TFR	*Tidsskrift for Rettsvitenskap*
TIAS	*Treaties and Other International Acts Series*
Tul. L Rev	*Tulane Law Review*
UKLR	*University of Kansas Law Review*
UKTS	*United Kingdom Treaty Series*

UN	United Nations
UNDRO	United Nations Disaster Relief Office
UNEP	United Nations Environmental Programme
UNESCO	United Nations Educational, Scientific and Cultural Organization
UN GAOR	United Nations General Assembly *Official Records*
UN JYB	*United Nations Juridical Yearbook*
UNTS	*United Nations Treaty Series*
US	United States Supreme Court *Reports*
USSR Proposed Programme	1986 USSR Proposed Programme for Establishing an International Regime for the Safe Development of Nuclear Energy
UST	*United States Treaties and other International Instruments*
UTLJ	*University of Toronto Law Journal*
Vienna Convention	1963 Vienna Convention on Civil Liability for Nuclear Damage
Virg. J Int'l L	*Virginia Journal of International Law*
WHO	World Health Organization
Yale LJ	*Yale Law Journal*
Ybk ILC	*Yearbook* of the International Law Commission
Ybk UN	United Nations *Yearbook*
1972 Convention	1972 Convention on International Liability for Damage Caused by Space Objects
1972 Stockholm Declaration	1972 Stockholm Declaration of the United Nations Conference on the Human Environment
1974 Nordic Convention	1974 Nordic Convention on the Protection of the Environment
1974 OECD Recommendation	1974 OECD Council Recommendation on Principles Concerning Transfrontier Pollution
1977 OECD Recommendation	1977 OECD Council Recommendation for the Implementation of a Regime of Equal Right of Access and Non-discrimination in relation to Transfrontier Pollution
1979 Convention	1979 Convention on Long-Range Transboundary Air Pollution

INTRODUCTION

Transboundary Nuclear Pollution: International Legal Issues

1. Background Information

This Introduction identifies and examines some of the principal international legal issues arising out of the accident at the Chernobyl nuclear power plant, setting out briefly the applicable law and describing the principal legal developments subsequent to the accident. It does this with less clarity and decisiveness than the author would have wished, for the issues are complex and changing. All the conclusions are inevitably tentative: this is the penalty of topicality.

1.1 The Accident at the Chernobyl Nuclear Power Plant

On 27 April 1986 Sweden, and then Denmark, Finland and Poland, detected significant increases in radioactivity levels.[1] Immediate steps were taken to discover the source. Within a few hours it became clear that this was somewhere in the USSR. Faced with a pointing finger the Soviet government at first denied that any leak had occurred and then maintained a steadfast silence. As significantly increased levels of radioactivity were detected all over Europe and beyond, the gravity of the situation became apparent.

It was only during the evening of 28 April 1986, some 72 hours after the accident had occurred, that the Soviet Representative to the International Atomic Energy Agency (IAEA) informed the Director General of the IAEA, Dr Hans Blix, that an accident had occurred at 1.23 a.m. on 26 April 1986 during the testing of a turbo-generator in the fourth unit of the Chernobyl

[1] See Salo, "Information Exchange After Chernobyl", 28 *IAEA Bulletin*, No. 3, p. 18 (1986). Increased radiation levels were subsequently observed, *inter alia*, in Austria, German Democratic Republic, Hungary, Italy, Norway, Yugoslavia (29 April); Federal Republic of Germany, Switzerland, Turkey (30 April); France (1 May); Belgium, Greece, Netherlands, United Kingdom (2 May); and Iceland (7 May) (see map at p. 290). Low-level increases were also detected in Japan and the United States. Significant increases of particular danger to human health were observed in the levels of Iodine-131, Caesium-134 and Caesium-137 immediately after the accident: see Summary Report of 22 July 1986 of the Working Group on Assessment of Radiation Dose Commitment in Europe due to the Chernobyl Accident, noted in 28 *IAEA Bulletin*, No. 3, at p. 27 (1986).

Nuclear Power Plant.[2] The scale of the disaster became clearer when the world learnt that in the 36 hours after the accident more than 100,000 people had been evacuated from a radius of some 20 miles around the reactor. The full effects of the accident on people, property and the environment are still difficult to assess. In the USSR 31 people died as a direct result within a few weeks and a further three during 1987 as a result of on-site exposure.[3] The United Kingdom National Radiation Protection Board has estimated that in the EEC countries 1,000 people will die and 3,000 will contract non-fatal cancers because of the accident.[4] Many States, as well as the EEC, took measures to minimize the effects,[5] measures sometimes costly in themselves (as, for example, the protective medication undertaken in Poland) but which also caused losses to dairy and agricultural farmers, fish and meat producers and the tourist industries.[6] The effects in the Federal Republic of Germany have been described as follows:

The widespread radioactive contamination of the air, water and soil entailed direct damage to spring vegetables; milk-producing cattle had to be kept from grazing; the consumption of milk and other foodstuffs had to be supervised; import restrictions became necessary; the fixing of state intervention levels led to a change in consumers' eating and buying habits; travel agencies and transport undertakings specialising in Eastern Europe business lost their clientele; and finally, seasonal workers in agriculture lost their jobs.[7]

The measures taken have become a source of controversy. The USSR claims that they were unnecessary and implemented to spread untrue information and to attack the USSR. For other States they may become the basis for compensation claims. They have also been seen as principally a protectionist device to block competitive imports.

---

[2] For a detailed description of the circumstances and evolution of the accident see International Nuclear Safety Advisory Group (INSAG), Summary Report on the Post-Accident Review Meeting on the Chernobyl Accident, *Safety Series* No. 75-INSAG-1-STI/PUB/740 (1987); and NEA-OECD, *Chernobyl and the Safety of Nuclear Reactors in OECD Countries*, 1987 (NEA-OECD Report).

[3] *The Financial Times*, 5 December 1987.

[4] See NRPB, *A Preliminary Assessment of the Chernobyl Reactor Accident on the Population of the European Community* (1987).

[5] See below at pp. 16-17.

[6] See *The Financial Times*, 11 July 1986, at p. 36; 22 May 1986, at p. 3; 15 May 1986, at p. 2; *The Economist*, 16 August 1986, at p. 28.

[7] 38 *NLB* 21 (1986).

1.2   Subsequent Developments at the IAEA

Once it realised the political damage caused by the 72 hour vacuum of information about a matter of great public concern, the USSR acted swiftly. In a joint communiqué, following the visit by an IAEA delegation to the USSR in early May, the USSR stated its willingness to provide information on the accident as it became available[8] and undertook to provide the IAEA with daily information on radiation levels at a number of meteorological stations located close to the Chernobyl plant.[9] Readings were received from 9 May 1986 and transmitted to radiation protection authorities in affected Member States of the IAEA, first on a daily basis and then, as the levels stabilized, twice a week.[10]

Thereafter the IAEA played an important role in channelling information between the various affected States and in the remarkably swift chain of events which followed. It made informal contact with radiation protection authorities in a number of European Member States in order to obtain a more complete picture of the extent of the affected areas, receiving information on radiological measurements and protective measures from 23 Member States.

At the end of May 1986 the IAEA Board of Governors agreed a programme of action including a Post-Accident Review Meeting, the sponsoring of international conventions for improved emergency response and assistance, a special conference of governmental representatives on a full range of nuclear safety issues, and the establishment of an expert working group to review nuclear safety standards.[11] Two months later a meeting of governmental experts was convened to draft two international conventions: the Convention on Early Notification of a Nuclear Accident (Notification Convention) and the Convention on Assistance in the Case of a Nuclear Accident or Radiological Emergency (Assistance Convention).[12]

The Post-Accident Review Meeting, held from 25 to 29 August 1986, was attended by some 600 technical experts from 62 countries and national and

[8] See Petrosyants, "The Soviet Union and the Development of Nuclear Power", 28 *IAEA Bulletin*, Vol. 3, at p. 8 (1986).
[9] Leningrad, Riga, Vilnyus, Brest, Rakhov and Kishinev (see map at p. 290).
[10] See Salo, *supra* n. 1 at p. 19.
[11] The summary of decisions taken by the Board of Governors on 22 May 1986 is reprinted below at No. 19.
[12] The meeting took place from 21 July to 15 August 1987. It was attended by 286 participants from 62 Member States and 10 international organizations. The summary record of the Final Plenary Meeting is reproduced as Annex V to *IAEA Doc.* GC(SPL.I)/2.

international organizations.[13] The Soviet delegation presented a Report on the Chernobyl accident describing the reactor, the circumstances of the accident and response measures taken by the USSR.[14] According to the Report

the prime cause of the accident was an extremely improbable combination of violation of instructions and operating rules committed by the staff of the unit.[15]

The USSR has not accepted that the accident was due to design or operation flaws. It has nevertheless identified several measures to improve the safety of reactors such as those operating at the Chernobyl plant.[16] The NEA-OECD Report concludes that:

the design of the engineered safeguards was sound in principle for the design basis accidents (failure of a single pressure tube within the reactor, or of a large steam pipe apart from the reactor) and for the allowable range of operating conditions. However, it appears that insufficient accident analysis was done to develop the design of the shutdown system to enhance its capability to compensate for failures elsewhere in the safety structure, such as the possibility that operating rules would be grossly breached. Similarly the containment design left limited margin for demands which exceeded the design basic events.[17]

The Notification and Assistance Conventions were opened for signature at the end of the Special Session of the IAEA 30th Regular Session of the General Conference, convened from 24 to 26 September 1986 to consider measures related to nuclear safety and radiological protection.[18]

1.3   International Law

It came as a considerable shock to the world that an accident in a nuclear power plant could have significant effects thousands of miles away. The

---

[13] See the Report of the meeting prepared by the IAEA's INSAG, *supra* n. 2.

[14] USSR State Committee on the Utilization of Atomic Energy, *The Accident at the Chernobyl Nuclear Power Plant and its Consequences*, August 1986 (Vienna).

[15] As quoted in the NEA-OECD Report, *supra* n. 2, at p. 29. On 29 July 1987 the former Director, Chief Engineer and Deputy Chief Engineer of the Chernobyl plant were convicted and sentenced, under Article 220 of the Ukrainian Criminal Code, to ten years in a labour camp for gross violations of safety regulations, which led to the accident: see *The Guardian*, 30 July 1987.

[16] NEA-OECD Report, *supra* n. 2, at p. 34.

[17] *Id.* at p. 33.

[18] The Special Session was attended by 639 delegates from 94 countries and 27 national and international organizations.

accident exposed, in the most serious manner possible, the way in which traditional notions of sovereignty and national frontiers have been transformed by the modern technological and industrial world. Modern technology permitted such an accident to occur. But it also penetrated the sovereignty of the USSR, via satellite, to identify the source of the accident. Faced with the irrefutable evidence picked up by satellites, the USSR was forced to provide its own information to the world.

The Chernobyl Report acknowledges that the accident gave rise to significant international consequences, recognizing the international character of the dangers of the development of the world's nuclear power resources, including the risk of transfers of radioactivity across borders, especially in large scale radiation accidents.[19] These international effects have raised a number of international legal issues of considerable complexity relating to the prevention of nuclear accidents, the provision of information should they occur, assistance in connection with them and liability. Does international law impose upon States any obligation:

(1)   to prevent the transboundary release of radioactive material;

(2)   to repair any damage resulting from such a release;

(3)   to inform other States of an actual or potential transborder release of radioactive material;

(4)   to provide assistance to States affected by such a release?

As one consequence of the Chernobyl accident these four issues are now recognized by international society, both public and private, as the core of any arrangement for the establishment of an international nuclear safety regime. They form the basis for the Proposed Programme for Establishing an International Regime for the Safe Development of Nuclear Energy (USSR Proposed Programme) put forward recently by the USSR.[20]

There is no single multilateral treaty which establishes comprehensive rules covering all these issues. To ascertain what the present law is one must have general recourse to the traditional sources of international legal obligation as set out in Article 38 of the Statute of the International Court of Justice (ICJ),[21] i.e., multilateral and bilateral treaties, custom, general principles of law recognized by civilized nations, judicial decisions and the teachings of publicists.[22]

[19] *The New York Times*, 22 August 1986, at pp. A1, A4.
[20] Reprinted below at No. 20.
[21] *UKTS* 67 (1946), Cmnd. 7015.
[22] Article 38 provides, *inter alia*:
"1. The Court, whose function it is to decide in accordance with international law such disputes as are submitted to it, shall apply:

As will be seen, all these sources are defective. The rules existing at the time of the accident were neither comprehensive nor well developed, a demonstration of the difficulties of applying traditional rules of international law to a problem related to the use of new technologies. It is for this reason that States and the IAEA acted with such speed to identify and address the problems.

2. Prevention and Liability

2.1 Introduction

The principle of State sovereignty, recognized as the cornerstone of international society, allows States, within limits established by international law, to conduct such activities as they choose within their territories, including peaceful nuclear activity. The right to engage in such activity is recognized by a large number of treaties encouraging nuclear cooperation between States. Article IV of the 1968 Treaty on the Non-Proliferation of Nuclear Weapons (Non-Proliferation Treaty)[23] affirms ''the inalienable right of all the Parties to the Treaty to develop research production and use of nuclear energy for peaceful uses''. In 1977 the United Nations (UN) General Assembly, by consensus, specifically recognized the right of States,

in accordance with the principle of sovereign equality, to develop their programme for the peaceful use of nuclear technology for economic and social development, in conformity with their priorities, interests and needs.[24]

The right to engage in nuclear activity is not, however, unlimited. The Chernobyl accident showed that the radioactive material produced by nuclear technology may have effects beyond national boundaries. What are the limits international law places on States engaged in nuclear activities? More specifically:

(²² continued)
(a) international conventions, whether general or particular, establishing rules expressly recognized by the contesting States;
(b) international custom, as evidence of a general practice accepted as law;
(c) the general principles of law recognized by civilized nations;
(d) . . . judicial decisions and the teachings of the most highly qualified publicists of the various nations as subsidiary means for the determination of rules of law.''
[23] 729 *UNTS* 161.
[24] See Resolution 3250 of 8 December 1977, 31 *Ybk UN* 1977 at 107; *UN Doc.* A/32/L.15/Rev.1.

(1) Does international law lay on States an obligation to prevent a transboundary release of nuclear material? If so,

    (a) are States under an obligation to prevent any transboundary nuclear release, or only transboundary nuclear releases having serious or significant consequences? If the latter is the rule, what international standards are applicable to determine whether serious or significant consequences have occurred? and

    (b) is the obligation imposed upon States absolute, or is it a defence to show due diligence and absence of fault?

(2) If an obligation does exist and a transboundary release of nuclear material occurs, is the State liable to repair any damage it so causes? If so, what is the extent of that liability?

2.2 The Obligation to Prevent Transboundary Nuclear Pollution

The ICJ has stated that the principle of sovereignty embodies "the obligation of every State not to allow its territory to be used for acts contrary to the rights of other States".[25]

In the *Lac Lanoux* arbitration, involving the diversion of an international river by an upstream State, the Arbitral Tribunal affirmed that a State has an obligation not to exercise its rights to the extent of ignoring the rights of another:

France is entitled to exercise her rights; she cannot ignore the Spanish interests. Spain is entitled to demand that her rights be respected and that her interests be taken into consideration.[26]

Since the early 1970s States have become generally more aware of the damage caused by industrial and other pollution to the environment. They have acted internationally, regionally and bilaterally to encourage a reduction of transboundary air pollution.[27] In 1972 a UN Conference was held in Stockholm on the Human Environment and this produced a Declaration of

---

[25] *Corfu Channel* case (*UK* v. *Albania*), 1949, *ICJ Rep.* pp. 4, 22.

[26] (*Spain* v. *France*), *RIAA*, Vol. XII, p. 285.

[27] Air pollution is defined in Article 1 of the 1979 Convention on Long-Range Transboundary Air Pollution, reprinted below at No. 10, as: "the introduction by man, directly or indirectly, of substances or energy into the air resulting in deleterious effects of such a nature as to endanger human health, harm living resources and ecosystems and material property and impair or interfere with amenities and other legitimate uses of the environment".

This definition has achieved general acceptance by States and is wide enough to include within its scope radioactive material.

Principles (1972 Stockholm Declaration)[28] to preserve and enhance the human environment. That same year the United Nations Environment Programme (UNEP) was established by the UN General Assembly[29] and in 1978 it produced Draft Principles for the Guidance of States in the Conservation and Harmonious Utilization of Natural Resources Shared by Two or More States (1978 UNEP Principles).[30]

The UN Economic Commission for Europe (ECE) sponsored the 1979 Convention on Long-Range Transboundary Air Pollution (1979 Convention),[31] to which almost all States in both Eastern and Western Europe are now Parties. The Organization for Economic Co-operation and Development (OECD) has also been active. Among its more important contributions are the 1974 Recommendation on Principles Concerning Transfrontier Pollution (1974 OECD Recommendation)[32] and the 1977 Recommendation for the Implementation of a Regime of Equal Right of Access and Non-Discrimination in Relation to Transfrontier Pollution (1977 OECD Recommendation).[33]

A number of regional treaties have also been concluded. These include the 1974 Nordic Convention for the Protection of the Environment (1974 Nordic Convention)[34] and several relating to the protection of the marine environment.[35]

[28] Reprinted below at No. 6. The USSR did not participate at this Conference due to the exclusion of the German Democratic Republic. Nevertheless it has expressly accepted the Principles set out in the Declaration by its ratification of the 1979 Convention, the Preamble to which incorporates by reference those Principles: see *supra* n. 27.

The Austrian delegate in the UN General Assembly's Second Committee discussion of the Stockholm Declaration stated that, ''it represented the first comprehensive international political consensus on environmental issues and, although it was not legally binding, it had been the subject of intensive negotiations and should thus be generally acceptable'': cited in Handl, ''Territorial Sovereignty and the Problem of Transnational Pollution'', 69 *AJIL* 50 (1975) at p. 67.

[29] By Resolution 2997 (XXVII) of 15 December 1972. The Resolution was adopted by 112 votes in favour, 0 against and 10 abstentions. See also Dupuy, ''United Nations Environment Programme'', in Bernhardt (ed.), *Encyclopaedia of International Law*, Vol. 5, p. 319.

[30] Reprinted in 17 *ILM* 1097.

[31] Reprinted below at No. 10.

[32] Reprinted below at No. 8.

[33] Reprinted below at No. 9.

[34] Reprinted below at No. 7.

[35] 1983 Cartagena de Indas Convention for the Protection and Development of the Marine Environment of the Wider Caribbean Region, 22 *ILM* 227; 1981 Abidjan

Nuclear pollution causes particular concern in relation to the rights of other States: release of radioactive material into the atmosphere will invariably cross international boundaries and by its nature may cause substantial or serious injury. Recognizing the potential dangers, some States have attempted to limit atmospheric nuclear pollution[36] in a variety of ways. There are, for example, multilateral treaties banning atmospheric nuclear weapons tests,[37] and placing special obligations and requirements on the operation of nuclear ships,[38] the maritime carriage of nuclear materials[39] and the physical protection of nuclear materials.[40]

Many States have concluded bilateral treaties for cooperation in the peaceful uses of nuclear energy, some of which stress the need to protect the environment from radioactive contamination.[41] States have also acted through the IAEA and established, under the Non-Proliferation Treaty,[42] a system to prevent the diversion of nuclear energy from peaceful uses to nuclear weapons or other nuclear explosive devices.[43]

Convention for the Cooperation on the Protection and Development of the Marine and Coastal Environment of the West and Central African Region, 20 *ILM* 746; 1980 Athens Protocol for the Protection of the Mediterranean Sea against Pollution from Land-Based Sources, 19 *ILM* 869; 1978 Kuwait Regional Convention for Cooperation on the Protection of the Marine Environment from Pollution, 17 *ILM* 511; 1976 Barcelona Convention for the Protection of the Mediterranean Sea against Pollution, 15 *ILM* 290; 1974 Helsinki Convention on the Protection of the Marine Environment of the Baltic Sea Area, 13 *ILM* 546.

[36] See generally Ioannou, "Peaceful Uses of Nuclear Energy", in Bernhardt (ed.), *Encyclopaedia of Public International Law*, Vol. 9 (1985), p. 290.

[37] See the 1963 Treaty Banning Nuclear Weapon Testing in the Atmosphere, in Outer Space and Under Water, 480 *UNTS* 43.

[38] See the 1962 Brussels Convention on the Liability of Operators of Nuclear Ships, reprinted below at No. 2.

[39] See the 1971 Convention Relating to Civil Liability in the Field of Maritime Carriage of Nuclear Material, 1971 *UN JYB* 100.

[40] See the 1980 Convention on the Physical Protection of Nuclear Material, 18 *ILM* 1419.

[41] See for example the 1985 Agreement for Co-operation between the Government of the United States of America and the Government of the People's Republic of China Concerning Peaceful Uses of Nuclear Energy, reprinted below at No. 17. The Preamble and Article 9 both refer to the need to protect the environment from radioactive contamination.

[42] *Supra* n. 23.

[43] See for example the 1985 Agreement between the USSR and the IAEA for the Application of Safeguards in the USSR, reprinted in 24 *ILM* 1411 (1985).

The IAEA has developed special safety standards to govern nuclear activities. The Director of the IAEA's Division of Nuclear Safety has summarized recent developments:[44] during the 1970s a Nuclear Safety Standards programme was developed to establish an internationally agreed frame of reference for the safety of nuclear power plants;[45] in 1983 an Incident Reporting System was established to share operational safety experience among Member States; also in 1983 an Operational Safety Review Team programme (OSART)[46] was created to provide advice to nuclear power plant operators on safety enhancement; and in 1985 an International Nuclear Safety Advisory Group (INSAG) was established to review activities in nuclear safety and to provide advice on further directions.

All this activity has produced a bewildering array of standards, some binding, others not, and leaves unanswered the question whether States are under a duty to prevent any increase in levels of radioactivity in neighbouring States, or only increased levels which are harmful. In view of the paucity of acts specially aimed at nuclear activity, this question has to be addressed according to the standards developed in relation to pollution generally.

Transboundary pollution, and the disputes it causes between States, is not a new phenomenon. In the much-cited *Trail Smelter* case[47] the United States brought a claim against Canada for damage to property in the State of Washington caused by sulphuric and other noxious fumes drifting over the frontier from a smelter in British Columbia, Canada. The Tribunal held that:

Under the principles of international law . . . no State has the right to use or permit the use of territory in such a manner as to cause injury by fumes in or to the territory

---

[44] See Rosen, "New Directions in Nuclear Safety", 28 *IAEA Bulletin*, No. 3, p. 13 (1986). On the IAEA, see Szasz, *The Law and Practice of the International Atomic Energy Agency* (1970).

[45] The recommendations relate to nuclear power plant safety in siting, design, operation and quality assurance. See Adede & Phuong, "Perception from the Standpoint of a Worldwide International Organization", in Pelzer (ed.), *Status, Prospects and Possibilities of International Harmonization in the Field of Nuclear Energy Law* (1986) at p. 563.

[46] Small teams of experts perform in-depth reviews of local operating practices, covering such areas as maintenance, operations, technical support, radiation protection, training and emergency planning. The IAEA has inspected 23 reactors so far under this programme. In September 1987 the USSR invited the IAEA, for the first time, to inspect the safety and management of a pressurised water reactor under the OSART programme. The inspection is expected to take place in mid-1988 at the Zajorozhe reactor in the Ukraine to placate local feelings about reactor safety following the Chernobyl accident: *The Financial Times*, 23 September 1987.

[47] *United States* v. *Canada*, 3 RIAA p. 1907 (1941).

of another of the properties or persons therein, when the case is of serious consequence and the injury is established by clear and convincing evidence.[48]

Most writers have accepted this formulation as a rule of customary international law[49] and it was cited, with apparent approval, by Judge de Castro in his dissent in the *Nuclear Tests* case.[50] In that case Australia had asked the ICJ to adjudge and declare that the carrying out of further atmospheric nuclear tests was not consistent with applicable rules of international law and would be unlawful "in so far as it involves modification of the physical conditions of and over Australian territory [and] pollution of the atmosphere and of the resources of the seas".[51] The Rapporteur of the International Law Association (ILA) Committee on Legal Aspects of the Environment has examined recent State practice and has concluded that it is founded upon this rule.[52] The *Trail Smelter* decision has been rightly criticized, however, for the manner in which it transformed what was nothing more than a maxim into a principle of international law,[53] especially as that very principle was applicable *a priori* by virtue of the arbitral *compromis* between the United States and Canada.[54] The Tribunal in the *Trail Smelter*

[48] *Id.* at p. 1965.

[49] See for example Goldie, "A General View of International Environmental Law—A Survey of Capabilities, Trends and Limits", in *Colloque La Haye*, pp. 66-9 (1973); Kirgis, "Technological Challenge of the Shared Environment: US Practise", 66 *AJIL* 291 (1974); Kiss, "La Lutte contre la Pollution de l'Air sur le Plan International", *Colloque La Haye*, pp. 169-74 (1973). The principle has also been applied to inter-State practice in the United States by the US Supreme Court in *Georgia v. Tennessee Copper Co.*, 206 *US* 230 (1906).

[50] *Australia* v. *France*, 1974 *ICJ Rep.* pp. 253, 389. He stated: "If it is admitted as a general rule that there is a right to demand prohibition of the emission by neighbouring properties of noxious fumes, the consequence must be drawn, by an obvious analogy, that the Applicant is entitled to ask the Court to uphold its claim that France should put an end to the deposit of radio-active fall-out on its territory".

[51] ICJ Pleadings, *Nuclear Tests Cases*, I, p. 27. The ICJ held that in view of the unilateral declaration made by the French Government concerning its intention to terminate atmospheric tests, Australia's claim no longer had any object and no decision was called upon to be given by the ICJ.

[52] See ILA, Report of the Committee on Legal Aspects of the Environment, *60th Conference Report*, p. 157 at 163.

[53] See Mirfendereski, Book Review, 18 *Bos. Coll. Int'l & Comp. L Rev*, p. 267 at 279 (1985).

[54] Convention for the Final Settlement of the Difficulties Arising Through the Complaints of Damage Done in the State of Washington by Fumes discharged from the Smelter of the Consolidated Mining and Smelting Company, Trail, British Columbia, 15 April 1935, United States-Canada, 162 *LNTS* 73 (1935-36).

case reached its decision in a pre-nuclear age. Nevertheless, there is no reason in principle why the rule the Tribunal relied upon should not apply to nuclear pollution; such pollution will often be carried by air, like fumes, and may well lead to serious consequences. Moreover, the difficulties of establishing injury by clear and convincing evidence are considerable but, as will be discussed later, by no means insurmountable.

The UN General Assembly has recognized the applicability of general principles of international law to nuclear issues. In 1961, by Resolution 1629 (XVI), it declared:

The fundamental principles of international law impose a responsibility on all states concerning actions which might have harmful biological consequences for the existing and future generations of peoples of other states, by increasing the levels of radioactive fallout.[55]

The 1972 Stockholm Declaration[56] broadly reflects the legal rule applied by the Tribunal in the *Trail Smelter* decision and set out in Resolution 1629. Principle 21 provides that:

States have . . . the responsibility to ensure that activities within their jurisdiction or control do not cause damage to the environment of other States or of areas beyond the limits of national jurisdiction.[57]

While the 1972 Stockholm Declaration is not legally binding, the terms of Principle 21 have received considerable support from States. The Principle was expressly recommended by UN General Assembly Resolution 2996 (XXVII) of 15 December 1972[58] as laying down the basic rules governing the international responsibility of States in regard to the environment. The USSR and a number of Eastern European States did not participate in the Stockholm Conference and abstained in the General Assembly vote, but their non-participation was due to the exclusion of East Germany from the Conference

---

[55] 16 *UN GAOR* (1043 Plenary Meeting) at 505-7, *UN Doc.* A/PV.1043 (1961). The Resolution was passed with 74 votes in favour, 0 against, 17 abstentions.

[56] *Supra* n. 28.

[57] *Id.* It is generally agreed that Principle 21 is ''an accurate statement of the present law'': per Akehurst, ''International Liability for Injurious Consequences Arising out of Acts not Prohibited by International Law'', 1985 *NYIL* p. 3 at 5; see also P.-M. Dupuy, *La Responsabilité des États pour les Dommages d'origine technologique et industrielle* (1976), p. 177.

[58] Reprinted below at No. 6. The Resolution received 112 votes in favour, 0 against, 10 abstentions.

and not to differences relating to its purpose. They have since supported the substance of Principle 21 in, for example, Article 30 of the Charter of Economic Rights and Duties of States, which provides, *inter alia*, that:

All States have the responsibility to ensure that activities within their jurisdiction or control do not cause damage to the environment of other States or of areas beyond the limits of national jurisdiction.[59]

The USSR and a number of Eastern European States are also Parties to the 1979 Convention[60] which refers, in the Preamble, to Principle 21 as expressing the "common conviction" of States. Under the 1979 Convention States undertake to "endeavour to limit and as far as possible, gradually reduce and prevent air pollution, including long range transboundary air pollution".[61] Support for Principle 21 is virtually universal. Whether, however, it or a similar principle has emerged into a rule of customary international law depends, in part, on whether it has received the requisite *opinio juris*[62] and this requires a closer analysis of State practice than is possible in this brief Introduction. However, the ILA[63] has concluded that a rule of custom does exist. Article 3(1) of the ILA Draft Rules on Transboundary Pollution (Montreal Rules) restates customary international law as requiring States

[59] UN General Assembly Resolution 3281 (XXIX), adopted on 12 December 1974, *Ybk UN* 1974 at 402. The Resolution was passed with 120 votes in favour, 6 against, and 10 abstentions. The USSR is a Signatory of the 1982 UN Convention on the Law of the Sea, Article 194(2) of which provides: "States shall take all measures necessary to ensure that activities under their jurisdiction or control are so conducted as not to cause damage by pollution to other States and their environment, and that pollution arising from incidents or activities under their jurisdiction or control does not spread beyond the areas where they exercise sovereign rights in accordance with this Convention." *UN Doc.* A/CONF.62/122, reprinted in 21 *ILM* 1261 (1982).

[60] *Supra* n. 31.

[61] *Id.* at Article 1.

[62] In the *North Sea Continental Shelf* cases (*Federal Republic of Germany v. Denmark*; *Federal Republic of Germany v. Netherlands*) 1969 *ICJ Rep.* p. 3, the ICJ stated that the acts emanating to settled practice "must also be such, or be carried out in such a way, as to be evidence of a belief that this practice is rendered obligatory by the existence of a rule of law requiring it. The need for such a belief, i.e. the existence of a subjective element, is implicit in the very notion of the *opinio juris sive necessitatis*", at p. 44.

[63] The ILA, founded in 1873, is a private organization of lawyers whose objects include "the study, elucidation and advancement of international law, public and private" (Article 2 of the Constitution).

to prevent . . . transfrontier air pollution to such an extent that no substantial injury is caused in the territory of another State.[64]

The obligation to refrain from causing pollution which might cause substantial injury is reinforced by Article 4, which provides, *inter alia*, that:

States shall refrain from causing transfrontier pollution by discharging into the environment substances generally considered as being highly dangerous to human health.[65]

The rule established by the Institut de Droit International (IDI) in its 1987 Resolution on Transboundary Pollution (IDI Resolution),[66] which does not purport to restate custom, is less strict. Article 2 provides that:

In the exercise of their sovereign right to exploit their resources pursuant to their own environmental policies, States shall be under a duty to take all appropriate and effective measures to ensure that their activities or those conducted within their jurisdiction or under their control cause no transboundary air pollution.[67]

The IAEA Secretariat, in its post-Chernobyl review of the principle of State responsibility for transboundary harm, takes a view of the applicable rule which is closer to that adopted by the ILA. It concluded that:

No State has the right to use its property or territory in such a way as to injure others—a principle of law rooted in the concept of harm and usually expressed in the maxim *sic utere tuo ut alienum non laedas* (use your own property in such a manner as not to damage that of another). One aspect of the duty which a State may be said to have under this principle is the duty to protect other States and their nationals from serious transboundary effects arising within its territory or jurisdiction.[68]

---

[64] Reprinted below at No. 12.

[65] *Id.*

[66] Reprinted below at No. 23. The IDI, founded in 1873, is a private association of scholars of public and private international law which aims to facilitate the progress of international law (Article 1(2) of Statute).

[67] *Id.* Article 10 establishes a stronger obligation on States ''to prohibit, prevent and refrain from carrying out any nuclear explosions likely to cause transboundary air pollution of a radioactive nature''. The words ''carrying out'' do not, however, make it absolutely clear whether this obligation applies to an accidental explosion.

[68] IAEA, Note by Director General, ''The Question of International Liability for Damage Arising from a Nuclear Accident'', *IAEA Doc.* GOV/INF/509 at para. 14 (26 January 1987).

Following the accident many States, including some which suffered increased levels of radiation, were vague about the extent of the obligation, if any, which existed. This is reflected in the Statement of the Group of Seven Industrial Nations, issued after the Chernobyl accident:

For each country the maintenance of safety and security is an international responsibility, and each country engaged in nuclear power generation bears full responsibility for the safety of the design, manufacture, operation and maintenance of its installations.[69]

However, the *Trail Smelter* case, Resolution 1629, Principle 21, the 1979 Convention, the Charter of Economic Rights and Duties of States and the Montreal Rules together suggest that a universally accepted rule has emerged, and is applicable to transboundary nuclear pollution in the following way: international law imposes upon States an obligation not to increase levels of radioactivity in neighbouring States to a level capable of causing harm to persons, property and the environment.

2.3 Defining Harm

What constitutes harmful levels of radioactivity has long been a source of controversy, and at the time of the Chernobyl accident there were no legally binding international standards. This is a significant gap in the international arrangements for the protection of persons in the event of a nuclear accident and one which has caused problems in the wake of the Chernobyl accident.

The importance of harmonizing international norms of radionuclide concentrations and radioactive contamination levels under accident conditions has been widely recognized. The Secretariat of the IAEA has noted that:

harmonized international norms would provide an objective threshold both for triggering claims for damage and for determining whether they were justified . . . Within the context of a new international liability instrument, therefore, the possibility might be explored of using the intervention levels applicable in a State where a nuclear accident has occurred as a criterion for the presentation of claims for damage by other States which have been physically affected.[70]

The USSR, following the Chernobyl accident, has taken the same view:

[69] Reprinted below at No. 18.
[70] IAEA, Note by Director General, "The Question of Liability for Damage Arising from a Nuclear Accident", *IAEA Doc.* GOV/2306, Annex 2 at p. 6 (22 May 1987).

There is a need to agree upon common international standards for accident-induced concentrations of radionuclides and levels of radioactive contamination of the affected area. Such internationally agreed standards and norms could be used both for the adequate application of protective measures by all States as well as for the justification of claims for damages in connection with a transboundary release of radioactivity.[71]

Several international guidelines establish radiation dose limits for the whole human body or for specific organs or tissues. The Commission of the EEC has published recommendations on dose levels as guidelines for national authorities in setting specific levels at which products might be deemed unsafe (intervention levels).[72] Similar guidelines have also been prepared by the International Commission on Radiological Protection (ICRP),[73] whose standards are the most widely accepted, the World Health Organization (WHO)[74] and the IAEA.[75] At the time of the Chernobyl accident, however, little consideration had been given to the control of foodstuffs contaminated by an accidental release of radioactivity. Therefore, national authorities set their own intervention levels according to a variety of different standards.[76]

On 12 May 1986 the Commission of the EEC issued a Regulation suspending the import of certain agricultural products originating in certain third countries.[77] This Regulation was superseded on 30 May 1986 by a further Regulation laying down, until 30 September 1987, the maximum permitted radioactivity levels for products originating in third countries.[78]

---

[71] *Supra* n. 20.

[72] *Radiological Protection Criteria for Controlling Doses to the Public in the Event of Accidental Releases of Radioactive Material, A Guide on Emergency Reference Levels of Dose from the Group of Experts Convened under Article 41 of the EURATOM Treaty* (1982).

[73] See "Protection of the Public in the Event of Major Radiation Accidents: Principles for Planning", 40 *Annals of the ICRP*, No. 2 (1984), at pp. 5-7 and 12-14.

[74] *Nuclear Power: Principles of Public Health Actions for Accidental Releases* (1984).

[75] Principles for Establishing Intervention Levels for the Protection of the Public in the Event of a Nuclear Accident or Radiological Emergency, *IAEA Safety Series* No. 72, 1985.

[76] See FAO, *Report of the Expert Consultation on Recommended Limits for Radionuclide Contamination of Foods* (FAO Report), 1987, Table II, for examples of the varying post-Chernobyl "action levels" applied by some countries for certain radionuclides (in terms of becquerels per kilogram or litre (bq/kg or bq/l)) in imported foods, as at December 1986.

[77] Regulation (EEC) No. 1388/86, *OJ* No. L 127, 13.5.1986, p. 1. The third countries were Bulgaria, Czechoslovakia, Hungary, Poland, Romania, USSR and Yugoslavia.

[78] Council Regulation (EEC) No. 1707/86, on the Conditions Governing Imports of Agricultural Products Originating in Third Countries Following the Accident at

These Regulations had a significant effect on trade in agricultural and dairy products between Eastern and Western Europe.

On 21 May 1986 the Government of the Federal Republic of Germany, acting under the 1985 Atomic Energy Act,[79] issued an Equity Guideline establishing intervention levels and setting out rules for compensation for certain agricultural damage arising out of the Chernobyl accident.[80] On 2 June 1986 the Federal Government undertook to pay compensation for damage due to the introduction of official intervention levels for certain spring vegetables where damage occurred by 31 May 1986.[81] On 24 July 1986 the Federal Government and the *Länder* agreed to pay compensation of two-thirds and one-third respectively for insolvency or impending insolvency due to the Chernobyl accident, limited to a certain period of time and to certain fields of business, including protection of and trade in vegetables, transport enterprises, travel agencies specializing in Eastern European business, enterprises having suffered similar losses, dairies, and seasonal workers in agriculture and in food industries.[82]

On 20 June 1986 the Government of the United Kingdom, acting under the Food and Environmental Protection Act 1985,[83] restricted the movement and

the Chernobyl Nuclear Power Station, *OJ* No. L 146, 31.5.1986, p. 88. The Regulation was subsequently extended until 28 February 1987 by Council Regulation (EEC) No. 3020/86, *OJ* No. L 280, 1.10.1986, p. 79; and until 31 October 1987 by Council Regulation (EEC) No. 624/87, *OJ* No. L 58, 28.2.1987, p. 101.

[79] Reprinted below at Annex. Section 38(2) provides that the Federal State shall pay compensation for damage caused by a foreign nuclear installation and suffered in the territory of the Federal Republic of Germany (and where the applicable foreign law only provides for compensation which is short of that available under German law).

[80] *Bundesanzeiger* of 27 May 1986, No. 95, p. 6417. The Guideline sets out the damage to be compensated, including damage to property and prejudice to similar rights caused directly by the Chernobyl accident; seizure of products; restrictions concerning the use of milk and direct damage to enterprises within the meaning of section 823, paragraph 1 of the Civil Code.

[81] *Bundesanzeiger* of 12 June 1986, No. 105, p. 7237.

[82] *Bundesanzeiger* of 2 August 1986, No. 140, p. 10388. The information relating to the Federal Republic of Germany is taken from a Note in 38 *NLB* 22 (1986) by Dr Pelzer of the University of Göttingen.

[83] Section 1 of the Act provides:

''(1) If in the opinion of a designating authority—

(a) there has been an escape of substances of such descriptions and in such quantities and in such circumstances as are likely to create hazard to human health through human consumption of food; and

(b) in consequence food which is or may be in the future in an area—

slaughter of sheep for 21 days in certain areas of Cumbria in England and North Wales.[84] On 24 June 1986 restrictions were introduced for certain parts of Scotland[85] and, over a year later on 14 September 1987, with respect to certain parts of Northern Ireland.[86] The Restriction Orders provided for the payment of certain compensation to those affected.

The lack of generally accepted standards relating to safe levels of radioactivity in food made it difficult to assess whether all, or any, of these measures were justified. The UN Food and Agriculture Organization (FAO) Report states that events related to the Chernobyl accident

showed a serious lack of international communication, cooperation and harmony in the development of "acceptable" limits for possible radioactive contamination of food, feed and their ecological precursors.

This situation led to confusion, concern, and suspicion in the public mind and media. It also resulted in constraints or threats of constraints on food movement in international trade.[87]

Accordingly, the FAO has now proposed "Interim International Radionuclide Action Levels for Food" (IRALFs) moving in international

([83] continued)
  (i) of land in the United Kingdom;
  (ii) of sea within British fishery limits; or
  (iii) both of such land and of such sea, or which may be in the future derived from anything in such an area, is, or may be, or may become, unsuitable for human consumption, that designating authority may by statutory instrument make an order designating that area and containing emergency prohibitions."
[84] Food Protection (Emergency Prohibitions) (England) Order, 1986, *SI* 1986 No. 1411. The subsequent replacing and amending Orders have recently been consolidated by the Food Protection (Emergency Prohibitions) (England) Order, 1987, *SI* 1987 No. 1893.
Separate Orders were made for Wales with effect from August 1986. Current restrictions are imposed by the Food Protection (Emergency Prohibitions) (Wales) Order, 1987, *SI* 1987 Nos. 1893 and 1894.
[85] Food Protection (Emergency Prohibitions) (Scotland) Order, 1986, *SI* 1986 No. 1059. This Order was subsequently amended and replaced. Current restrictions are imposed by the Food Protection (Emergency Prohibitions) (Scotland) Order, 1987, *SI* 1987 Nos. 1165 and 1450.
[86] Food Protection (Emergency Prohibitions) (Northern Ireland) Order, 1987, *SI* 1987 Nos. 367 and 395. An Order has also recently been made restricting the export of sheep: *SI* 1987 No. 409.
[87] FAO Report, *supra* n. 76 at p. 3.

trade.[88] While these are non-binding and *ex post facto*, they might usefully be taken as the standard for assessing whether the increases in radioactivity caused by the Chernobyl accident were harmful to foodstuffs and whether the restrictions imposed by, *inter alia*, the UK, the Federal Republic of Germany and the EEC were justified under international law. The restrictions imposed by the EEC were based on radioactivity levels almost identical to the IRALFs proposed by the FAO.[89]

2.4   Standard of Care

If, as concluded above, there is an obligation to avoid harmful increase in levels of transboundary radioactivity, what is the standard of care applicable to this obligation? The various possibilities include fault (based upon intention or negligence), strict liability (''essentially a *prima facie* responsibility, and various defences or qualifications may be available'')[90] and absolute liability (''for which there can be no mode of exculpation'').[91]

This question has received much attention from writers,[92] but it is not the function of this Introduction to explore the role of fault in relation to State responsibility generally. In relation to nuclear activity, the special dangers it creates provide a compelling reason for ensuring that the standard of care is a high one. This has been recognized by some of the treaties regulating nuclear activities, which establish a principle of ''absolute'' liability.

The Paris Convention on Third Party Liability in the Field of Nuclear Energy (Paris Convention)[93] provides that the operator of a nuclear installation ''shall be liable'' for damage to or loss of life of any person and any property upon proof that such damage was caused by a nuclear incident involving that nuclear installation.[94] The 1963 IAEA Vienna Convention on Civil Liability for Nuclear Damage (Vienna Convention),[95] whose purpose is to establish some minimum standards to provide protection under national law against certain nuclear damage, provides that the ''liability of the operator . . .

---

[88] *Id.* at Table II.

[89] The IRALF for Iodine-131 is 400 bq/kg; the EEC imposed import restrictions on milk of 500 bq/kg and on vegetables of 350 bq/kg.

[90] Brownlie, *System of the Law of Nations*, State Responsibility, Part I (1983) at p. 44.

[91] *Id.*

[92] See the discussion by Brownlie, *id.* at pp. 40-6, and literature there cited.

[93] Reprinted below at No. 1.

[94] *Id.* at Article 3.

[95] Reprinted below at No. 3.

shall be absolute''.[96] Similarly, the 1962 Brussels Convention on the Liability of Operators of Nuclear Ships (Brussels Convention)[97] provides that:

> The operator of a nuclear ship shall be absolutely liable for any nuclear damage upon proof that such damage has been caused by a nuclear incident involving the nuclear fuel of, or radioactive products or waste produced in such ship.[98]

The word ''absolute'' is, however, used misleadingly since each of these Conventions provides exceptions to the rule. By way of example, Article 9 of the Paris Convention provides that the operator shall not be liable for nuclear incidents

> directly due to an act of armed conflict, hostilities, civil war, insurrection or . . . a grave natural disaster of an exceptional character.[99]

Moreover, these Conventions have not received widespread participation and a great many States, including the United States and the USSR, are Parties to none.

The principle of absolute liability is found in other treaties regulating ultra-hazardous, but non-nuclear, activities. Thus, the 1972 Convention on International Liability for Damage Caused by Space Objects (1972 Convention),[100] provides that:

> a launching State shall be absolutely liable to pay compensation for damage caused by its space objects on the surface of the earth.[101]

On the basis of this provision Canada successfully claimed compensation from the USSR for damage caused within Canadian territory by the accidental crash in 1978 of the USSR's Cosmos 954 satellite. In its Statement of Claim[102] the Canadian Government relied on Article 2 and on general principles of international law, submitting that ''international precedents recognized that a violation of sovereignty gives rise to an obligation to pay compensation'' and that ''the principle of absolute liability applies to fields of activity having in

---

[96] *Supra* n. 95 at Article IV(1).
[97] *Supra* n. 38.
[98] *Id.* at Article II(1).
[99] *Supra* n. 93. Further exceptions are set out in Article 4. See also Article IV of the Vienna Convention *supra* n. 95, and Article VIII of the Brussels Convention, *supra* n. 38.
[100] Reprinted below at No. 5.
[101] *Id.* at Article II.
[102] Reprinted in 18 *ILM* 902-30; and see below at pp. 30, 119-20.

common a high degree of risk . . . [and] had been accepted as a general principle of international law".[103]

The national law of many countries adopts a standard of strict liability for ultra-hazardous activities. By way of illustration, it is a principle of English law that if a person brings on to his land and keeps there anything which is likely to do mischief, "he is *prima facie* answerable for all the damage which is the natural consequence of its escape".[104]

The Parties to the Paris Convention, whose purpose is to harmonize national legislation with regard to third party liability and compensation for nuclear accidents, have introduced national legislation incorporating into national law the "absolute" liability provision contained in Article 3 of that Convention.[105] Many other States which are not Parties adopt a principle of absolute or strict liability in relation to ultra-hazardous activities.[106] In the USSR the Civil Code provides for an exception from the general rule that fault is a necessary precondition of liability where it is found that damage has been caused by a source of increased danger.[107]

What is the standard in customary law? It is certainly arguable that the pattern of treaties establishing a standard of "absolute" liability for nuclear harm and other ultra-hazardous activities, together with the general principle of "absolute" or strict liability established by municipal law in relation to ultra-hazardous activities, creates an absolute obligation on States to prevent transboundary nuclear harm. According to Jenks:

The principle that liability for 'nuclear' damage is absolute is generally accepted, but the expression is somewhat misleading in that it does not exclude the possibility of exceptions.[108]

Taking this into account the Montreal Rules[109] and the IDI Resolution[110]

---

[103] *Id.* at p. 907. On 2 April 1981 the USSR agreed to pay Canada Canadian $3 million in "full and final settlement" of the claim: see Brownlie, *op. cit.* n. 90 at p. 97, footnote 11.

[104] *Rylands and Another* v. *Fletcher* (1861-73), *All ER* 1, 7.

[105] The implementing legislation is set out at pp. 79-80 below.

[106] See Tunc (ed.), *International Encyclopaedia of Comparative Law*, Vol. XI, Chapter V.

[107] Civil Code of the Russian Soviet Federative Socialist Republic, 1964, at Article 454.

[108] See Jenks, "The Scope and Nature of Ultra-Hazardous Liability in International Law", 117 *RC* 99, at 144 (1966).

[109] *Supra* n. 63 at Article 4.

[110] *Supra* n. 66 at Articles 2 and 10.

both recognize an absolute obligation to prevent pollution by highly dangerous materials.

On the other hand, the 1979 Convention[111] and the 1974 OECD Recommendation[112] only require States to "endeavour to limit and . . . prevent air pollution" and to "take all appropriate measures to prevent and control transfrontier pollution" respectively. The Environment Committee of the OECD has also observed that there is a

custom based rule of *due diligence* imposed on all States in order that activities carried out within their jurisdiction do not cause damage to the environment of other States.[113]

These provisions may, however, be distinguished in that they were not specifically addressing ultra-hazardous activities. Whilst it cannot therefore be stated with certainty that, in the absence of an express treaty provision, States have an "absolute" or even strict obligation to prevent transboundary nuclear harm, such a conclusion receives considerable support from the authorities. It is also an acceptable conclusion on policy grounds: nuclear harm is likely to be particularly serious and an "absolute" duty acts as an incentive to States to take special precautions when engaging in nuclear activities.

2.5   Liability and Compensation[114]

2.5.1   Introduction

It is a well established principle of international law, now recognized in Article 1 of the ILC's Draft Articles on State Responsibility,[115] that every international wrongful act of a State entails the international responsibility of that State.

---

[111] *Supra* n. 31 at Article 2.

[112] *Supra* n. 32 at Title B, paragraph 2.

[113] OECD, Report by the Environment Committee, *Responsibility and Liability of States in Relation to Transfrontier Pollution* (1984) at p. 4.

[114] See e.g. Whiteman, *Damages in International Law*, 3 vols., 1937-1943; Mann, "The Consequences of an International Wrong in International and National Law", 48 *BYIL*, 1978, p. 1; Brownlie, *op. cit.* n. 90 at pp. 199-241, especially pp. 222-7; Dupuy & Smets, "Compensation for Damage due to Transfrontier Pollution", in OECD, *Compensation for Pollution Damage*, at pp. 181-208 (1981); OECD Environment Committee, *Responsibility and Liability of States in Relation to Transfrontier Pollution* (1984); IAEA, Note by the Director General, *supra* n. 68; IAEA, Note by the Director General, *supra* n. 70 at Annex 2.

[115] [1977] II *Ybk ILC* (*UN Doc.* A/CN.4/302).

The principle that a breach of an international legal obligation creates a further obligation, or a liability,[116] to make reparation is also well established. In the *Chorzów Factory* case the Permanent Court of International Justice (PCIJ) stated that:

> it is a principle of international law, and even a general conception of law, that any breach of an engagement involves an obligation to make reparation. In judgment no. 8 (1927) (PCIJ, Ser. A, No. 9, p. 21) . . . the Court had already said that reparation was the indispensable complement of a failure to apply a convention, and there is no necessity for this to be stated in the convention itself.[117]

States have recognized the role liability has in the international arrangements for the prevention of transboundary nuclear harm. The Paris and Vienna Conventions, discussed below, regulate the liability for risks arising out of the peaceful uses of nuclear energy by creating a framework within which persons affected by nuclear damage may recover compensation in municipal courts. Beyond these Conventions there are no formal arrangements regarding inter-State liability or, with the exception of the Nordic Convention, requiring protection of the environment not including persons and property. Principle 22 of the Stockholm Declaration recognizes these gaps:

> States shall co-operate to develop further the international law regarding liability and compensation for the victims of pollution and other environmental damage caused by activities within the jurisdiction or control of such States to areas beyond their jurisdiction.[118]

Since 1972 little has been done to further develop the international law of liability and compensation. The OECD has set out, in its 1974 and 1977 Recommendations,[119] guiding principles for the Members of the OECD for harmonizing environmental policies in relation to transboundary pollution by, *inter alia*, establishing a regime of access to affected persons without

---

[116]The term "liability" in international law has been described in a number of ways. For Dupuy and Smets it means "the international obligation to compensate": *supra* n. 114 at p. 182. For Goldie, the meaning is wider in that it designates more generally "the consequences of a failure to perform [a] duty, or to fulfill the standards of performance required. That is, liability connotes exposure to legal redress once responsibility and injury arising from a failure to fulfill that legal responsibility have been established": "Concepts of Strict and Absolute Liability and the Ranking of Liability in Terms of Relative Exposure to Risk", 1985 *NYIL* p. 175, at 180.

[117]1928 PCIJ, Ser. A, No. 17, at p. 47.

[118]*Supra* n. 28.

[119]*Supra* nn. 32 and 33.

discrimination on the grounds of nationality to the courts of polluting States. The unwillingness of States to further develop this area is exemplified by the 1979 Convention.[120] Article 8 provides that Contracting Parties shall exchange available information on, inter alia, "(f) physico-chemical and biological data relating to the effects of long-range transboundary air-pollution and the extent of damage". To that provision is appended a footnote which expressly provides: "The present Convention does not contain a rule on State liability as to damage".

In the absence of an inter-State liability treaty applicable to transboundary nuclear harm, any such liability will be governed by the ordinary principles of State responsibility.

2.5.2   Personal Claims

The Paris and Vienna Conventions both seek to harmonize the national legislation of Contracting Parties with regard to third party liability and insurance against nuclear risks and to establish minimum standards to provide financial protection against nuclear damage. The Conventions are very similar, the only significant differences being in relation to their geographical and subject-matter scope and their provisions limiting the extent of liability. Both Conventions provide for the payment of compensation for nuclear damage upon proof that the damage has been caused by the operator of a nuclear installation.[121] The Paris Convention establishes a maximum liability for the operator[122] and the Vienna Convention allows the installation State to limit the liability of the operator to a stated amount.[123]

---

[120] Supra n. 31.

[121] Paris Convention, supra n. 93, Article 3; Vienna Convention, supra n. 95, Article II. Differences of definition affect the application of the Convention; e.g. whereas the Paris Convention does not apply to radioisotopes outside a nuclear installation (Article 1(a)(iv)), the Vienna Convention does not apply, in practice, to any radioisotopes (Article I(i)(g)). Compare generally Article 1 of the Paris Convention with Article I of the Vienna Convention.

[122] Supra n. 93 at Article 7(a) and (b). The maximum liability of 15 million European Monetary Agreement units of account has now been revised by the Brussels Supplementary Convention, reprinted below at No. 1, which increases the total compensation available to 120 million units of account. Further Protocols to the Paris Convention and the Brussels Supplementary Convention were adopted in 1982. They change the unit of compensation to SDR of the IMF and increase the compensation by a State and by the Parties to the Brussels Convention to 175 million SDR and 300 million SDR. The 1982 Protocols are not yet in force.

[123] Supra n. 95 at Article V(1)-(4).

To ensure payment of sums awarded by national courts, both Conventions require the operator to maintain insurance or other financial security.[124] Only the national courts of the Contracting Party in whose territory the nuclear incident occurred have jurisdiction over actions arising under the Conventions.[125] In order to provide protection to persons affected by transboundary nuclear harm, national courts are expressly prohibited from discriminating in the application of the law on grounds of nationality, domicile or residence.[126] Moreover, the judgment of the competent court will be enforceable in the territory of any Contracting Party,[127] and the jurisdictional immunity of a defendant State may not be invoked except for execution of the judgment.[128]

As the USSR is not a Party to either Convention their provisions are not applicable to the Chernobyl accident. Even if they were, the limits of liability which they establish would clearly be inadequate to cope with claims from all over Europe. In order to encourage wider participation in the Paris and Vienna Conventions, and to avoid the danger of their simultaneous application, following the Chernobyl accident the IAEA Standing Committee on Civil Liability for Nuclear Damage has endorsed[129] a draft Preamble[130] and two draft articles[131] aimed at harmonizing the Paris and Vienna Conventions. The two draft articles provide for the application of one Convention, to the exclusion of the other Convention, to a nuclear accident involving Parties to both Conventions; a determination of the applicable Convention according to the location of the nuclear installation of the operator liable; and the enumeration of all the provisions of each Convention which would be made applicable to the Parties to the other Convention.

The Paris and Vienna Conventions can be compared to the 1974 Nordic Convention, which provides that:

Any person who is affected or may be affected by a nuisance caused by environmentally harmful activities in another Contracting State shall have the right to bring before the appropriate Court or Administrative Authority of that State the question of the

---

[124] Paris Convention, Article 10; Vienna Convention, Article VIII.
[125] Paris Convention, Article 13(a); Vienna Convention, Article XI (1).
[126] Paris Convention, Article 14(c); Vienna Convention, Article XIII.
[127] Paris Convention, Article 13(d); Vienna Convention, Article XII(1), (2).
[128] Paris Convention, Article 13(e); Vienna Convention, Article XIV.
[129] ''The Question of International Liability Arising from a Nuclear Accident'', *IAEA Doc.* GOV/2305 at para. 8, 19 May 1987.
[130] *Id.* at Annex B.
[131] *Id.* at Annex C.

permissibility of such activities, including the question of measures to prevent damage[132]
. . .

This provision is equally applicable ''in the case of proceedings concerning compensation for damage caused by environmentally harmful activities''.[133] The Nordic Convention seems to be unique in giving private persons a right of action in all Contracting States to protect the environment as well as to seek compensation. The Convention does not impose a limit on the amount of compensation, providing only that the question ''shall not be judged by rules which are less favourable to the injured party than the rules of compensation of the State in which the activities are being carried out''.[134]

Finally, it should be pointed out that, in theory, civil claims may also be brought against a polluting State under the rules of private international law. It is likely to prove difficult in practice to get results by this route. Following the Chernobyl accident at least two claims have been brought in the State courts of the Federal Republic of Germany.[135] In one, a Berlin gardener brought a claim against the USSR for compensation for damage suffered to his allotment as a result of radioactive contamination from the Chernobyl fall-out. His claim was rejected by the District Court of Bonn on the basis that the person he had named as the defendant, the Soviet Ambassador to the Federal Republic, was not the USSR's representative for the purposes of this, a fiscal matter, and therefore not a proper defendant. This decision has been subject to an appeal. Moreover, the District Court held, the Ambassador would have been entitled to claim diplomatic immunity. In the other case, the Regional Court of Munich forwarded a similar claim for compensation against the USSR's Industrial Union for Atomic Energy to the Union's Ministry for Energy and Electrification of the USSR, in Moscow, via the Embassy of the Federal Republic.

2.5.3 Inter-State Claims

A number of governments, including those of the Federal Republic of Germany, the United Kingdom and Sweden, are known to have paid large sums of compensation to persons affected within their jurisdiction by the fall-

---

[132] *Supra* n. 34 at Article 3.
[133] *Id.*
[134] *Id.*
[135] See Mansel, ''Zustellung einer Klage in Sachen 'Tschernobyl' '', *IPrax* 1987, p. 210.

out from Chernobyl.[136] The payment of such compensation may give rise to a
claim for damages, in the absence of an inter-State liability treaty such as the
1972 Convention,[137] under the traditional rules of State responsibility.[138]
Under these rules a State will need to point to a breach of an international legal
obligation in order to claim "reparation", which term commonly refers to all
measures which a State may be required to make in the event of such a breach.
It includes payment of compensation, apology, punishment of individuals
responsible, steps to prevent a recurrence, and any other terms of
satisfaction.[139]

In the context of nuclear activity, as has been shown above, difficulties exist
in terms of defining precisely the extent of the obligations owed by States,
including the extent of the harm which they are under an obligation to
prevent, and the standard of care which they must take. This is one reason
why, to date, no State has made a formal claim against the USSR following
the Chernobyl accident. According to the Swedish Government:

In terms of treaties there is no international agreement existing, whether bilateral or
multilateral, on the basis of which a Swedish claim for damages against the USSR
could be conceived.

Insofar as customary international law is concerned, principles exist which might be
invoked to support a claim against the USSR. The issues involved, however, are
complex from the legal as well as the technical point of view and warrant careful
consideration.

In the present circumstances, the Government has felt that priority should be given,
in the wake of the Chernobyl accident, to endeavors of another nature.[140]

A number of States, including the Federal Republic of Germany, are known

---

[136] By 1 December 1987 the Government of the United Kingdom had paid
£4,950,199 compensation under the scheme set up by the Food Protection Orders, see
supra nn. 84-86 (figure supplied by Ministry of Agriculture, Fisheries and Food); the
Government of the Federal Republic of Germany had paid DM390 million
compensation under the Equity Guidelines, see *supra* nn. 79-82 (figures supplied by
London Embassy of the Federal Republic of Germany). The Government of Sweden
had paid SK204 million compensation to farmers, up to 30 June 1987, and SK117
million to the reindeer industry during the budget year 1986/87 (figures supplied by
Swedish Embassy in London).
[137] *Supra* n. 100.
[138] See generally Brownlie, *op. cit.* n. 90; Eagleton, *The Responsibility of States in
International Law* (1928).
[139] Brownlie, *Principles of Public International Law*, 3rd ed. (1979) p. 457.
[140] Correspondence with the Swedish Embassy in London, 10 December 1987.

to have reserved their right to make a claim and have taken part in talks with the USSR on this question.[141]

The position of the Government of the United Kingdom is complicated by outstanding disputes relating to the problem of acid rain in Scandinavia, contamination of the Irish Sea by nuclear waste from the Windscale/Sellafield nuclear plant, and alleged damage to Australian territory from the nuclear tests carried out by the United Kingdom in the 1950s. On 21 July 1986 the Secretary of State for Foreign and Commonwealth Affairs in a written answer in the House of Commons said:

On 10 July we formally reserved our right with the Soviet Government to claim compensation on our own behalf on behalf of our citizens for any losses suffered as a consequence of the accident at Chernobyl. The presentation of a formal claim, should we decide to make one, would not take place until the nature and full extent of any damage suffered had been assessed.[142]

Three months later the Minister of State for Agriculture, Fisheries and Food stated that:

We have reserved our position on whether the USSR will be required—as it should be if the case is proved—to pay compensation.[143]

More recently the position has been put thus by the Parliamentary Under-Secretary of State for Scotland:

The USSR is not a party to any of the international conventions relating to third party liability in nuclear energy, and is therefore not subject to any specific treaty obligation to compensate for damage caused outside its national boundaries.[144]

The possibility of a claim against the USSR has been left open by these States. Some authority for the view that a claim for compensation will lie in the event of radioactive harm is to be found in diplomatic practice relating to atmospheric nuclear tests. In 1958 the Japanese Government stated in a Note that:

in the event the United States Government conducts nuclear tests in defiance of the request of the Japanese Government, the United States Government has the

---

[141] Communication between the Embassy of the Federal Republic of Germany in London and the Editor, 8 December 1987.
[142] Hansard, House of Commons, 21 July 1986, Vol. 102, c. 5 (W).
[143] Hansard, House of Commons, 24 October 1986, Vol. 102, c. 1455.
[144] Hansard, House of Commons, 16 November 1987, Vol. 122, c. 894.

responsibility of compensating for economic losses that may be caused by the establishment of a danger zone and for all losses and damages that may be inflicted on Japan and the Japanese people as a result of the nuclear tests.[145]

In 1966 the New Zealand Government reserved its right to hold the French Government "responsible for the damage or losses incurred as a result of" atmospheric nuclear tests carried out by France in the South Pacific.[146] While the difference between an atmospheric nuclear test, which is deliberate, and a nuclear accident, which is not, seems clear enough, the cause of action may well be the same: raising the levels of radioactivity in neighbouring States to a harmful level; liability will then turn, in part, on whether the obligation imposed by international law is absolute or dependent on fault.

In the event that a claim is made, the PCIJ in the *Chorzów Factory* case has established a measure of compensation which might be relied upon by States in assessing the quantum of the claim:

the essential principle contained in the actual notion of an illegal act—a principle which seems to be established by international practice and in particular by the decisions of arbitral tribunals—is that reparation must, as far as possible, wipe out all the consequences of the illegal act and establish the situation which would in all probability have existed if that act had not been committed.[147]

These consequences are not easy to show. The difficulties of proving damage and loss, in particular to human health over the long term, are considerable.[148] Three precedents, however, relating to compensation payments made for transboundary damage suffered as a result of an ultra-hazardous activity, suggest that it is possible to quantify some of the consequences in monetary terms.

In the *Trail Smelter* case, the Arbitral Tribunal awarded an indemnity of US $78,000 for damage to cleared and uncleared land used for crops and timber.[149] The Tribunal denied a US claim for damage to livestock and property in the town of Northport, holding that the US had failed to prove that the existence of fumes from the smelter had caused the damage.[150] The Tribunal similarly denied the US claim for damage to business enterprise as

---

[145] Whiteman, *Digest of International Law*, Vol. 4, p. 585.
[146] ICJ Pleadings, *Nuclear Test* cases, II (*New Zealand v. France*), p. 22.
[147] *Supra* n. 114 at 47.
[148] See the findings of the ICRP, *supra* n. 73, at pp. 12-14; also Moser, "Proof of Damage from Ionizing Radiation", 38 *NLB* 70 (1986) at pp. 71-7.
[149] *Supra* n. 47 at 1924-31.
[150] *Id.* at 1931.

being "too indirect, remote and uncertain to be appraised and not for such which an indemnity can be awarded".[151] The Tribunal also rejected the US claim for damage for "violation of sovereignty".[152]

In January 1955 the US Government paid $2 million to Japan for "purposes of compensation for the injuries or damage sustained" by Japanese nationals as a result of thermonuclear tests carried out by the US near the Marshall Islands in March 1954.[153] The payments were made "*ex gratia*" and "without reference to the question of legal liability".[154]

More recently, in April 1981, the USSR agreed to pay, and Canada to accept, Canadian $3 million in final settlement of the Canadian claim for damage incurred by way of expense in locating, recovering, removing and testing radioactive debris and cleaning up affected areas following the crash of Cosmos 954 in January 1978. In calculating the claims Canada relied partly on Article II of the 1972 Convention and partly on

general principles of international law according to which fair compensation is to be paid, by including in its claim only those costs that are reasonable, proximately caused by the intrusion of the satellite and deposit of debris and capable of being calculated with a reasonable degree of certainty.[155]

These precedents suggest that where a nuclear accident occurs international law requires the payment of compensation for damage and loss to persons and property in a neighbouring State which can reasonably be calculated to arise as a result of increased radioactivity levels caused by the accident. The German Equity Guideline of 2 June 1986[156] illustrates the type of damage to property for which compensation might be paid.

2.6   Recent Developments

Following the Chernobyl accident two views have emerged on how best to develop the law on international liability for nuclear damage.[157] The first is

[151] *Supra* n. 47 at 1931.

[152] *Id.* at 1932-3.

[153] See Margolis, "The Hydrogen Bomb Experiments and International Law", 64 *Yale LJ* 629 at pp. 638-9 (1955); Brownlie, "A Survey of International Customary Rules of Environmental Protection", in Teclaff and Utton, *International Environmental Law* (1974) p. 1 at 2-4.

[154] Margolis, *op. cit.* at p. 639.

[155] See *supra* at p. 20; and n. 102 at para. 23.

[156] *Supra* n. 81.

[157] See *IAEA Doc.* GOV/INF/509 at para. 2.

that the Paris and Vienna Conventions, if harmonized and perhaps simultaneously applied, are sufficient, and that wider acceptance of them should be encouraged. The second is that, as both Conventions address liability primarily under civil law, limiting themselves to the liability of individuals or juridical persons for damage resulting in loss of life or for damage to the property of individuals, there is

a need to consider the broader question of international liability for the injurious consequences of activities attributable to states in the context of their relations *inter se* and hence to elaborate—in a new multilateral instrument—the principle of international liability for nuclear damage under the law of State responsibility concerning international claims against States.[158]

The Board of Governors of the IAEA, having considered a background paper by the Secretariat on the question of international liability for nuclear damage,[159] in February 1987, asked the Secretariat, "to consider whether it was necessary to devise a new instrument on State liability for nuclear damage . . . full account being taken of the work of the [ILC]".[160]

The Secretariat concluded that "there seems to be no doctrinal obstacle to the elaboration of special rules intended to regulate international liability for nuclear damage".[161] The rules might result from the work of the ILC.[162] It suggested that a new international instrument

could have a double purpose: it could complement the existing civil law conventions on nuclear liability . . . in those areas where their regimes are incomplete because of legal lacunae (claims between States, damage to the environment) and it could provide the necessary framework for possibly combining international liability aspects and the issues already covered by the Vienna and Paris Conventions into a comprehensive nuclear liability regime, giving the parties to either of these instruments the option of providing remedies in accordance with appropriate procedures to be embodied within the framework.[163]

---

[158] *Id.*

[159] *Id.* The Secretariat's analysis is set out in the Annex, Parts I ("The Civil Law Regimes of the Paris and Vienna Conventions") and II ("International Liability Regime Based on the Law of State Responsibility").

[160] *IAEA Doc.* GOV/2306 at para. 1. The ILC work referred to is on "International Liability for Injurious Consequences Arising Out of Acts not Prohibited by International Law". See below at pp. 183-4, 190-1.

[161] *Supra* n. 157, Annex 2 at para. 3.

[162] *Id.*, Annex 2 at para. 2.

[163] *Id.*, Annex 2 at para. 4.

The Secretariat suggested that any such liability convention should address the following issues: State liability for damage caused by private activities; a procedural mechanism for the presentation of claims; the form of liability;[164] the extent of liability;[165] intervention levels; responsibility for political and moral damage; and damage to the environment. The Chernobyl accident has given fresh impetus to these proposals, which have widespread support. In its Proposal[166] the USSR has also suggested that:

A possible multilateral legal instrument could envisage the liability of States for international damage in terms of the transboundary effects of nuclear accidents, as well as for material, moral and political damage caused by unwarranted action taken under the pretext of protection against the consequences of nuclear accidents (the spreading of untrue information, introduction of unjustified restrictive measures, etc.).

Much of this work will be drawn from the ILC study, begun in 1978, of ''International Liability for Injurious Consequences Arising out of Acts not Prohibited by International Law''.[167] The Special Rapporteur, Robert Quentin-Baxter, produced, as an Annex to the Fourth Report, a Schematic Outline[168] which contains the ILC primary obligations covering the prevention and minimizing of physical transboundary harm and the provision of reparation. The Schematic Outline was clearly developed with Chernobyl-type situations in mind and is now being relied upon by the Secretariat of the IAEA:

It had become a common place that scientific and technological advances had multiplied the circumstances in which legitimate activities entailed the possibility—or even the certainty—of transboundary harm.[169]

These legitimate activities included the ''development and use of nuclear energy, including the operation of nuclear installations.''[170]

[164] The Secretariat considers that this could only be strict, objective or absolute liability: id. at para. 9. For the literature on the standard of care, see supra n. 92.
[165] The choice is seen to be between a high ceiling or strict liability, and a general limitation on liability in view of the fact that the former might make it impossible for operators to obtain financial security (insurance) coverage: id. at paras. 11-14.
[166] Supra n. 20.
[167] For the background and literature relating to this study, see below at pp. 183-4, 190-1.
[168] Reprinted below at No. 13.
[169] Quentin-Baxter (Special Rapporteur), ''Fourth Report on International Liability for Injurious Consequences arising out of Acts not Prohibited by International Law'', Ybk ILC 1983, Vol. II (Part One), p. 201 at para. 1.
[170] Id. at p. 202, footnote 8.

The Schematic Outline has as its aim the establishment of a regime consisting of a network of simple rules that yield reasonably clear answers; . . . the second aim is to provide for a method of settlement that is reasonably fair, and that does not frighten States, when there is no applicable or agreed regime.[171]

It governs activities within the territory and control of a State which

give rise or may give rise to loss or injury to persons or things within the territory or control of another State.[172]

In such circumstances the acting State is obligated to provide all relevant and available information to the affected State.[173] Unless the States concerned agree otherwise, they are to establish joint fact finding machinery designed to produce a non-binding report containing recommended solutions.[174] In the absence of such machinery, States concerned have a duty to begin the negotiations, "with a view to determining whether a regime is necessary and what form it should take".[175] In the event of loss or injury:

Reparation shall be made by the acting State to the affected State . . . unless it is established that the making of reparation for a loss or injury of that kind or character is not in accordance with the shared expectations of those States.[176]

The Schematic Outline also sets out a number of factors which should be considered when assessing the activities of States[177] and the matters, including compensation as a means of reparation, which might be relevant in negotiations concerning prevention and reparation in relation to transboundary harm.[178]

3. Information[179]

3.1 Introduction

The Chernobyl accident raises a number of questions relating to the

[171] Id. at para. 69.
[172] Supra n. 168 at Section 1.1.
[173] Id. at Section 2.1.
[174] Id. at Section 2.6.
[175] Id. at Section 3.1.
[176] Id. at Section 4.
[177] Id. at Section 6.
[178] Id. at Section 7.
[179] See Dominick, "Notification", in Bernhardt (ed.), Encyclopaedia of Public International Law, Vol. 9 (1985) p. 288.

provision of information by States establishing or operating nuclear installations to States which are or may be affected by the establishment or operation of such installations. The most important is whether a State is under any obligation to warn all other States which are or might be affected by a nuclear accident causing transboundary radioactive harm and, if so, what is the extent of that obligation. This has been described as "the main legal issue involved in the Chernobyl nuclear disaster".[180]

A related question is whether a State is under any obligation to provide neighbouring States with information on the planned or actual operation of a nuclear installation.

3.2   Pre-accident Information

Since the early 1970s States have increasingly recognized the need to protect the environment. UN General Assembly Resolution 2995[181] on "Co-operation between States in the Field of the Environment" recognizes that such cooperation towards the implementation of Principles 21 and 22 of the Stockholm Declaration:[182]

will be effectively achieved if official and public knowledge is provided of the technical data relating to the work to be carried out by States within their national jurisdiction, with a view to avoiding significant harm that may occur in the environment of the adjacent area.

Similarly the 1974 OECD Recommendation[183] provides that:

Prior to the initiation in a country of works or undertakings which might create a significant risk of transfrontier pollution, this country should provide early information to other countries which are or may be affected.

The 1977 OECD Recommendation also recommends the provision of prior information.[184] A number of treaties require prior information and

---

[180] Provisional Report of the Rapporteur, 20th Commission IDI, "Air Pollution Across National Frontiers", 62 *Annuaire IDI*, I, p. 178 (1987).

[181] Reprinted below at No. 6. The Resolution received 112 votes in favour, 0 against and 10 abstentions.

[182] *Supra* n. 28.

[183] *Supra* n. 32 at para. 6.

[184] *Supra* n. 33 at para. 8.

consultation in relation to potentially harmful activities. The 1974 Nordic Convention requires consultations to take place between States concerned by the "permissibility of environmentally harmful activities which entail or may entail considerable nuisance in another Contracting State".[185] In addition a number of States have entered into bilateral treaties relating to nuclear safety in border areas.[186] By way of example, the 1980 Agreement between Spain and Portugal on Co-operation in Matters Affecting the Safety of Nuclear Installations in the Vicinity of the Frontier[187] provides (Article 2) that:

The competent authorities of the constructor country shall notify the neighbouring country of applications for licences for the siting, construction or operation of nuclear installations in the vicinity of the frontier which are submitted to them . . .

Article 3 provides that comments and observations by the neighbouring country must be taken into account before the licence is issued.

Is the provision of prior information now required by customary international law? The Montreal Rules[188] and the IDI Resolution[189] both take the view, respectively, that customary law does, and should, require States planning activities which might entail a significant risk of transfrontier pollution to give early notice to States likely to be affected and to enter into good faith consultations at the request of such a State. However, the present writer does not share the view of the ILA. While it may be desirable, it is not yet supported by the requisite State practice or by *opinio juris*.

3.3   Post-accident Information

The provision of immediate information following a nuclear accident is crucial in reducing to a minimum the harm from a radioactive release and thereby the loss in the event of a claim for damage. The ICRP has identified three time phases which are common to all accidents: the early, intermediate and recovery phases.[190] The early phase includes the first few hours after the accident and the intermediate phase "covers that period of time from the first

---

[185] *Supra* n. 34 at Article 11.
[186] See list set out at p. 178 below.
[187] Reprinted below at No. 11.
[188] *Supra* n. 64 at Articles 6 and 7. The Rapporteur, Professor Dietrich Rauschning, concluded that "recent State practice shows that information is not usually withheld": ILA, *Report of the 59th Conference* (1982, London) at p. 545.
[189] *Supra* n. 66 at Article 8(1).
[190] *Supra* n. 73 at p. 3.

few hours to a few days after the onset of the accident".[191] It is only during these two phases that countermeasures against radiation damage, such as the provision of shelter, administering stable iodine and evacuating the threatened population, are possible.[192] A failure to provide immediate information after an accident creates confusion, increases the difficulty of knowing what appropriate measures affected States ought to take, and may lead to biologically serious consequences.[193]

The advent of new technologies, in particular international communication systems, has made possible the fast and efficient flow of information between States. Moreover, States have established emergency notification systems in other contexts:

> The provision of early warning procedures for the timely implementation of measures to protect the public against both natural and man-made hazards and accidents is a well-established practice. Typhoons, dam failure, and high volume storage of toxic gaseous materials are typical of the potential hazards for which pre-established warning and emergency measures exist in many countries. Similar provisions should be expected for any nuclear facility or activity where there exists the possibility of harm in the event of a serious plant malfunction, nuclear accident, or radiological emergency. As with other industrial or natural hazards, it is necessary, when planning an appropriate emergency response and notification system, to take into account the consequences of the event at various distances from its initiating point, including, where relevant, any effect in neighbouring or other countries.[194]

The question arises: are States under an international legal obligation to provide immediate information of a radioactive release which may have transboundary effects?

Members are required to provide the IAEA with such information which could, in the Members' judgment, be helpful to the IAEA,[195] and to provide the WHO with "such additional information pertaining to health as may be practicable".[196]

In relation to the Chernobyl accident the only applicable treaty is the 1979 Convention, which provides, in Article 5, that:

[191] *Supra* n. 73 at p. 4.
[192] *Id.* at Table 1, p. 8.
[193] *Id.* at p. 16.
[194] Collins, Emmerson & Phuong, "Information Exchange and Mutual Emergency Assistance", 28 *IAEA Bulletin*, No. 3, p. 16 (1986).
[195] Statute of the IAEA, 276 *UNTS* 3, at Article 8.
[196] Statute of the WHO, 14 *UNTS* 185, at Article 65.

Consultations shall be held, upon request, at an early stage between, on the one hand, Contracting Parties which are actually affected by or exposed to a significant risk of long-range transboundary air pollution and, on the other hand, Contracting Parties within which and subject to whose jurisdiction a significant contribution to long-range transboundary air pollution originates, or could originate, in connexion with activities carried on or contemplated therein.[197]

Articles 4 and 8 of that Convention also require only exchanges of information and again these are of a general nature.

None of these provisions are usefully applicable to Chernobyl-type situations. They leave to States a significant degree of discretion in relation to the quantity, type and nature of the information to be provided, as well as its timing, and none could be interpreted as creating an obligation to provide immediate information.

A number of treaties lay down a duty to warn potentially affected States in case of nuclear and other emergencies,[198] and several States have entered into bilateral agreements creating a framework within which emergency information is to be provided in the event of a nuclear accident.[199] Thus, the 1983 Exchange of Notes between the United Kingdom and France Concerning Exchanges of Information in the Event of Emergencies Occurring in One of the Two States which could have Radiological Consequences for the Other State[200] provides that:

Each State-Party shall inform the other without delay of any emergency which occurs in its State as a result of civil activities which may have radiological consequences liable to affect the other State.

The information is to be communicated through reciprocal warning centres which are capable of receiving and transmitting information 24 hours a day.

---

[197] *Supra* n. 31.
[198] See for example the 1972 Agreement between the United States and Canada concerning the Great Lakes' Water Quality, 508 *UNTS* 26; 1983 Agreement between Federal Republic of Germany and the German Democratic Republic on Principles Covering Damage at the Border, *Bulletin Presse und Informationsamt der Bundesregierung*, No. 115 (September 1983).
[199] See the list set out at p. 198 below.
[200] Reprinted below at No. 14. The United Kingdom has signed similar agreements with Denmark, on 19 November 1987, and with Norway, on 24 November 1987, and is currently engaged in talks with the Irish Republic and the USSR. The Portugal-Spain Agreement contains a similar provision; *supra* n. 187 at Article 9.

Does customary law require the provision of immediate information in the event of a nuclear emergency? Again, both the Montreal Rules[201] and the IDI Resolution[202] refer to such a rule although the evidence of State practice is hardly overwhelming. Certainly there are a number of non-binding guidelines and recommendations which require the provision of such information. The OECD has recommended that:

Countries should promptly warn other potentially affected countries of any situation which may cause any sudden increase in the level of pollution in areas outside the country of origin of pollution . . .[203]

Principle 9 of the UNEP Principles makes similar provision.[204]

In 1985 the IAEA drew up its Guidelines on Reportable Events, Integrated Planning and Information Exchange in a Transboundary Release of Radioactive Materials (Information Guidelines).[205] These recommend that in the event of a potential or actual release of radioactive material, which might or has crossed an international boundary and which could be of radiological safety significance,[206] there should be a timely exchange of adequate information between the competent national authorities of the State in which the plant is situated and the authorities in neighbouring States.[207] This information should relate to the site, the facility, the emergency response plan and the response to an emergency,[208] and in the event of an off-site emergency should include the nature and time of the accident, the characteristics of the release and meteorological and hydrological conditions.[209]

Following the Chernobyl accident many States maintained that the obligation to provide emergency information was a rule of international law. Much of the criticism of the USSR's failure to provide information immediately after the accident was couched in legal terms.[210] The Director

---

[201] *Supra* n. 64 at Article 7.
[202] *Supra* n. 66 at Article 9(1)(a).
[203] *Supra* n. 32.
[204] *Supra* n. 30.
[205] Reprinted below at No. 16.
[206] *Id.* at para. 3.1.
[207] *Id.* at para. 4.1.1.
[208] *Id.* at para. 4.1.2.
[209] *Id.* at para. 4.3.2.
[210] See for example the US Secretary of State: ''When an incident has cross border implications, there is an obligation under international law to inform others and do it promptly'', in Final Report of the Rapporteur (do Nascimento e Silva), Twentieth

General of the IAEA noted the failure of the Soviet system to inform its own citizens and neighbouring countries of a release which would affect them, the late implementation of the emergency measures and the apparent failure to warn immediately.[211] And during the negotiation of the Notification Convention, support for the view that there was a legal obligation to provide information under customary law was expressed on a number of occasions.[212] It is almost impossible to find a writer who reaches an opposite conclusion:

> The duty to inform in cases of emergency involving a risk of transfrontier damage is an undeniable rule of international law. Therefore, its existence does not depend on a future treaty as envisaged in the framework of the [IAEA].[213]

> The duty of the emitting State to promptly warn all potentially affected States in the case of suddenly aggravating environmental pollution might be considered as a duty to reduce the damage based on customary international law . . . at least in those cases where pollution presents a substantial and present danger to the nationals of the neighbouring State. In the case of accidents in nuclear reactors this requirement might always be met if radio-active radiation is released to a large extent. The necessary safety measures can be taken only if the warning is effected promptly. Insofar, an ultra hazardous activity implies at least a duty to promptly warn in cases of emergency.[214]

Humanitarian principles also require the provision of information to people who might be affected by a nuclear accident. The ICJ has recently reaffirmed

---

Commission IDI, ''Air Pollution across National Frontiers'', 62 *Annuaire IDI*, I at p. 259. See also the Statement of the Group of Seven: ''Each country . . . is responsible for prompt provision of detailed and complete information on nuclear emergencies and accidents, in particular those with potential transboundary consequences. Each of our countries accepts that responsibility . . .'', *supra* n. 69 at para. 2.

[211] Speech by the Director General of the IAEA to the International Press Institute, Vienna, 13 May 1986. Transcript provided by the IAEA.

[212] See Statement of US representative at Final Plenary Meeting of Governmental Experts on 15 August 1986, *supra* n. 18 at p. 4; Chinese representative at p. 5; Japanese representative at p. 21. The Chairman of the meeting of Governmental Experts at the Final Plenary Session on 15 August 1986 stated, in his summing up, that ''the [Notification and Assistance] conventions are not intended to derogate from any international obligations on early notification and assistance that may already exist under international law''. *Id.*, Annex VI at p. 2.

[213] Professor Dietrich Rauschning, as quoted in Final Report, Twentieth Commission IDI, *supra* n. 210 at p. 259.

[214] *Id.* at p. 280 per Mr Walter Rudolf.

the view that a substantive legal rule can be derived from the principle of humanity:[215]

if a State lays mines in any waters whatever in which the vessels of another State have rights of access or passage, and fails to give any warning or notification whatsoever, in disregard of the security of peaceful shipping, it commits a breach of the principles of humanitarian law.[216]

While these facts differ from those relating to a nuclear accident, most notably in relation to the matter of the intent of the acting State, a similar principle of humanity, requiring notification, could be said to apply to the danger to the security of citizens in foreign countries arising from a transboundary release of radioactive material.

3.4 1986 Notification Convention

The failure of the USSR to provide immediate information led to prompt action. Under the auspices of the IAEA the Notification Convention[217] was drawn up and opened for signature within six months of the Chernobyl accident.

The Convention incorporates many of the recommendations set out in the Information Guidelines and applies in the event of any "accident involving facilities or activities of a State Party or of persons or legal entities under its jurisdiction or control".[218] In the event of such an accident States Parties are required to notify, directly or through the IAEA, those States which are or may be physically affected with details of the accident, its nature, time of occurrence and exact location.[219] They are also to promptly provide the States, directly or through the IAEA, and the IAEA with such available information as relevant to minimize the radiological consequences in those

---

[215] *Case Concerning Military and Paramilitary Activities In and Against Nicaragua* (*Nicaragua* v. *United States*) (Merits), *ICJ Rep.* 1986, p. 1.

[216] *Id.* at p. 112. The principles of humanity were expressed by the ICJ in the earlier *Corfu Channel* case, *supra* n. 25, p. 22.

[217] Reprinted below at No. 21.

[218] *Id.* at Article 1(i). The Convention only applies to certain "facilities and activities": see Article 1(2). In October 1987 an accident occurred in Brazil when abandoned radiotherapy equipment was broken open by a scrap metal dealer. This led to widespread radioactive contamination and the death of a number of people: see *The Financial Times*, 8 October 1987. It is unclear whether the Convention applies to such "activities": see Article 1(2)(e).

[219] *Id.* at Article 2.

States.[220] This includes the cause and foreseeable development of the accident, the general characteristics of the radioactive release (including its nature, form, quantity, composition and effective weight), current and future meteorological and hydrological conditions, planned or taken protective measures, and the predicted behaviour over time of the release.[221] Such information is to be supplemented at "appropriate intervals" by the provision of relevant information including the foreseeable or actual termination of the emergency situation.[222] States should also respond "promptly" to a request for further information or consultations sought by an affected State.[223]

According to one writer the substantive provisions of the Notification Convention, imposing a clear obligation on States to provide immediate, regular and detailed information relating to the actual or potential transborder release of radioactive material, merely reflect pre-existing customary international law and in some parts are less stringent.[224] The significance of the Convention is that it is the first multilateral agreement to provide a detailed framework for the application of clearly identified rules requiring the provision of information in emergency situations, involving a role for the national authorities of States Parties[225] and the IAEA, as well as a binding dispute settlement mechanism.[226]

It is not, however, exhaustive, nor immune from a number of important criticisms. First, the Convention applies only to non-military nuclear accidents.[227] Second, certain of the recommendations contained in the Information Guidelines were not included.[228] In particular, the recommendation in Chapter III that "intervention levels for the introduction of protective measures such as sheltering and evacuation be set in advance by

---

[220] Id.

[221] Id. at Article 5(1).

[222] Id. at Article 5(2).

[223] Id. at Article 6.

[224] See Silagi, "Völkerrechtliche Verpflichtungen des Genehmigungsstaates bei Stör- und Unfällen", in Pelzer (ed.), Friedliche Kernenergienutzung und Staatsgrenzen in Mitteleuropa (1987).

[225] Id. at Article 7.

[226] Id. at Article 11.

[227] The five nuclear weapons States have declared that they will voluntarily apply the Convention to all nuclear accidents, irrespective of origin: see Statement of Voluntary Application, reprinted below at No. 21. On 6 October 1986, shortly after the Notification Convention was opened for signature, the USSR provided information about an accident on board one of its nuclear-powered submarines which might have radiological consequences: see The Independent, 7 October 1987, at p. 1.

[228] Supra n. 205.

competent national authorities''[229] has not been included in the Convention. In addition the whole of Chapter V, on "Integrated Planning" has been excluded. Third, the reference in Article 1(1) to an accident that "could be of radiological safety significance for another State" leaves it to the discretion of the State in whose territory or under whose jurisdiction or control the accident has occurred to determine what is or is not of radiological safety significance and what are the chances that another State would be affected.[230] Given the dangers of radioactivity it would have been preferable that all radioactive releases be notified to the IAEA. Failing that, there should be an agreed level which would trigger the obligation to provide information. Fourth, a number of States have entered reservations restricting the application of the Convention.[231] Most relate to the non-applicability of the dispute settlement provision, but some relate to the substantive provisions. Thus, the Government of the People's Republic of China stated that the Convention did not apply to cases caused by "gross negligence".[232]

Finally, the Convention does not establish any obligation on States giving or receiving information to make it available to members of the public. The 1985 IAEA Guidelines noted that:

Dissemination of information to the public is an important responsibility of the appropriate authorities in each State. Particular arrangements ensuring the necessary co-ordination across international borders should be established.[233]

The 1974 Nordic Convention also recognizes the need to inform the public and requires certain information to be published ''in the local newspaper or in some other suitable manner'' where necessary on account of public or private interests.[234]

Nuclear operators have also recognized the need for closer cooperation and the sharing of information among themselves. On 6 October 1987 representatives of almost all nuclear electricity producers in the world resolved

---

[229] *Supra* n. 205 at para. 3.5.

[230] On 4 December 1987 the Communist Party of the USSR announced that radiation exposure was still a problem at the Chernobyl plant and that during 1987 three fatal accidents had occurred: see *The Financial Times*, 5 December 1987. The USSR appears to have taken the view that the dangers leading to these fatalities were not of ''radiological safety significance to other States'' and therefore did not require immediate notification under the Convention.

[231] See below at pp. 246-60.

[232] *Id.* at p. 248.

[233] *Supra* n. 205 at para. 4.5.1.

[234] *Supra* n. 34 at Article 7.

to establish the Association of Nuclear Operators (ANO) whose mission would be to maximize the safe operation of nuclear power stations by, *inter alia*, "exchanging information, encouraging comparison, and stimulating emulation among nuclear power station operators".[235] The ANO will work closely with the IAEA. Among its more innovative proposals are the establishment of (1) direct communication links between nuclear operators; (2) information exchange on event and plant performance data; and (3) regional centres for the facilitation of information flows in Atlanta, Moscow, Paris and Tokyo.[236]

A final point concerning the provision of information relates to the responsibility of the mass media in the reporting of matters such as the Chernobyl accident. The reporting in the Western press was criticized by the USSR as being untruthful and creating mistrust. This point has been taken by the Director General of the IAEA, who has questioned the media's handling of the Chernobyl accident and noted the responsibility of the news reporter:

The Soviet reporting was late, meagre but probably not untrue. The Western reporting was fast, massive and often misleading, notably in casualty figures. Can there not be anything in between?[237]

The USSR has since proposed that the spreading of untrue information might entail the liability of States[238] and the IAEA Secretariat has noted the possibility of including in a new instrument "an obligation to refrain from actions which might exacerbate the consequences of a nuclear accident".[239]

4. Assistance

4.1 Introduction

The need for information is related to the response of third States in

---

[235] Resolution of the International Nuclear Utility Executive Meeting in Paris, 5/6 October 1987, in CEGB Document, December 1987.

[236] See generally *ANO Doc.* SC/P2 of 2 December 1987. The ANO is due to come into existence on 1 January 1989. Its legal status is currently under consideration.

[237] *Supra* n. 211.

[238] *Supra* n. 20.

[239] *Supra* n. 157 at paras. 18-19. Any State which feels particularly aggrieved at the treatment it has received at the hands of a foreign news report might wish to consider adhering to the 1953 Convention on the International Right of Correction (435 *UNTS* 191). This Convention provides States directly affected by a report, which they consider false or distorted and which is disseminated by an information agency, the possibility of securing commensurate publicity for its correction.

providing assistance to States affected by a radioactive release. The need to provide such assistance has been recognized and characterizes most significant radioactive releases:

A serious nuclear accident may require a substantial response effort to effect the recovery of both the plant and the off-site situation. This effort could tax the resources of the country in which the accident occurs, and in some countries might well be beyond their capability to mount an effective response . . . Arrangements for enhancing the national capability through the provision of advisory, technical, or material assistance from other countries having the requisite expertise appears, therefore, to be highly desirable.[240]

Desirable as it may be, there is no obligation under international law for a State to provide assistance in the event of a major disaster, nuclear or otherwise. States may, of course, offer assistance on humanitarian grounds, as was the case after the Chernobyl accident. The provision of such assistance nevertheless raises certain legal questions. The most important relate to the direction and control of the assistance; the reimbursement of any costs incurred; the attribution of liability in the event of damage being suffered by the assisting State in the course of assistance; and the liability of the assisting State for damage it might cause during the course of assistance, including any privileges and immunities attaching to the assisting State. These questions require clear answers if the provision of assistance is to be encouraged.

It is in this context that some States have entered into treaties intended to facilitate the provision of assistance by third States. The earliest such treaty is the 1963 Nordic Mutual Emergency Assistance Agreement in connection with Radiation Accidents.[241] It contains provisions relating to the general terms of assistance,[242] the advisory and coordinating role of the IAEA,[243] financing,[244] liability,[245] and privileges and immunities.[246] Assisting Parties undertake not to make public or communicate information relating to the accident without the consent of the requesting State.[247]

---

[240] Collins, Emmerson & Phuong, *supra* n. 194 at p. 16.
[241] Reprinted below at No. 4.
[242] *Id.* at Article I.
[243] *Id.* at Article II.
[244] *Id.* at Article III.
[245] *Id.* at Article IV.
[246] *Id.* at Article VI.
[247] *Id.* at Article VII.

To encourage the provision of assistance at times of disaster, in 1971 the UN General Assembly, by Resolution 2816 (XXVI),[248] established a Disaster Relief Co-ordinator and endorsed the UN Secretary-General's proposals for a permanent office. The UN Disaster Relief Office (UNDRO) became operational on 1 March 1972. It has provided general assistance in pre-disaster planning and has taken limited action when national disasters have occurred. Resolution 2816 also invites potential donor governments to "consider and to continue offering on a wider basis, emergency assistance in disaster situations" and "to inform the Disaster Relief Co-ordinator in advance about the facilities and services they might be in a position to provide immediately".[249]

The IAEA has recognized for some time that "the speed of initial response to a nuclear accident or radiological emergency could be crucial in minimizing the extent of the physical damage and the subsequent release of radioactive material".[250] In 1977 the IAEA concluded an agreement with the UNDRO for close coordination of their activities in providing assistance in connection with nuclear accidents;[251] and in 1984 it drew up the Guidelines for Mutual Emergency Assistance Arrangements in Connection with a Nuclear Accident or Radiological Emergency (Assistance Guidelines).[252] These are designed for use as the basis for the negotiation of bilateral or regional arrangements to encourage the provision of assistance and contain very similar provisions to the Nordic Assistance Agreement, including the establishment of channels for communication and, if appropriate, the designation of working languages.[253]

4.2   The 1986 Assistance Convention

The Chernobyl accident gave fresh impetus for the further development of a legal framework for assistance. Within six months a new multilateral instrument had been drawn up and opened for signature. The 1986 Assistance Convention,[254] which is closely modelled on the Assistance Guidelines, seeks to

facilitate prompt assistance in the event of a nuclear accident or radiological emergency

[248] Adopted on 14 December 1971 by 86 votes in favour, 0 against and 10 abstentions: reprinted in *Ybk UN* 1971 p. 477.

[249] *Id.* at Articles 9(b) and (c).

[250] IAEA Information Guidelines, *supra* n. 205, Technical Annex, para. 4.

[251] See 28 *IAEA Bulletin*, No. 3 at p. 70 (1986).

[252] Reprinted below at No. 15.

[253] *Id.* at para. 3.

[254] Reprinted below at No. 22.

to minimize its consequences and to protect life, property and the environment from the effects of radioactive releases.[255]

The Convention applies whether or not the accident occurred within the requesting State's territory or jurisdiction[256] and it extends to the provision of assistance in relation to medical treatment or the temporary relocation of displaced persons.[257]

Requesting States are required to specify the scope and type of assistance they require and, where practicable, to provide any necessary information.[258] A State receiving such a request is under an obligation to

promptly decide and notify the requesting State Party . . . whether it is in a position to render the assistance requested, and the scope and terms of the assistance that might be rendered.[259]

States Parties are under an obligation

within the limits of their capabilities [to] identify and notify the [IAEA] of experts, equipment and materials which could be made available . . . as well as the terms, especially financial, under which such assistance could be provided.[260]

The IAEA is to make available appropriate resources allocated for emergency purposes, to transmit information relating to resources and, if asked by the requesting State, to coordinate available assistance at the national level.[261]

The Convention contains provisions for the establishment of the direction and control of assistance,[262] the competent national authorities and points of contact[263] and the reimbursement of costs.[264] It also requires the assisting State to maintain the confidentiality of certain information,[265] and establishes rules on privileges and immunities[266] and claims and compensation relating to persons or property injured or damaged in the course of providing the

[255] *Supra* n. 254 at Article 1(1).
[256] *Id.*
[257] *Id.* at Article 2(5).
[258] *Id.* at Article 2(2).
[259] *Id.* at Article 2(3).
[260] *Id.* at Article 2(4).
[261] *Id.* at Article 2(6).
[262] *Id.* at Article 3.
[263] *Id.* at Article 4.
[264] *Id.* at Article 7.
[265] *Id.* at Article 6.
[266] *Id.* at Article 8.

assistance requested.[267] It also sets out a binding dispute settlement provision.[268]

The Convention is a significant contribution to international cooperation in the event of a nuclear accident. Significantly, it establishes an important role for the IAEA, as a channel for the provision of information and assistance to the States Parties or Member States.[269] However, the Convention can be criticized on a number of grounds. It clearly emphasizes the protection of the assisting State. As the Argentinian representative at the Special Session noted, under Article 10(2) the State receiving assistance is to be held responsible for all damage suffered by the assisting State, but the assisting State apparently assumes no responsibility for any damage which it might cause.[270] Furthermore Article 7, on the reimbursement of costs, has the result that a State which has caused a nuclear accident and which agrees to provide assistance to another affected State has the right to require reimbursement of assistance costs. This seems most unsatisfactory, and led the representative from Luxembourg to conclude that the fundamental question of responsibility had not been properly resolved.[271] Moreover, a number of States have entered reservations and declarations restricting the application of the provisions relating to dispute settlement, privileges and immunities, and claims and compensation.[272]

5. Conclusions

A straightforward examination of the international law relating to transboundary nuclear pollution suggests that the legal issues are clear enough. It is their resolution which causes difficulties. This is due partly to the nature of the traditional notions of international law, one of which treats international society in terms of the relations between sovereign and equal States; and partly to the special problems of radioactive material, and in particular the unseen and apparently unquantifiable potential dangers it poses to people, property and the environment when it is released into the atmosphere.

[267] *Id.* at Article 10.
[268] *Id.* at Article 13. A number of Signatories and Parties have entered reservations limiting the applicability of this provision: see pp. 246-60 below.
[269] *Id.* at Article 5.
[270] See comment of the representative of Argentina at the Final Plenary Meeting of the Governmental Experts on 15 August 1986, *supra* n. 18 at p. 19.
[271] *Id.* at p. 28.
[272] See below at pp. 246-60.

The Chernobyl accident, which starkly illustrated the fact that nuclear pollution does not respect the boundaries between sovereign States, blended these two strands of difficulty and threw up a multitude of questions for international lawyers. Are States under an obligation to prevent transboundary nuclear accidents? If such accidents occur, are States under an obligation to provide immediate information to their neighbours and, in the event of damage, are they under an obligation to make reparation? Finally, what legal obligations exist in relation to the provision of assistance? In general, international law is not found entirely wanting. This Introduction suggests that at the time of the Chernobyl accident international law did provide some limited answers to these questions as well as the potential for further development: there are obligations to, *inter alia*, prevent nuclear harm to your neighbours and, in the event of a nuclear accident which might affect them, to provide them with certain immediate information. But the answers are subject to a number of important limitations: the definition of harm is yet to be settled; the standard of care applicable to the obligation to prevent harm is unclear; and there are open questions in regard to the extent of the obligation to repair damage.

In relation to Chernobyl the USSR did not provide immediate information and it seems unlikely to pay compensation for any of the damage which other States claim to have suffered as a result of the accident. That does not mean that international law has been ineffective. As a result of the accident the international law regulation of nuclear activity has been considerably developed. Within a few months two important treaties, the Notification and Assistance Conventions, were drawn up and opened for signature: both are now in force; the USSR had presented a formal proposal, which has received widespread support, for the further elaboration of a complete legal regime, including the development of the rules on liability; and nuclear operators around the world had laid the foundations for the establishment of an Association to share information through regional centres on four continents. It was possible to achieve these results largely because many States, indeed, almost all States engaged in peaceful nuclear activity, recognized the same legal issues and spoke a similar legal language: the new Conventions are the result of a process of international legal development over the last thirty years. This process was helped by the perception of all nuclear power States that the Chernobyl accident was a threat to their own nuclear industries: international law, and the possibilities it presents to produce binding rules according to a more or less common language, provided the means for States to take measures to strengthen nuclear safety.

However, the Chernobyl accident has also had other effects which may, in turn, influence the development of international law in this and other areas.

For the USSR the accident provided an opportunity to open itself up to the world and show that *glasnost* could produce tangible results. The initial 72 hour silence was followed by a steady and fairly detailed flow of information from the USSR and the opening for signature of the Notification Convention. The USSR was the first State to ratify that Convention and the first to provide information about a nuclear accident in the spirit of its terms. The Convention will be a model for the establishment of information networks in relation to other disaster situations, both man-made and natural. It may well be that the era in which a State can shut itself off from the rest of the world and fail to provide information on a matter of global public concern is now politically and legally past.

The role of the IAEA, and perhaps of other international organizations, has been strengthened by the common perception that it fulfilled its tasks effectively in the aftermath of the accident and provided a forum within which the response of States could be worked out. States have shown that, where their common interests require, they are willing and able to act decisively within the framework of an international organization. But perhaps the biggest impact of the accident will be on the traditional notion of State sovereignty. New technologies, in the form of nuclear reactors and satellites, have broken down some of the barriers between States and created a change in the political and legal environment. In particular, certain activities which might previously have been considered the internal affairs of States, namely nuclear accidents and the provision of information relating to them, have been treated as matters of legitimate concern for neighbouring States and for the international community collectively.

1.1 PARIS CONVENTION ON THIRD PARTY LIABILITY IN THE FIELD OF NUCLEAR ENERGY
29 July 1960

1.2 BRUSSELS SUPPLEMENTARY CONVENTION TO THE PARIS CONVENTION ON THIRD PARTY LIABILITY IN THE FIELD OF NUCLEAR ENERGY
31 January 1963

Editorial Note

The Paris Convention, concluded under the auspices of the OEEC (now OECD), was the first international convention to regulate the liability for risks arising out of the peaceful use of nuclear energy. In February 1956 the OEEC established a "Special Committee on Atomic Energy" which charged two sub-committees with the task of studying the insurance and liability aspects of atomic energy. The reports of these two bodies were transmitted to a group of experts who drew up a draft set of regulations on nuclear energy, which formed the basis for the Convention.

The purpose of the Paris Convention is to harmonize national legislation with regard to third party liability and insurance against atomic risks and to establish a regime for liability and compensation in the event of a "nuclear incident" as defined in Article 1(a)(i). The Convention generally applies only to nuclear incidents occurring, and damage suffered, in the territory of Contracting States (Article 2).

By Article 3 the operator of the nuclear installation (as defined in Article 1(a)(ii)-(vi)) is liable for personal injury or damage to property as a result of a nuclear incident. That operator may be a private entity or the State itself. This applies not only to incidents occurring in the operator's installation but also to incidents involving nuclear substances in the course of carriage to or from that installation. The operator's liability may be established simply by proving the causal connection between the loss and the nuclear incident; proof of fault on the part of the operator is not required (Article 3). Certain limited exceptions to liability are provided for in Articles 4 and 9. Liability for general environmental harm, and the regulation of inter-State actions, lie outside the Convention.

Unless a longer period is provided by national legislation, claims must be brought within 10 years from the date of the nuclear incident (Article 8). The general rule is that jurisdiction over actions lies only with the courts of the Contracting State in whose territory the nuclear incident occurred (Article 13(a)). If an action is brought against a State itself, it may not, except in respect of measures of execution, invoke any jurisdictional immunities (Article 13(e)). Judgments are enforceable in the territory of any of the Contracting States (Article 13 (d)) and the Convention is to be applied without discrimination as to nationality, domicile or residence (Article 14).

The Convention stipulates that the maximum liability of an operator for damage caused by any one nuclear incident is 15 million European Monetary Agreement units of account (Article 7(b)) (i.e. US $15 million). Any Contracting State may establish by legislation a greater or lesser amount, but in no event less than 5 million units of account (Article 7(b)). To cover potential liability the operator is required to have and maintain insurance or other financial security (Article 10). Recognizing that in many cases the damage suffered might exceed the operator's liability, a majority of the Contracting States have ratified the Brussels Supplementary Convention of 1963. Initially sponsored by Euratom, the Brussels Convention increases the total compensation available to 120 million units of account (Article 3(a)). The operator's liability remains unchanged but the Contracting State in whose territory the operator's installation is situated is required to provide additional compensation up to 70 million units of account (Article 3(b)(ii)). Should the damage exceed this amount further compensation up to 120 million units of account is to be paid jointly by the Parties to the Brussels Convention according to the formula prescribed in Article 12 (Article 3(b)(iii)).

The texts of the Paris Convention and the Brussels Convention reproduced below incorporate the provisions of amending Protocols adopted in 1964 (*UKTS* 69 (1968), Cmnd. 3755). These Protocols do not change the substance of the liability regimes; rather, they were intended to harmonize the provisions of the Paris and Brussels Conventions with those of the Vienna Convention on Civil Liability for Nuclear Damage adopted in 1963 (reprinted below at No. 3). Further efforts at harmonization are currently being undertaken within the framework of the IAEA. These are directed at eliminating difficulties which might result from the simultaneous application of the Paris and Vienna Conventions and at establishing a link between the two.

In 1982 further Protocols to the Paris and Brussels Conventions were adopted. They change the unit of compensation to Special Drawing Rights ("SDR") of the IMF and they increase the compensation payable by a State and by the Parties to the Brussels Convention jointly to 175 million SDR and 300 million SDR respectively. These Protocols are not yet in force.

PARIS CONVENTION ON THIRD PARTY LIABILITY IN THE FIELD OF NUCLEAR ENERGY

Date of signature:	29 July 1960
Entry into force:	1 April 1968
Depositary:	Secretary General of OECD
Authentic languages:	English, French, German, Spanish, Italian and Dutch
Text reprinted from:	956 *UNTS* 251 (as amended by 1964 Protocol)
Also published in:	55 *AJIL* 1082
	12 *Rüster* 5972

Text

THE GOVERNMENTS of the Federal Republic of Germany, the Republic of Austria, the Kingdom of Belgium, the Kingdom of Denmark, Spain, the French Republic, the Kingdom of Greece, the Italian Republic, the Grand Duchy of Luxembourg, the Kingdom of Norway, the Kingdom of the Netherlands, the Portuguese Republic, the United Kingdom of Great Britain and Northern Ireland, the Kingdom of Sweden, the Swiss Confederation and the Turkish Republic;

CONSIDERING that the European Nuclear Energy Agency, established within the framework of the Organization for European Economic Co-operation (hereinafter referred to as the "Organization"), is charged with encouraging the elaboration and harmonization of legislation relating to nuclear energy in participating countries, in particular with regard to third party liability and insurance against atomic risks;

DESIROUS of ensuring adequate and equitable compensation for persons who suffer damage caused by nuclear incidents whilst taking the necessary steps to ensure that the development of the production and uses of nuclear energy for peaceful purposes is not thereby hindered;

CONVINCED of the need for unifying the basic rules applying in the various countries to the liability incurred for such damage, whilst leaving these countries free to take, on a national basis, any additional measures which they deem appropriate, including the application of the provisions of this Convention to damage caused by incidents due to ionizing radiations not covered therein;

HAVE AGREED as follows:

Article 1
(a) For the purposes of this Convention:
  (i) "A nuclear incident" means any occurrence or succession of occurrences having the same origin which causes damage, provided that such occurrence or succession of occurrences, or any of the damage caused, arises out of or results from the radioactive properties, or a combination of radioactive properties with toxic, explosive, or other hazardous properties of nuclear fuel or radioactive products or waste or with any of them.
  (ii) "Nuclear installation" means reactors other than those comprised in any means of transport; factories for the manufacture or processing of nuclear substances; factories for the separation of

isotopes of nuclear fuel; factories for the reprocessing of irradiated nuclear fuel; facilities for the storage of nuclear substances other than storage incidental to the carriage of such substances; and such other installations in which there are nuclear fuel or radioactive products or waste as the Steering Committee of the European Nuclear Energy Agency (hereinafter referred to as the "Steering Committee") shall from time to time determine.

(iii) "Nuclear fuel" means fissionable material in the form of uranium metal, alloy, or chemical compound (including natural uranium), plutonium metal, alloy, or chemical compound, and such other fissionable material as the Steering Committee shall from time to time determine.

(iv) "Radioactive products or waste" means any radioactive material produced in or made radioactive by exposure to the radiation incidental to the process of producing or utilizing nuclear fuel, but does not include (1) nuclear fuel, or (2) radioisotopes outside a nuclear installation which are used or intended to be used for any industrial, commercial, agricultural, medical or scientific purpose.

(v) "Nuclear substances" means nuclear fuel (other than natural uranium and other than depleted uranium) and radioactive products or waste.

(vi) "Operator" in relation to a nuclear installation means the person designated or recognized by the competent public authority as the operator of that installation.

(b) The Steering Committee may, if in its view the small extent of the risks involved so warrants, exclude any nuclear installation, nuclear fuel, or nuclear substances from the application of this Convention.

Article 2

This Convention does not apply to nuclear incidents occurring in the territory of non-Contracting States or to damage suffered in such territory, unless otherwise provided by the legislation of the Contracting Party in whose territory the nuclear installation of the operator liable is situated, and except in regard to rights referred to in Article 6(e).

Article 3

(a) The operator of a nuclear installation shall be liable, in accordance with this Convention, for:

(i) damage to or loss of life of any person; and

(ii) damage to or loss of any property other than

(1) the nuclear installation itself and any property on the site of that installation which is used or to be used in connection with that installation.

(2) in the cases within Article 4, the means of transport upon which the nuclear substances involved were at the time of the nuclear incident, upon proof that such damage or loss (hereinafter referred to as "damage") was caused by a nuclear incident involving either nuclear fuel or radioactive products or waste in, or nuclear substances coming from such installation, except as otherwise provided for in Article 4.

(b) Where the damage or loss is caused jointly by a nuclear incident and by an incident other than a nuclear incident, that part of the damage or loss which is caused by such other incident shall, to the extent that it is not reasonably separable from the damage or loss caused by the nuclear incident, be considered to be damage caused by the nuclear incident. Where the damage or loss is caused jointly by a nuclear incident and by an emission of ionizing radiation not covered by this Convention, nothing in this Convention shall limit or otherwise affect the liability of any person in connection with that emission of ionizing radiation.

(c) Any Contracting Party may by legislation provide that the liability of the operator of a nuclear installation situated in its territory shall include liability for damage which arises out of or results from ionizing radiations emitted by any source or radiation inside that installation, other than those referred to in paragraph (a) of this Article.

Article 4

In the case of carriage of nuclear substances, including storage incidental thereto, without prejudice to Article 2:

(a) The operator of a nuclear installation shall be liable, in accordance with this Convention, for damage upon proof that it was caused by a nuclear incident outside that installation and involving nuclear substances in the course of carriage therefrom, only if the incident occurs:

(i) before liability with regard to nuclear incidents involving the nuclear substances has been assumed, pursuant to the express terms of a contract in writing, by the operator of another nuclear installation;

(ii) in the absence of such express terms, before the operator of another nuclear installation has taken charge of the nuclear substances; or

(iii) where the nuclear substances are intended to be used in a reactor comprised in a means of transport, before the person duly authorized to operate that reactor has taken charge of the nuclear substances; but

(iv) where the nuclear substances have been sent to a person within the territory of a non-Contracting State, before they have been unloaded from the means of transport by which they have arrived in the territory of that non-Contracting State.

(b) The operator of a nuclear installation shall be liable, in accordance with this Convention, for damage upon proof that it was caused by a nuclear incident outside that installation and involving nuclear substances in the course of carriage thereto, only if the incident occurs:

(i) after liability with regard to nuclear incidents involving the nuclear substances has been assumed by him, pursuant to the express terms of a contract in writing, from the operator of another nuclear installation;

(ii) in the absence of such express terms, after he has taken charge of the nuclear substances; or

(iii) after he has taken charge of the nuclear substances from a person operating a reactor comprised in a means of transport; but

(iv) where the nuclear substances have, with the written consent of the operator, been sent from a person within the territory of a non-Contracting State, after they have been loaded on the means of transport by which they are to be carried from the territory of that State.

(c) The operator liable in accordance with this Convention shall provide the carrier with a certificate issued by or on behalf of the insurer or other financial guarantor furnishing the security required pursuant to Article 10. The certificate shall state the name and address of that operator and the amount, type and duration of the security, and these statements may not be disputed by the person by whom or on whose behalf the certificate was issued. The certificate shall also indicate the nuclear substances and the carriage in respect of which the security applies and shall include a statement by the competent public authority that the person named is an operator within the meaning of this Convention.

(d) A Contracting Party may provide by legislation that, under such terms as may be contained therein and upon fulfilment of the requirements of Article 10(a), a carrier may, at his request and with the consent of an operator of a nuclear installation situated in its territory, by decision of the competent public authority, be liable in accordance with this Convention in place of that operator. In such case for all the purposes of this Convention the carrier shall be considered, in respect of nuclear incidents occurring in the course of carriage of nuclear substances, as an operator of a nuclear installation on the territory of the Contracting Party whose legislation so provides.

Article 5

(a) If the nuclear fuel or radioactive products or waste involved in a nuclear incident have been in more than one nuclear installation and are in a nuclear installation at the time damage is caused, no operator of any nuclear installation in which they have previously been shall be liable for the damage.

(b) Where, however, damage is caused by a nuclear incident occurring in a nuclear installation and involving only nuclear substances stored therein incidentally to their carriage, the operator of the nuclear installation shall not be liable where another operator or person is liable pursuant to Article 4.

(c) If the nuclear fuel or radioactive products or waste involved in a nuclear incident have been in more than one nuclear installation and are not in a nuclear installation at the time damage is caused, no operator other than the operator of the last nuclear installation in which they were before the damage was caused or an operator who has subsequently taken them in charge shall be liable for the damage.

(d) If damage gives rise to liability of more than one operator in accordance with this Convention, the liability of these operators shall be joint and several: provided that where such liability arises as a result of damage caused by a nuclear incident involving nuclear substances in the course of carriage in one and the same means of transport, or, in the case of storage incidental to the carriage, in one and the same nuclear installation, the maximum total amount for which such operators shall be liable shall be the highest amount established with respect to any of them pursuant to Article 7 and provided that in no case shall any one operator be required, in respect of a nuclear incident, to pay more than the amount established with respect to him pursuant to Article 7.

Article 6

(a) The right to compensation for damage caused by a nuclear incident may be exercised only against an operator liable for the damage in accordance with this Convention, or, if a direct right of action against the insurer or other financial guarantor furnishing the security required pursuant to Article 10 is given by national law, against the insurer or other financial guarantor.

(b) Except as otherwise provided in this Article, no other person shall be liable for damage caused by a nuclear incident, but this provision shall not affect the application of any international agreement in the field of transport in force or open for signature, ratification or accession at the date of this Convention.

(c) (i) Nothing in this Convention shall affect the liability:

   (1) of any individual for damage caused by a nuclear incident for which the operator, by virtue of Article 3(a)(ii)(1) and (2) or Article 9, is not liable under this Convention and which results from an act or omission of that individual done with intent to cause damage;

   (2) of a person duly authorized to operate a reactor comprised in a means of transport for damage caused by a nuclear incident when an operator is not liable for such damage pursuant to Article 4(a)(iii) or (b)(iii).

   (ii) The operator shall incur no liability outside this Convention for damage caused by a nuclear incident except where use has not been made of the right provided for in Article 7(c), and then only to the extent that national legislation or the legislation of the Contracting Party in whose territory the nuclear installation of the operator liable is situated has made specific provisions concerning damage to the means of transport.

(d) Any person who has paid compensation in respect of damage caused by a nuclear incident under any international agreement referred to in paragraph (b) of this Article or under any legislation of a non-Contracting State shall, up to the amount which he has paid, acquire by subrogation the rights under this Convention of the person suffering damage whom he has so compensated.

(e) Any person who has his principal place of business in the territory of a Contracting Party or who is the servant of such a person and who has paid compensation in respect of damage caused by a nuclear incident occurring in the territory of a non-Contracting State or in respect of damage suffered in such territory shall, up to the amount which he has paid, acquire the rights which the person so compensated would have had against the operator but for the provisions of Article 2.

(f) The operator shall have a right of recourse only:

   (i) if the damage caused by a nuclear incident results from an act or omission done with intent to cause damage, against the individual acting or omitting to act with such intent;

   (ii) if and to the extent that it is so provided expressly by contract.

(g) If the operator has a right of recourse to any extent pursuant to paragraph (f) of this Article against any person, that person shall not, to that extent, have a right against the operator under paragraphs (d) or (e) of this Article.

(h) Where provisions of national or public health insurance, social security, workmen's compensation or occupational disease compensation systems include compensation for damage caused by a nuclear incident, rights of beneficiaries of such systems and rights of recourse by virtue of such systems shall be determined by the law of the Contracting Party or by the regulations of the inter-governmental organization which has established such systems.

Article 7

(a) The aggregate of compensation required to be paid in respect of damage caused by a nuclear incident shall not exceed the maximum liability established in accordance with this Article.

(b) The maximum liability of the operator in respect of damage caused by a nuclear incident shall be 15,000,000 European Monetary Agreement units of account as defined at the date of this Convention (hereinafter referred to as "units of account"): provided that any Contracting Party, taking into account the possibilities for the operator of obtaining the insurance or other financial security required pursuant to Article 10 may establish by legislation a greater or less amount, but in no event less than 5,000,000 units of account. The sums mentioned above may be converted into national currency in round figures.

(c) Any Contracting Party may by legislation provide that the exception in Article 3(a)(ii)(2) shall not apply: provided that in no case shall the inclusion of damage to the means of transport result in reducing the liability of the operator in respect of other damage to an amount less than 5,000,000 units of account.

(d) The amount of liability of operators of nuclear installations in the territory of a Contracting Party established in accordance with paragraph (b) of this Article as well as the provisions of any legislation of a Contracting Party pursuant to paragraph (c) of this Article shall apply to the liability of such operators wherever the nuclear incident occurs.

(e) A Contracting Party may subject the transit of nuclear substances through its territory to the condition that the maximum amount of liability of the foreign operator concerned be increased, if it considers that such amount does not adequately cover the risks of a nuclear incident in the course of the transit: provided that the maximum amount thus increased shall not exceed the maximum amount of liability of operators of nuclear installations situated in its territory.

(f) The provisions of paragraph (e) of this Article shall not apply:

(i) to carriage by sea where, under international law, there is a right of entry in cases of urgent distress into the ports of such Contracting Party or a right of innocent passage through its territory; or

(ii) to carriage by air where, by agreement or under international law there is a right to fly over or land on the territory of such Contracting Party.

(g) Any interest and costs awarded by a court in actions for compensation under this Convention shall not be considered to be compensation for the purposes of this Convention and shall be payable by the operator in addition to any sum for which he is liable in accordance with this Article.

Article 8

(a) The right of compensation under this Convention shall be extinguished if an action is not brought within ten years from the date of the nuclear incident. National legislation may, however, establish a period longer than ten years if measures have been taken by the Contracting Party in whose territory the nuclear installation of the operator liable is situated to cover the liability of that operator in respect of any actions for compensation begun after the expiry of the period of ten years and during such longer period: provided that such extension of the extinction period shall in no case affect the right of compensation under this Convention of any person who has brought an action in respect of loss of life or personal injury against the operator before the expiry of the period of ten years.

(b) In the case of damage caused by a nuclear incident involving nuclear fuel or radioactive products or waste which, at the time of the incident have been stolen, lost, jettisoned or abandoned and have not yet been recovered, the period established pursuant to paragraph (a) of this Article shall be computed from the date of that nuclear incident, but the period shall in no case exceed twenty years from the date of the theft, loss, jettison or abandonment.

(c) National legislation may establish a period of not less than two years for the extinction of the right or as a period of limitation either from the date at which the person suffering damage has knowledge or from the date at which he ought reasonably to have known of both the damage and the operator liable: provided that the period established pursuant to paragraphs (a) and (b) of this Article shall not be exceeded.

(d) Where the provisions of Article 13(c)(ii) are applicable, the right of compensation shall not, however, be extinguished if, within the time provided for in paragraph (a) of this Article,

(i) prior to the determination by the Tribunal referred to in Article 17, an action has been brought before any of the courts from which the Tribunal can choose; if the Tribunal determines that the competent court is a court other than that before which such action has already been brought, it may fix a date by which such action has to be brought before the competent court so determined; or

(ii) a request has been made to a Contracting Party concerned to initiate a determination by the Tribunal of the competent court pursuant to

Article 13(c)(ii) and an action is brought subsequent to such determination within such time as may be fixed by the Tribunal.

(e) Unless national law provides to the contrary, any person suffering damage caused by a nuclear incident who has brought an action for compensation within the period provided for in this Article may amend his claim in respect of any aggravation of the damage after the expiry of such period provided that final judgment has not been entered by the competent court.

Article 9

The operator shall not be liable for damage caused by a nuclear incident directly due to an act of armed conflict, hostilities, civil war, insurrection or, except in so far as the legislation of the Contracting Party in whose territory his nuclear installation is situated may provide to the contrary, a grave natural disaster of an exceptional character.

Article 10

(a) To cover the liability under this Convention, the operator shall be required to have and maintain insurance or other financial security of the amount established pursuant to Article 7 and of such type and terms as the competent public authority shall specify.

(b) No insurer or other financial guarantor shall suspend or cancel the insurance or other financial security provided for in paragraph (a) of this Article without giving notice in writing of at least two months to the competent public authority or in so far as such insurance or other financial security relates to the carriage of nuclear substances, during the period of the carriage in question.

(c) The sums provided as insurance, reinsurance or other financial security may be drawn upon only for compensation for damage caused by a nuclear incident.

Article 11

The nature, form and extent of the compensation within the limits of this Convention, as well as the equitable distribution thereof, shall be governed by national law.

Article 12

Compensation payable under this Convention, insurance and reinsurance premiums, sums provided as insurance, reinsurance, or other financial security required pursuant to Article 10, and interest and costs referred to in Article

7(g), shall be freely transferable between the monetary areas of the Contracting Parties.

Article 13

(a) Except as otherwise provided in this Article, jurisdiction over actions under Articles 3, 4, 6(a) and 6(e) shall lie only with the courts of the Contracting Party in whose territory the nuclear incident occurred.

(b) Where a nuclear incident occurs outside the territory of the Contracting Parties, or where the place of the nuclear incident cannot be determined with certainty, jurisdiction over such actions shall lie with the courts of the Contracting Party in whose territory the nuclear installation of the operator liable is situated.

(c) Where jurisdiction would lie with the courts of more than one Contracting Party by virtue of paragraphs (a) or (b) of this Article, jurisdiction shall lie,

(i) if the nuclear incident occurred partly outside the territory of any Contracting Party and partly in the territory of a single Contracting Party, with the courts of that Contracting Party; and

(ii) in any other case, with the courts of the Contracting Party determined, at the request of a Contracting Party concerned, by the Tribunal referred to in Article 17 as being the most closely related to the case in question.

(d) Judgments entered by the competent court under this Article after trial, or by default, shall, when they have become enforceable under the law applied by that court, become enforceable in the territory of any of the other Contracting Parties as soon as the formalities required by the Contracting Party concerned have been complied with. The merits of the case shall not be the subject of further proceedings. The foregoing provisions shall not apply to interim judgments.

(e) If an action is brought against a Contracting Party under this Convention, such Contracting Party may not, except in respect of measures of execution, invoke any jurisdictional immunities before the court competent in accordance with this Article.

Article 14

(a) This Convention shall be applied without any discrimination based upon nationality, domicile, or residence.

(b) ''National law'' and ''national legislation'' mean the national law or the national legislation of the court having jurisdiction under this Convention over claims arising out of a nuclear incident, and that law or legislation shall apply to all matters both substantive and procedural not specifically governed by this Convention.

(c) That law and legislation shall be applied without any discrimination based upon nationality, domicile, or residence.

Article 15

(a) Any Contracting Party may take such measures as it deems necessary to provide for an increase in the amount of compensation specified in this Convention.

(b) In so far as compensation for damage involves public funds and is in excess of the 5,000,000 units of account referred to in Article 7, any such measure in whatever form may be applied under conditions which may derogate from the provisions of this Convention.

Article 16

Decisions taken by the Steering Committee under Article 1(a)(ii), 1(a)(iii) and 1(b) shall be adopted by mutual agreement of the members representing the Contracting Parties.

Article 17

Any dispute arising between two or more Contracting Parties concerning the interpretation or application of this Convention shall be examined by the Steering Committee and in the absence of friendly settlement shall, upon the request of a Contracting Party concerned, be submitted to the Tribunal established by the Convention of 20 December 1957 on the Establishment of a Security Control in the Field of Nuclear Energy.

Article 18

(a) Reservations to one or more of the provisions of this Convention may be made at any time prior to ratification of or accession to this Convention or prior to the time of notification under Article 23 in respect of any territory or territories mentioned in the notification, and shall be admissible only if the terms of these reservations have been expressly accepted by the Signatories.

(b) Such acceptance shall not be required from a Signatory which has not itself ratified this Convention within a period of twelve months after the date of notification to it of such reservation by the Secretary-General of the Organization in accordance with Article 24.

(c) Any reservation admitted in accordance with this Article may be withdrawn at any time by notification addressed to the Secretary-General of the Organization.

Article 19

(a) This Convention shall be ratified. Instruments of ratification shall be deposited with the Secretary-General of the Organization.

(b) This Convention shall come into force upon the deposit of instruments of ratification by not less than five of the Signatories. For each Signatory ratifying thereafter, this Convention shall come into force upon the deposit of its instrument of ratification.

Article 20

Amendments to this Convention shall be adopted by mutual agreement of all the Contracting Parties. They shall come into force when ratified or confirmed by two-thirds of the Contracting Parties. For each Contracting Party ratifying or confirming thereafter, they shall come into force at the date of such ratification or confirmation.

Article 21

(a) The Government of any Member or Associate country of the Organization which is not Signatory to this Convention may accede thereto by notification addressed to the Secretary-General of the Organization.

(b) The Government of any other country which is not a Signatory to this Convention may accede thereto by notification addressed to the Secretary-General of the Organization and with the unanimous assent of the Contracting Parties. Such accession shall take effect from the date of such assent.

Article 22

(a) This Convention shall remain in effect for a period of ten years as from the date of its coming into force. Any Contracting Party may, by giving twelve months' notice to the Secretary-General of the Organization, terminate the application of this Convention to itself at the end of the period of ten years.

(b) This Convention shall, after the period of ten years, remain in force for a period of five years for such Contracting Parties as have not terminated its application in accordance with paragraph (a) of this Article, and thereafter for successive periods of five years for such Contracting Parties as have not terminated its application at the end of one of such periods of five years by giving twelve months' notice to that effect to the Secretary-General of the Organization.

(c) A conference shall be convened by the Secretary-General of the Organization in order to consider revisions to this Convention after a period of five years as from the date of its coming into force or, at any other time, at the request of a Contracting Party, within six months from the date of such request.

Article 23

(a) This Convention shall apply to the metropolitan territories of the Contracting Parties.

(b) Any Signatory or Contracting Party may, at the time of signature or ratification of or accession to this Convention or at any later time, notify the Secretary-General of the Organization that this Convention shall apply to those of its territories, including the territories for whose international relations it is responsible, to which this Convention is not applicable in accordance with paragraph (a) of this Article and which are mentioned in the notification. Any such notification may in respect of any territory or territories mentioned therein be withdrawn by giving twelve months' notice to that effect to the Secretary-General of the Organization.

(c) Any territories of a Contracting Party, including the territories for whose international relations it is responsible, to which this Convention does not apply shall be regarded for the purposes of this Convention as being a territory of a non-Contracting State.

Article 24

The Secretary-General of the Organization shall give notice to all Signatories and acceding Governments of the receipt of any instrument of ratification, accession, withdrawal, notification under Article 23, and decisions of the Steering Committee under Article 1(a)(ii), 1(a)(iii) and 1(b). He shall also notify them of the date on which this Convention comes into force, the text of any amendment thereto, and of the date on which such amendment comes into force, and any reservation made in accordance with Article 18.

Annex I

The following reservations were accepted either at the time of signature of the Convention or at the time of signature of the Additional Protocol:
1. *Article 6(b) and (c) and (d):*
   Reservation by the Government of the Federal Republic of Germany, the Government of the Republic of Austria and the Government of the Kingdom of Greece.
   Reservation of the right to provide, by national law, that persons other than the operator may continue to be liable for damage caused by a nuclear incident

on condition that these persons are fully covered in respect of their liability, including defence against unjustified actions, by insurance or other financial security obtained by the operator or out of State funds.

2. *Article 6(b) and (d):*
Reservation by the Government of the Republic of Austria, the Government of the Kingdom of Greece, the Government of the Kingdom of Norway and the Government of the Kingdom of Sweden.

Reservation of the right to consider their national legislation which includes provisions equivalent to those included in the international agreements referred to in Article 6(b) as being international agreements within the meaning of Article 6(b) and (d).

3. *Article 8(a):*
Reservation by the Government of the Federal Republic of Germany and the Government of the Republic of Austria.

Reservation of the right to establish, in respect of nuclear incidents occurring in the Federal Republic of Germany and in the Republic of Austria respectively, a period longer than ten years if measures have been taken to cover the liability of the operator in respect of any actions for compensation begun after the expiry of the period of ten years and during such longer period.

4. *Article 9:*
Reservation by the Government of the Federal Republic of Germany and the Government of the Republic of Austria.

Reservation of the right to provide, in respect of nuclear incidents occurring in the Federal Republic of Germany and in the Republic of Austria respectively, that the operator shall be liable for damage caused by a nuclear incident directly due to an act of armed conflict, hostilities, civil war, insurrection or a grave natural disaster of an exceptional character.

5. *Article 19:*
Reservation by the Government of the Federal Republic of Germany, the Government of the Republic of Austria, and the Government of the Kingdom of Greece.

Reservation of the right to consider ratification of this Convention as constituting an obligation under international law to enact national legislation on third party liability in the field of nuclear energy in accordance with the provisions of this Convention.

Annex II

This Convention shall not be interpreted as depriving a Contracting Party, on whose territory damage was caused by a nuclear incident occurring in the territory of another Contracting Party, of any recourse which might be available to it under international law.

Parties

Date of Ratification or Accession (A)

State	Convention	1964 Additional Protocol
Belgium	3 August 1966	3 August 1966
Denmark	4 September 1974	4 September 1974
Finland	16 June 1972 (A)	16 June 1972 (A)
France	9 March 1966	9 March 1966
Germany, Federal Republic	30 September 1975	30 September 1975
Greece	12 May 1970	12 May 1970
Italy	17 September 1975	17 September 1975
Netherlands	28 December 1979	28 December 1979
Norway	2 July 1973	2 July 1973
Portugal	29 September 1977	29 September 1977
Spain	31 October 1961	30 April 1965
Sweden	1 April 1968	1 April 1968
Turkey	10 October 1961	5 April 1968
United Kingdom	23 February 1966	23 February 1966

BRUSSELS SUPPLEMENTARY CONVENTION TO THE PARIS CONVENTION ON THIRD PARTY LIABILITY IN THE FIELD OF NUCLEAR ENERGY

Date of signature: 31 January 1963
Entry into force: 4 December 1974
Depositary: Belgian Government
Authentic languages: English, Dutch, French, German, Italian and Spanish
Text reprinted from: 1041 *UNTS* 358
(as amended by 1964 Protocol)
Also published in: *UKTS* 44 (1975), Cmnd. 5948
12 *Rüster* 5990
2 *ILM* 685

Text

THE GOVERNMENTS of the Federal Republic of Germany, the Republic of Austria, the Kingdom of Belgium, the Kingdom of Denmark, Spain, the French Republic, the Italian Republic, the Grand Duchy of Luxembourg, the Kingdom of Norway, the Kingdom of the Netherlands, the United Kingdom of Great Britain and Northern Ireland, the Kingdom of Sweden and the Swiss Confederation;

BEING PARTIES to the Convention of 29 July 1960 on Third Party Liability in the Field of Nuclear Energy, concluded within the framework of the Organization for European Economic Co-operation, now the Organization for Economic Co-operation and Development and as modified by the Additional Protocol concluded in Paris on 28 January 1964 (hereinafter referred to as the "Paris Convention");

DESIROUS of supplementing the measures provided in that Convention with a view to increasing the amount of compensation for damage which might result from the use of nuclear energy for peaceful purposes;

HAVE AGREED as follows:

Article 1

The system instituted by this Convention is supplementary to that of the Paris Convention, shall be subject to the provisions of the Paris Convention, and shall be applied in accordance with the following Articles.

Article 2

(a) The system of this Convention shall apply to damage caused by nuclear incidents, other than those occurring entirely in the territory of a State which is not a Party to this Convention:

(i) for which an operator of a nuclear installation, used for peaceful purposes, situated in the territory of a Contracting Party to this Convention (hereinafter referred to as a "Contracting Party"), and which appears on the list established and kept up to date in accordance with the terms of Article 13, is liable under the Paris Convention, and

(ii) suffered

(1) in the territory of a Contracting Party; or

(2) on or over the high seas on board a ship or aircraft registered in the territory of a Contracting Party; or

(3) on or over the high seas by a national of a Contracting Party, provided that, in the case of damage to a ship or an aircraft, the

ship or aircraft is registered in the territory of a Contracting Party;
provided that the courts of a Contracting Party have jurisdiction pursuant to the Paris Convention.

(b) Any Signatory or acceding Government may, at the time of signature of, or accession to, this Convention or on the deposit of its instrument of ratification, declare that, for the purposes of the application of paragraph (a)(ii) of this Article, individuals or certain categories thereof, considered under its law as having their habitual residence in its territory, are assimilated to its own nationals.

(c) In this Article, the expression "a national of a Contracting Party" shall include a Contracting Party or any of its constituent sub-divisions, or a partnership, or any public or private body whether corporate or not established in the territory of a Contracting Party.

Article 3

(a) Under the conditions established by this Convention, the Contracting Parties undertake that compensation in respect of the damage referred to in Article 2 shall be provided up to the amount of 120 million units of account per incident.

(b) Such compensation shall be provided:
  (i) up to an amount of at least 5 million units of account, out of funds provided by insurance or other financial security, such amount to be established by the legislation of the Contracting Party in whose territory the nuclear installation of the operator liable is situated;
  (ii) between this amount and 70 million units of account, out of public funds to be made available by the Contracting Party in whose territory the nuclear installation is situated;
  (iii) between 70 million and 120 million units of account, out of public funds to be made available by the Contracting Parties according to the formula for contributions specified in Article 12.

(c) For this purpose, each Contracting Party shall either:
  (i) establish the maximum liability of the operator, pursuant to Article 7 of the Paris Convention, at 120 million units of account, and provide that such liability shall be covered by all the funds referred to in paragraph (b) of this Article; or
  (ii) establish the maximum liability of the operator at an amount at least equal to that established pursuant to paragraph (b)(i) of this Article and provide that, in excess of such amount and up to 120 million units of account, the public funds referred to in paragraph (b)(ii) and (iii) of this Article shall be made available by some means other

than as cover for the liability of the operator, provided that the rules of substance and procedure laid down in this Convention are not thereby affected.

(d) The obligation of the operator to pay compensation, interest or costs out of public funds made available pursuant to paragraphs (b)(ii) and (iii), and (f) of this Article shall only be enforceable against the operator as and when such funds are in fact made available.

(e) The Contracting Parties, in carrying out this Convention, undertake not to make use of the right provided for in Article 15(b) of the Paris Convention to apply special conditions:

(i)   in respect of compensation for damage provided out of the funds referred to in paragraph (b)(i) of this Article;

(ii) other than those laid down in this Convention in respect of compensation for damage provided out of the public funds referred to in paragraph (b)(ii) and (iii) of this Article.

(f) The interest and costs referred to in Article 7(g) of the Paris Convention are payable in addition to the amounts referred to in paragraph (b) of this Article and shall be borne in so far as they are awarded in respect of compensation payable out of the funds referred to in:

(i)   paragraph (b)(i) of this Article, by the operator liable;

(ii) paragraph (b)(ii) of this Article, by the Contracting Party in whose territory the nuclear installation of that operator is situated;

(iii) paragraph (b)(iii) of this Article, by the Contracting Parties together.

(g) For the purposes of this Convention, "unit of account" means the unit of account of the European Monetary Agreement as defined at the date of the Paris Convention.

Article 4

(a) If a nuclear incident causes damage which gives rise to liability of more than one operator, the aggregate liability provided for in Article 5(d) of the Paris Convention shall not, to the extent that public funds have to be made available pursuant to Article 3(b)(ii) and (iii), exceed 120 million units of account.

(b) The total amount of the public funds made available pursuant to Article 3(b)(ii) and (iii) shall not, in such event, exceed the difference between 120 million units of account and the sum of the amounts established with respect to such operators pursuant to Article 3(b)(i) or, in the case of an operator whose nuclear installation is situated in the territory of a State which is not a Party to this Convention, the amount established pursuant to Article 7 of the Paris Convention. If more than one Contracting Party is required to make available public funds pursuant to Article 3(b)(ii), such funds shall be made available by them in proportion to the number of nuclear installations situated in their respective territories, which are involved in the nuclear incident and of which the operators are liable.

Article 5

(a) Where the operator liable has a right of recourse pursuant to Article 6(f) of the Paris Convention, the Contracting Party in whose territory the nuclear installation of that operator is situated shall take such legislative measures as are necessary to enable both that Contracting Party and the other Contracting Parties to benefit from this recourse to the extent that public funds have been made available pursuant to Article 3(b)(ii) and (iii), and (f).

(b) Such legislation may provide for the recovery of public funds made available pursuant to Article 3(b)(ii) and (iii), and (f) from such operator if the damage results from fault on his part.

Article 6

In calculating the public funds to be made available pursuant to this Convention, account shall be taken only of those rights to compensation exercised within ten years from the date of the nuclear incident. In the case of damage caused by a nuclear incident involving nuclear fuel or radioactive products or waste which, at the time of the incident have been stolen, lost, jettisoned, or abandoned and have not yet been recovered, such period shall not in any case exceed 20 years from the date of the theft, loss, jettison or abandonment. It shall also be extended in the cases and under the conditions laid down in Article 8(d) of the Paris Convention. Amendments made to claims after the expiry of this period, under the conditions laid down in Article 8(e) of the Paris Convention, shall also be taken into account.

Article 7

Where a Contracting Party makes use of the right provided for in Article 8(c) of the Paris Convention, the period which it establishes shall be a period of prescription of three years either from the date at which the person suffering damage has knowledge or from the date at which he ought reasonably to have known of both the damage and the operator liable.

Article 8

Any person who is entitled to benefit from the provisions of this Convention shall have the right to full compensation in accordance with national law for damage suffered, provided that, where the amount of damage exceeds or is likely to exceed:

(i)   120 million units of account; or

(ii) if there is aggregate liability under Article 5(d) of the Paris Convention and a higher sum results therefrom, such higher sum, any Contracting Party may establish equitable criteria for apportionment. Such criteria shall be applied whatever the origin of the funds and, subject to the provisions of Article 2, without discrimination based on the nationality, domicile or residence of the person suffering the damage.

Article 9

(a) The system of disbursements by which the public funds required under Article 3(b)(ii) and (iii), and (f) are to be made available shall be that of the Contracting Party whose courts have jurisdiction.

(b) Each Contracting Party shall ensure that persons suffering damage may enforce their rights to compensation without having to bring separate proceedings according to the origin of the funds provided for such compensation.

(c) No Contracting Party shall be required to make available the public funds referred to in Article 3(b)(ii) and (iii) so long as any of the funds referred to in Article 3(b)(i) remain available.

Article 10

(a) The Contracting Party whose courts have jurisdiction shall be required to inform the other Contracting Parties of a nuclear incident and its circumstances as soon as it appears that the damage caused by such incident exceeds, or is likely to exceed, 70 million units of account. The Contracting Parties shall, without delay, make all the necessary arrangements to settle the procedure for their relations in this connection.

(b) Only the Contracting Party whose courts have jurisdiction shall be entitled to request the other Contracting Parties to make available the public funds required under Article 3(b)(ii) and (f) and shall have exclusive competence to disburse such funds.

(c) Such Contracting Party shall, when the occasion arises, exercise the right of recourse provided for in Article 5 on behalf of the other Contracting Parties who have made available public funds pursuant to Article 3(b)(iii) and (f).

(d) Settlements effected in respect of the payment of compensation out of the public funds referred to in Article 3(b)(ii) and (iii) in accordance with the conditions established by national legislation shall be recognized by the other Contracting Parties, and judgments entered by the competent courts in respect of such compensation shall become enforceable in the territory of the other Contracting Parties in accordance with the provisions of Article 13(d) of the Paris Convention.

Article 11

(a) If the courts having jurisdiction are those of a Contracting Party other than the Contracting Party in whose territory the nuclear installation of the operator liable is situated, the public funds required under Article 3(b)(ii) and (f) shall be made available by the first-named Contracting Party. The Contracting Party in whose territory the nuclear installation of the operator liable is situated shall reimburse to the other Contracting Party the sums paid. These two Contracting Parties shall agree on the procedure for reimbursement.

(b) In adopting all legislative, regulatory or administrative provisions, after the nuclear incident has occurred, concerning the nature, form and extent of the compensation, the procedure for making available the public funds required under Article 3(b)(ii) and, if necessary, the criteria for the apportionment of such funds, the Contracting Party whose courts have jurisdiction shall consult the Contracting Party in whose territory the nuclear installation of the operator liable is situated. It shall further take all measures necessary to enable the latter to intervene in proceedings and to participate in any settlement concerning compensation.

Article 12

(a) The formula for contributions according to which the Contracting Parties shall make available the public funds referred to in Article 3(b)(iii) shall be determined as follows:

(i) as to 50 per cent, on the basis of the ratio between the gross national product at current prices of each Contracting Party and the total of the gross national products at current prices of all Contracting Parties as shown by the official statistics published by the Organization for Economic Co-operation and Development for the year preceding the year in which the nuclear incident occurs;

(ii) as to 50 per cent, on the basis of the ratio between the thermal power of the reactors situated in the territory of each Contracting Party and the total thermal power of the reactors situated in the territories of all the Contracting Parties. This calculation shall be made on the basis of the thermal power of the reactors shown at the date of the nuclear incident in the list referred to in Article 2(a)(i): provided that a reactor shall only be taken into consideration for the purposes of this calculation as from the date when it first reaches criticality.

(b) For the purposes of this Convention, "thermal power" means

(i) before the issue of a final operating licence, the planned thermal power;

(ii) after the issue of such licence, the thermal power authorized by the competent national authorities.

Article 13

(a) Each Contracting Party shall ensure that all nuclear installations used for peaceful purposes situated in its territory, and falling within the definition in Article 1 of the Paris Convention, appear in the list referred to in Article 2(a)(i).

(b) For this purpose, each Signatory or acceding Government shall, on the deposit of its instrument of ratification or accession, communicate to the Belgian Government full particulars of such installations.

(c) Such particulars shall indicate:

(i) in the case of installations not yet completed, the expected date on which the risk of a nuclear incident will exist;

(ii) and further, in the case of reactors, the expected date on which they will first reach criticality, and also their thermal power.

(d) Each Contracting Party shall also communicate to the Belgian Government the exact date of the existence of the risk of a nuclear incident and, in the case of reactors, the date on which they first reached criticality.

(e) Each Contracting Party shall also communicate to the Belgian Government all modifications to be made to the list. Where such modifications include the addition of a nuclear installation, the communication must be made at least three months before the expected date on which the risk of a nuclear incident will exist.

(f) If a Contracting Party is of the opinion that the particulars, or any modification to be made to the list, communicated by another Contracting Party do not comply with the provisions of Article 2(a)(i) and of this Article, it may raise objections thereto only by addressing them to the Belgian Government within three months from the date on which it has received notice pursuant to paragraph (h) of this Article.

(g) If a Contracting Party is of the opinion that a communication required in accordance with this Article has not been made within the time prescribed in this Article, it may raise objections only by addressing them to the Belgian Government within three months from the date on which it knew of the facts which, in its opinion, ought to have been communicated.

(h) The Belgian Government shall give notice as soon as possible to each Contracting Party of the communications and objections which it has received pursuant to this Article.

(i) The list referred to in Article 2(a)(i) shall consist of all the particulars and modifications referred to in paragraphs (b), (c), (d) and (e) of this Article, it being understood that objections submitted pursuant to paragraphs (f) and (g) of this Article shall have effect retrospective to the date on which they were raised, if they are sustained.

(j) The Belgian Government shall supply any Contracting Party on demand with an up-to-date statement of the nuclear installations covered by this Convention and the details supplied in respect of them pursuant to this Article.

Article 14

(a) Except in so far as this Convention otherwise provides, each Contracting Party may exercise the powers vested in it by virtue of the Paris Convention, and any provisions made thereunder may be invoked against the other Contracting Parties in order that the public funds referred to in Article 3(b)(ii) and (iii) be made available.

(b) Any such provisions made by a Contracting Party pursuant to Articles 2, 7(c) and 9 of the Paris Convention as a result of which the public funds referred to in Article 3(b)(ii) and (iii) are required to be made available may not be invoked against any other Contracting Party unless it has consented thereto.

(c) Nothing in this Convention shall prevent a Contracting Party from making provisions outside the scope of the Paris Convention and of this Convention, provided that such provisions shall not involve any further obligation on the part of the other Contracting Parties in so far as their public funds are concerned.

Article 15

(a) Any Contracting Party may conclude an agreement with a State which is not a Party to this Convention concerning compensation out of public funds for damage caused by a nuclear incident.

(b) To the extent that the conditions for payment of compensation under any such agreement are not more favourable than those which result from the measures adopted by the Contracting Party concerned for the application of the Paris Convention and of this Convention, the amount of damage caused by a nuclear incident covered by this Convention and for which compensation is payable by virtue of such an agreement may be taken into consideration, where the proviso to Article 8 applies, in calculating the total amount of damage caused by that incident.

(c) The provisions of paragraphs (a) and (b) of this Article shall in no case affect the obligations under Article 3(b)(ii) and (iii) of those Contracting Parties which have not given their consent to such agreement.

(d) Any Contracting Party intending to conclude such an agreement shall notify the other Contracting Parties of its intention. Agreements concluded shall be notified to the Belgian Government.

Article 16

(a) The Contracting Parties shall consult each other upon all problems of common interest raised by the application of this Convention and of the Paris Convention, especially Articles 20 and 22(c) of the latter Convention.

(b) They shall consult each other on the desirability of revising this Convention after a period of five years from the date of its coming into force, and at any other time upon the request of a Contracting Party.

Article 17

Any dispute arising between two or more Contracting Parties concerning the interpretation or application of this Convention shall, upon the request of a Contracting Party concerned, be submitted to the European Nuclear Energy Tribunal established by the Convention of 20 December 1957 on the Establishment of a Security Control in the Field of Nuclear Energy.

Article 18

(a) Reservations to one or more of the provisions of this Convention may be made at any time prior to ratification of this Convention if the terms of these reservations have been expressly accepted by all Signatories or, at the time of accession or of the application of the provisions of Articles 21 and 24, if the terms of these reservations have been expressly accepted by all Signatories and acceding Governments.

(b) Such acceptance shall not be required from a Signatory which has not itself ratified this Convention within a period of twelve months after the date of notification to it of such reservation by the Belgian Government in accordance with Article 25.

(c) Any reservation accepted in accordance with the provisions of paragraph (a) of this Article may be withdrawn at any time by notification addressed to the Belgian Government.

Article 19

No State may become or continue to be a Contracting Party to this Convention unless it is a Contracting Party to the Paris Convention.

Article 20

(a) The Annex to this Convention shall form an integral part thereof.

(b) This Convention shall be ratified. Instruments of ratification shall be deposited with the Belgian Government.

(c) This Convention shall come into force three months after the deposit of the sixth instrument of ratification.

(d) For each Signatory ratifying this Convention after the deposit of the sixth instrument of ratification, it shall come into force three months after the date of the deposit of its instrument of ratification.

Article 21

Amendments to this Convention shall be adopted by agreement among all the Contracting Parties. They shall come into force on the date when all Contracting Parties have ratified or confirmed them.

Article 22

(a) After the coming into force of this Convention, any Contracting Party to the Paris Convention which has not signed this Convention may request accession to this Convention by notification addressed to the Belgian Government.

(b) Such accession shall require the unanimous assent of the Contracting Parties.

(c) Once such assent has been given, the Contracting Party to the Paris Convention requesting accession shall deposit its instrument of accession with the Belgian Government.

(d) The accession shall take effect three months from the date of deposit of the instrument of accession.

Article 23

(a) This Convention shall remain in force until the expiry of the Paris Convention.

(b) Any Contracting Party may, by giving twelve months' notice to the Belgian Government, terminate the application of this Convention to itself after the end of the period of ten years specified in Article 22(a) of the Paris Convention. Within six months after receipt of such notice, any other Contracting Party may, by notice to the Belgian Government, terminate the application of this Convention to itself as from the date when it ceases to have effect in respect of the Contracting Party which first gave notice.

(c) The expiry of this Convention or the withdrawal of a Contracting Party shall not terminate the obligations assumed by each Contracting Party under this Convention to pay compensation for damage caused by nuclear incidents occurring before the date of such expiry or withdrawal.

(d) The Contracting Parties shall, in good time, consult each other on what measures should be taken after the expiry of this Convention or the withdrawal of one or more of the Contracting Parties, to provide compensation comparable to that accorded by this Convention for damage caused by nuclear incidents occurring after the date of such expiry or withdrawal and for which the operator of a nuclear installation in operation before such date within the territories of the Contracting Parties is liable.

Article 24

(a) This Convention shall apply to the metropolitan territories of the Contracting Parties.

(b) Any Contracting Party desiring the application of this Convention to one or more of the territories in respect of which, pursuant to Article 23 of the Paris Convention, it has given notification of application of that Convention, shall address a request to the Belgian Government.

(c) The application of this Convention to any such territory shall require the unanimous assent of the Contracting Parties.

(d) Once such assent has been given, the Contracting Party concerned shall address to the Belgian Government a notification which shall take effect as from the date of its receipt.

(e) Such notification may, as regards any territory mentioned therein, be withdrawn by the Contracting Party which has made it by giving 12 months' notice to that effect to the Belgian Government.

(f) If the Paris Convention ceases to apply to any such territory, this Convention shall also cease to apply thereto.

Article 25

The Belgian Government shall notify all Signatories and acceding Governments of the receipt of any instrument of ratification, accession or withdrawal, and shall also notify them of the date on which this Convention comes into force, the text of any amendment thereto and the date on which such amendment comes into force, any reservations made in accordance with Article 18, and all notifications which it has received.

Annex

THE GOVERNMENTS OF THE CONTRACTING PARTIES declare that compensation for damage caused by a nuclear incident not covered by the Supplementary Convention solely by reason of the fact that the relevant nuclear installation, on account of its utilization, is not on the list referred to in Article 2 of the Supplementary Convention (including the case where such installation is considered by one or more but not all of the Governments to be outside the Paris Convention):

—shall be provided without discrimination among the nationals of the Contracting Parties to the Supplementary Convention; and

—shall not be limited to less than 120 million units of account.

In addition, if they have not already done so, they shall endeavour to make the rules for compensation of persons suffering damage caused by such incidents as similar as possible to those established in respect of nuclear incidents occurring in connection with nuclear installations covered by the Supplementary Convention.

Parties

Date of Ratification or Accession (A)

State	Convention	1964 Additional Protocol
Belgium	20 August 1985	20 August 1985
Denmark [1]	4 September 1974	4 September 1974
Finland [4]	16 December 1974 (A)	16 December 1974 (A)
France	30 March 1966	30 March 1966
Germany, Federal Republic [2]	1 October 1975	1 October 1975
Italy	3 February 1976	3 February 1976
Netherlands [3]	28 September 1979	28 September 1979
Norway	9 July 1973	9 July 1973
Spain	27 July 1966	27 July 1966
Sweden	3 April 1968	3 April 1968
United Kingdom [5]	24 March 1966	24 March 1966

Implementing Legislation

National legislation implementing the Paris and Brussels Conventions includes the following:

Belgium, Act of 18 July 1966 on Third Party Liability in Field of Nuclear Energy, *Moniteur Belge,* 23 August 1966.

---

[1] Not applicable to the Faroe Islands; applicable to Greenland.

[2] Ratification accompanied by two declarations, one made in conformity with Article 2(b) of the Supplementary Convention and the other declaring the Convention to be applicable to West Berlin.

[3] Ratification accompanied by the following declaration: ''I am charged to declare that, with a view to the application of Article 2(a)(ii), my Government considers within its jurisdiction natural persons who have their habitual residence on its territory in the sense of the legislation, or certain categories of them.'' (Editor's translation).

[4] Accession accompanied by the following declaration: ''In order to apply Article 2(a)(ii) of the Convention, natural persons having their habitual residence in Finland, in accordance with Finnish Legislation, are within Finnish jurisdiction.'' (Editor's translation).

[5] Extended to the Isle of Man (24 November 1978), Guernsey (8 April 1982) and Jersey (9 May 1983).

Denmark, Act No. 332 of 19 June 1974 on Compensation for Nuclear Damage, 15 *NLB* (English translation).

Finland, Nuclear Liability Act of 8 June 1972 (Decree No. 484), 8 *NLB (Supplement)* (English translation); entered into force by Decree No. 486 of 16 June 1972.

France, Act No. 68-943 of 30 October 1968 on Third Party Liability in the Field of Nuclear Energy, *JORF*, 31 October 1968.

Federal Republic of Germany, Atomic Energy Act of 31 October 1976, *BGBl.* 1976 Part I, p. 3053 (as amended by Atomic Energy Act of 1985, reprinted below at Annex).

Italy, Act No. 1860 of 31 December 1962 on the Peaceful Uses of Nuclear Energy, as amended by Act No. 109 of 12 February 1974, 16 *NLB* (English translation).

Netherlands, Act of 17 March 1979 on Nuclear Third Party Liability, 24 *NLB* (English translation).

Norway, Act of 12 May 1972 Concerning Nuclear Energy Activities, *Norsk Lovtidend* of 23 June 1972, p. 606.

Spain, Act No. 25 of 29 April 1964 on Nuclear Energy, *Official State Gazette,* 4 May 1964; amended by Decree No. 2177 of 22 July 1967 and Decree No. 742 of 28 March 1968.

Sweden, Nuclear Liability Act No. 46 of 8 March 1968, *Svensk Författningsamling* of 25 March 1968, as amended by Decree No. 706 of 18 October 1974.

United Kingdom, Nuclear Installations Act 1965 as amended by Nuclear Installations Act 1969 and extended by Congenital Disabilities (Civil Liability) Act 1976.

Select Bibliography

Arangio-Ruiz, "Some International Legal Problems of the Civil Uses of Nuclear Energy", 107 *RC* 499 (1962).

Berman & Hyderman, "A Convention on Third Party Liability for Damage from Nuclear Incidents", 55 *AJIL* 966 (1969).

Bette, Didier, Fornassier & Stein, *Compensation of Nuclear Damage in Europe* (1965).

Cigoj, "International Regulation of Civil Liability for Nuclear Risks", 14 *ICLQ* 809 (1965).

Fornassier, "Une Expérience de Solidarité Internationale: la Convention Complémentaire à la Convention de Paris du 29 juillet 1960 sur la Responsabilité Civile dans la Domaine de l'Energie Nucléaire", 8 *AFDI* 762 (1962).

Hardy, "Nuclear Liability: the General Principles of Law and Further Proposals", 36 *BYIL* 223 (1960).

Hardy, "International Protection Against Nuclear Risks", 10 *ICLQ* 739 (1961).

Hebert, *Historique du Droit Nouveau de la Responsabilité en Matière Nucléaire: Analyse des Dispositions de la Convention OECE et de ses Compléments* (1962).

Jenks, "Liability for Ultra-Hazardous Activities in International Law", 117 *RC* 105 (1966, I) at pp. 133-7.

Pelzer, "On Modernising the Paris Convention", 12 *NLB* 46 (1973).

Pfaffelhuber, "New Trends in Atomic Law", 10 *NLB* 43 (1972).

Picard, "La Convention sur la Responsabilité Civile dans la Domaine de l'Energie Nucléaire", 2 *JDI* 344 (1962).

Reyners, "Compensation for Nuclear Damage in the OECD Member Countries", in OECD, *Compensation for Pollution Damage* (1981), p. 93.

Spleth, "The Simultaneous Application of the Paris and Vienna Conventions in the Danish Draft Act", 6 *NLB* 56 (1970).

Strohl, "The Concept of Nuclear Third Party Liability and Its Implementation by Legislation in OECD Member Countries", 8 *IAEA Leg. Ser.* 69 (1972).

IAEA, Note by Director General, "The Question of International Liability for Damage Arising from a Nuclear Accident", *Doc.* GOV/INF/509, 26 January 1987 (restricted distribution).

IAEA, Report of the Sixth Meeting of the Standing Committee on Civil Liability for Nuclear Damage, "The Question of International Liability for Damage Arising from a Nuclear Accident", *Doc.* GOV/2305, 19 May 1987 (restricted distribution).

OECD, NEA—"The Field of Application of the Nuclear Conventions", 5 *NLB* 22 (1970).

OECD, *Nuclear Third Party Liability: Nuclear Legislation* (1976).

OECD, *Legal Aspects of Transfrontier Pollution* (1977).

OECD, *Paris Convention: Decisions, Recommendations, Interpretations* (1984).

OECD, *Report by the Environment Committee on "Responsibility and Liability of States in Relation to Transfrontier Pollution"* (1984).

OECD, NEA—*Fifteenth Activity Report* (1987) p. 29.

UNEP, "Report of the Group of Experts on Liability for Pollution and Other Environmental Damage and Compensation of such Damage", *Doc.* UNEP/WG.8/3 (1977).

2. BRUSSELS CONVENTION ON THE LIABILITY OF OPERATORS OF NUCLEAR SHIPS
25 May 1962

Editorial Note

This Convention is based on a draft prepared in 1959 by the International Maritime Committee and then revised in 1960 by a panel of experts organized by the IAEA. It was adopted at the 1961/62 Brussels Diplomatic Conference on Maritime Law. The Conference was conscious that the development of nuclear-powered shipping and, in particular, the willingness of States to receive nuclear ships into their territorial waters and ports, was dependent on the existence of a satisfactory, uniform regime of liability for damage caused by such ships.

The Convention, whose purpose is to harmonize national legislation concerning the liability of operators of nuclear ships, applies to all nuclear-powered ships, whether merchant or naval (Article I(1)). Provisions are included in Article XV which prohibit the operation of such ships without a licence from the flag State and which also prohibit the operation of licensed nuclear ships under flags of convenience.

By Article II all liability for damage to persons and property caused by a nuclear incident occurring anywhere in the world and involving the nuclear fuel of, or radioactive products or waste produced in, a nuclear ship flying the flag of a Contracting State, is channelled to the operator of the ship. This liability is absolute and, subject only to a right of recourse in certain limited situations, is exclusive of the liability of any other person (Article II(1) and II(6)).

The limit of the operator's liability under the Convention is 1500 million gold Francs (US $100 million) in respect of any one nuclear incident (Article III(1)). The operator is required to maintain insurance or other financial security in an amount specified by the flag State (Article III(2)). To the extent that the claims in respect of a nuclear incident exceed the proceeds of this insurance or security, the flag State is required to make up the deficiency up to the above-mentioned limit (Article III(2)).

Article V provides that claims for compensation must be brought within ten years from the date of the incident, unless a longer period is provided by applicable national legislation. Claims may be brought, at the option of the claimant, either in the courts of the flag State or in the courts of any Contracting State in the territory of which damage has been sustained (Article X(1)). In this connection immunities from legal process are waived, except in respect of nuclear warships (Article X(3)). These are not subject to the jurisdiction of foreign courts and are also not subject to arrest, attachment or seizure. Final judgments of courts having jurisdiction under the Convention are required to be recognized and enforced in the territory of all Contracting States (Article XI(4)).

Where it appears that the claims in respect of a nuclear incident will exceed the limit of the operator's liability, a procedure is established in Article XI whereby the courts of the flag State may be called upon to establish, and supervise the distribution of, a fund comprising sums provided by the operator and/or the flag State equal to the amount of the operator's liability.

Significantly, the Convention has not received the support of the United States and the USSR, owing to the inclusion within its scope of nuclear-powered warships.

Date of signature:	25 May 1962
Entry into force:	Not yet in force
Depositary:	Belgian Government
Authentic languages:	English and French
Text reprinted from:	Text provided by Belgian Ministry of Foreign Affairs
Also published in:	57 *AJIL* 268 (1963)
	1 *Rüster* 405
	66 *RGDIP* 894

Text

BRUSSELS CONVENTION ON THE LIABILITY OF OPERATORS OF NUCLEAR SHIPS

THE CONTRACTING PARTIES,

HAVING RECOGNIZED the desirability of determining by agreement certain uniform rules concerning the liability of operators of nuclear ships,

HAVE DECIDED to conclude a Convention for this purpose, and thereto agreed as follows:

Article I

For the purpose of this Convention:

1. "Nuclear ship" means any ship equipped with a nuclear power plant.

2. "Licensing State" means the Contracting State which operates or which has authorized the operation of a nuclear ship under its flag.

3. "Person" means any individual or partnership, or any public or private body whether corporate or not, including a State or any of its constituent subdivisions.

4. "Operator" means the person authorized by the licensing State to operate a nuclear ship, or where a Contracting State operates a nuclear ship, that State.

5. "Nuclear fuel" means any material which is capable of producing energy by a self-sustaining process of nuclear fission and which is used or intended for use in a nuclear ship.

6. "Radioactive products or waste" means any material, including nuclear fuel, made radioactive by neutron irradiation incidental to the utilization of nuclear fuel in a nuclear ship.

7. "Nuclear damage" means loss of life or personal injury and loss or damage to property which arises out of or results from the radioactive properties or a combination of radioactive properties with toxic, explosive or other hazardous properties of nuclear fuel or of radioactive products or waste; any other loss, damage or expense so arising or resulting shall be included only if and to the extent that the applicable national law so provides.

8. "Nuclear incident" means any occurrence or series of occurrences having the same origin which causes nuclear damage.

9. "Nuclear power plant" means any power plant in which a nuclear reactor is, or is to be used as, the source of power, whether for propulsion of the ship or for any other purpose.

10. "Nuclear reactor" means any installation containing nuclear fuel in such an arrangement that a self-sustained chain process of nuclear fission can occur therein without an additional source of neutrons.

11. "Warship" means any ship belonging to the naval forces of a State and bearing the external marks distinguishing warships of its nationality, under the command of an officer duly commissioned by the Government of such State and whose name appears in the Navy List, and manned by a crew who are under regular naval discipline.

12. "Applicable national law" means the national law of the court having jurisdiction under the Convention including any rules of such national law relating to conflict of laws.

Article II

1. The operator of a nuclear ship shall be absolutely liable for any nuclear damage upon proof that such damage has been caused by a nuclear incident involving the nuclear fuel of, or radioactive products or waste produced in such ship.

2. Except as otherwise provided in this Convention no person other than the operator shall be liable for such nuclear damage.

3. Nuclear damage suffered by the nuclear ship itself, its equipment, fuel or stores shall not be covered by the operator's liability as defined in this Convention.

4. The operator shall not be liable with respect to nuclear incidents occurring before the nuclear fuel has been taken in charge by him or after the nuclear fuel or radioactive products or waste have been taken in charge by

another person duly authorized by law and liable for any nuclear damage that may be caused by them.

5. If the operator proves that the nuclear damage resulted wholly or partially from an act or omission done with intent to cause damage by the individual who suffered the damage, the competent courts may exonerate the operator wholly or partially from his liability to such individual.

6. Notwithstanding the provisions of paragraph 1 of this Article, the operator shall have a right of recourse:

(a) If the nuclear incident results from a personal act or omission done with intent to cause damage, in which event recourse shall lie against the individual who has acted, or omitted to act, with such intent;

(b) If the nuclear incident occurred as a consequence of any wreck-raising operation, against the person or persons who carried out such operation without the authority of the operator or of the State having licensed the sunken ship or of the State in whose waters the wreck is situated;

(c) If recourse is expressly provided for by contract.

Article III

1. The liability of the operator as regards one nuclear ship shall be limited to 1500 million francs in respect of any one nuclear incident, notwithstanding that the nuclear incident may have resulted from any fault of privity of that operator; such limit shall include neither any interest nor costs awarded by a court in actions for compensation under this Convention.

2. The operator shall be required to maintain insurance, or other financial security covering his liability for nuclear damage, in such amount, of such type and in such terms as the licensing State shall specify. The licensing State shall ensure the payment of claims for compensation for nuclear damage established against the operator by providing the necessary funds up to the limit laid down in paragraph 1 of this Article to the extent that the yield of the insurance or the financial security is inadequate to satisfy such claims.

3. However, nothing in paragraph 2 of this Article shall require any Contracting State or any of its constituent subdivisions, such as States, Republics or Cantons, to maintain insurance or other financial security to cover their liability as operators of nuclear ships.

4. The franc mentioned in paragraph 1 of this Article is a unit of account constituted by sixty-five and one half milligrams of gold of millesimal fineness nine hundred. The amount awarded may be converted into each national currency in round figures. Conversion into national currencies other than gold shall be effected on the basis of their gold at the date of payment.

Article IV

Whenever both nuclear damage and damage other than nuclear damage have been caused by a nuclear incident or jointly by a nuclear incident and one or more other occurrences and the nuclear damage and such other damage are not reasonably separable, the entire damage shall, for the purposes of this Convention, be deemed to be nuclear damage exclusively caused by the nuclear incident. However, where damage is caused jointly by a nuclear incident covered by this Convention and by an emission of ionizing radiation or by an emission of ionizing radiation in combination with the toxic, explosive or other hazardous properties of the source of radiation not covered by it, nothing in this Convention shall limit or otherwise affect the liability, either as regards the victims or by way of recourse or contribution, of any person who may be held liable in connection with the emission of ionizing radiation or by the toxic, explosive or other hazardous properties of the source of radiation not covered by this Convention.

Article V

1. Rights of compensation under this Convention shall be extinguished if an action is not brought within ten years from the date of the nuclear incident. If, however, under the law of the licensing State the liability of the operator is covered by insurance or other financial security or State indemnification for a period longer than ten years, the applicable national law may provide that rights of compensation against the operator shall only be extinguished after a period which may be longer than ten years but shall not be longer than the period for which his liability is covered under the law of the licensing State. However, such extension of the extinction period shall in no case affect the right of compensation under this Convention of any person who has brought an action for loss of life or personal injury against the operator before the expiry of the aforesaid period of ten years.

2. Where nuclear damage is caused by nuclear fuel, radioactive products or waste which were stolen, lost, jettisoned, or abandoned, the period established under paragraph 1 of this Article shall be computed from the date of the nuclear incident causing the nuclear damage, but the period shall in no case exceed a period of twenty years from the date of the theft, loss, jettison or abandonment.

3. The applicable national law may establish a period of extinction or prescription of not less than three years from the date on which the person who claims to have suffered nuclear damage had knowledge or ought reasonably to have had knowledge of the damage and of the person responsible for the damage, provided that the period established under paragraphs 1 and 2 of this Article shall not be exceeded.

4. Any person who claims to have suffered nuclear damage and who has brought an action for compensation within the period applicable under this Article may amend his claim to take into account any aggravation of the damage, even after the expiry of that period, provided that final judgment has not been entered.

Article VI

Where provisions of national health insurance, social security, workmen's compensation or occupational disease compensation systems include compensation for nuclear damage, rights of beneficiaries under such systems and rights of subrogation, or of recourse against the operator, by virtue of such systems, shall be determined by the law of the Contracting State having established such systems. However, if the law of such Contracting State allows claims of beneficiaries of such systems and such rights of subrogation and recourse to be brought against the operator in conformity with the terms of this Convention, this shall not result in the liability of the operator exceeding the amount specified in paragraph 1 of Article III.

Article VII

1. Where nuclear damage engages the liability of more than one operator and the damage attributable to each operator is not reasonably separable, the operators involved shall be jointly and severally liable for such damage. However, the liability of any one operator shall not exceed the limit laid down in Article III.

2. In the case of a nuclear incident where the nuclear damage arises out of or results from nuclear fuel or radioactive products or waste of more than one nuclear ship of the same operator, that operator shall be liable in respect of each ship up to the limit laid down in Article III.

3. In case of joint and several liability, and subject to the provisions of paragraph 1 of this Article:

(a) Each operator shall have a right of contribution against the others in proportion to the fault attaching to each of them;

(b) Where circumstances are such that the degree of fault cannot be apportioned, the total liability shall be borne in equal parts.

Article VIII

No liability under this Convention shall attach to an operator in respect to nuclear damage caused by a nuclear incident directly due to an act of war, hostilities, civil war or insurrection.

Article IX

The sums provided by insurance, by other financial security or by State indemnification in conformity with paragraph 2 of this Article III shall be exclusively available for compensation due under this Convention.

Article X

1. Any action for compensation shall be brought, at the option of the claimant, either before the courts of the licensing State or before the courts of the Contracting State or States in whose territory nuclear damage has been sustained.

2. If the licensing State has been or might be called upon to ensure the payment of claims for compensation in accordance with paragraph 2 of Article III of this Convention, it may intervene as party in any proceedings brought against the operator.

3. Any immunity from legal processes pursuant to rules of national or international law shall be waived with respect to duties or obligations arising under, or for the purpose of, this Convention. Nothing in this Convention shall make warships or other State-owned or State-operated ships on non-commercial service liable to arrest, attachment or seizure or confer jurisdiction in respect of warships on the courts of any foreign State.

Article XI

1. When, having regard to the likelihood of any claims arising out of a nuclear incident exceeding the amount specified in Article III of this Convention, a court of the licensing State, at the request of the operator, a claimant or the licensing State, so certifies, the operator or the licensing State shall make that amount available in that court to pay any such claims; that amount shall be regarded as constituting the limitation fund in respect of that incident.

2. The amount may be made available for the purposes of the preceding paragraph by payment into court or by the provision of security or guarantees sufficient to satisfy the court that the money will be available when required to meet any established claim.

3. After the fund has been constituted in accordance with paragraph 1 of this Article the court of the licensing State shall be exclusively competent to determine all matters relating to the apportionment and distribution of the fund.

4. (a) A final judgment entered by a court having jurisdiction under Article X shall be recognized in the territory of any other Contracting State, except:

(i) where the judgment was obtained by fraud; or

(ii) the operator was not given a fair opportunity to present his case;

(b) A final judgment which is recognized shall, upon being presented for enforcement in accordance with the formalities required by the law of the Contracting State where enforcement is sought, be enforceable as if it were a judgment of a court of that State;

(c) The merits of a claim on which the judgment has been given shall not be subject to further proceedings.

5. (a) If a person who is a national of a Contracting State, other than the operator, has paid compensation for nuclear damage under an International Convention or under the law of a non-Contracting State, such person shall, up to the amount which he has paid, acquire by subrogation the rights which the person so compensated would have enjoyed under this Convention. However, no rights shall be so acquired by any person if and to the extent that the operator has a right of recourse or contribution against such person under this Convention;

(b) If a limitation fund has been set up and

(i) the operator has paid, prior to its being set up, compensation for nuclear damage; or

(ii) the operator has paid, after it has been set up, compensation for nuclear damage under an International Convention or the law of a non-Contracting State, he shall be entitled to recover from the fund, up to the amount which he has paid, the amount which the person so compensated would have obtained in the distribution of the fund;

(c) If no limitation fund is set up, nothing in this Convention shall preclude an operator, who has paid compensation for nuclear damage out of funds other than those provided pursuant to paragraph 2 of Article III, from recovering from the person providing financial security under paragraph 2 of Article III or from the licensing State, up to the amount he has paid, the sum which the person so compensated would have obtained under this Convention;

(d) In this paragraph the expression ''a national of a Contracting State'' shall include a Contracting State or any of its constituent subdivisions or a partnership or any public or private body whether corporate or not established in a Contracting State.

6. Where no fund has been constituted under the provisions of this Article, the licensing State shall adopt such measures as are necessary to ensure that adequate sums provided by it or by insurance or other financial security in accordance with paragraph 2 of Article III, shall be available for the satisfaction of any claim established by a judgment of a court of any other

Contracting State which would be recognized under paragraph 4 of this Article; the sums shall be made available, at the option of the claimant, either in the licensing State or in the Contracting State in which the damage was sustained or in the Contracting State in which the claimant is habitually resident.

7.   After the limitation fund has been constituted in accordance with paragraph 1 of this Article or, where no such fund has been constituted, if the sums provided by the licensing State, or by insurance, or other financial security are available in accordance with paragraph 6 of this Article to meet a claim for compensation, the claimant shall not be entitled to exercise any right against any other asset of the operator in respect of his claim for nuclear damage, and any bail or security (other than security for costs) given by or on behalf of that operator in any Contracting State shall be released.

Article XII

1.   The Contracting States undertake to adopt such measures as are necessary to ensure implementation of the provisions of this Convention, including any appropriate measures for the prompt and equitable distribution of the sums available for compensation for nuclear damage.

2.   The Contracting States undertake to adopt such measures as are necessary to ensure that insurance and reinsurance premiums and sums provided by insurance, reinsurance or other financial security, or provided by them in accordance with paragraph 2 of Article III, shall be freely transferable into the currency of the Contracting State in which the damage was sustained, of the Contracting State in which the claimant is habitually resident or, as regards insurance and reinsurance premiums and payments, in the currencies specified in the insurance or reinsurance contract.

3.   This Convention shall be applied without discrimination based upon nationality, domicile or residence.

Article XIII

This Convention applies to nuclear damage caused by a nuclear incident occurring in any part of the world and involving the nuclear fuel of, or radioactive products or waste produced in, a nuclear ship flying the flag of a Contracting State.

Article XIV

This Convention shall supersede any International Conventions in force or open for signature, ratification or accession at the date on which this Convention is opened for signature, but only to the extent that such Conventions would be in conflict with it; however, nothing in this Article shall affect the obligations of Contracting States to non-Contracting States arising under such International Conventions.

Article XV

1.   Each Contracting State undertakes to take all measures necessary to prevent a nuclear ship flying its flag from being operated without a licence or authority granted by it.

2.   In the event of nuclear damage involving the nuclear fuel of, or radioactive products or waste produced in a nuclear ship flying the flag of a Contracting State, the operation of which was not at the time of the nuclear incident licensed or authorized by such Contracting State, the owner of the nuclear ship at the time of the nuclear incident shall be deemed to be the operator of the nuclear ship for all the purposes of this Convention, except that his liability shall not be limited in amount.

3.   In such an event, the Contracting State whose flag the nuclear ship flies shall be deemed to be the licensing State for all the purposes of this Convention and shall, in particular, be liable for compensation for victims in accordance with the obligations imposed on a licensing State by Article III and up to the limit laid down therein.

4.   Each Contracting State undertakes not to grant a licence or authority to operate a nuclear ship flying the flag of another State. However, nothing in this paragraph shall prevent a Contracting State from implementing the requirements of its national law concerning the operation of a nuclear ship within its internal waters and territorial sea.

Article XVI

This Convention shall apply to a nuclear ship from the date of her launching. Between her launching and the time she is authorized to fly a flag, the nuclear ship shall be deemed to be operated by the owner and to be flying the flag of the State in which she was built.

Article XVII

Nothing in this Convention shall affect any right which a Contracting State may have under international law to deny access to its waters and harbours to nuclear ships licensed by another Contracting State, even when it has formally complied with all the provisions of this Convention.

Article XVIII

An action for compensation for nuclear damage shall be brought against the operator; it may also be brought against the insurer or any person other than the licensing State who has provided financial security to the operator pursuant to paragraph 2 of Article III, if the right to bring an action against the insurer or such other person is provided under the applicable national law.

Article XIX

Notwithstanding the termination of this Convention or the termination of its application to any Contracting State pursuant to Article **XXVII**, the provisions of the Convention shall continue to apply with respect to any nuclear damage caused by a nuclear incident involving the nuclear fuel of, or radioactive products or waste produced in, a nuclear ship licensed or otherwise authorized for operation by any Contracting State prior to the date of such termination, provided the nuclear incident occurred prior to the date of such termination or, in the event of a nuclear incident occurring subsequent to the date of such termination, prior to the expiry of a period of twenty-five years after the date of such licensing or other authorization to operate such ship.

Article XX

Without prejudice to Article **X**, any dispute between two or more Contracting Parties concerning the interpretation or application of this Convention which cannot be settled through negotiation, shall, at the request of one of them, be submitted to arbitration. If within six months from the date of the request for arbitration the Parties are unable to agree on the organization of the arbitration, any one of those Parties may refer the dispute to the International Court of Justice by request in conformity with the Statute of the Court.

Article XXI

1.   Each Contracting Party may at the time of signature or ratification of this Convention or accession thereto, declare that it does not consider itself bound by Article **XX** of the Convention. The other Contracting Parties shall not be bound by this Article with respect to any Contracting Party having made such a reservation.

2.   Any Contracting Party having made a reservation in accordance with paragraph 1 may at any time withdraw this reservation by notification to the Belgian Government.

Article XXII

This Convention shall be open for signature by the States represented at the eleventh session (1961—1962) of the Diplomatic Conference on Maritime Law.

Article XXIII

This Convention shall be ratified and the instruments of ratification shall be deposited with the Belgian Government.

Article XXIV

1. This Convention shall come into force three months after the deposit of an instrument of ratification by at least one licensing State and one other State.

2. This Convention shall come into force, in respect of each signatory State which ratifies it after its entry into force as provided in paragraph 1 of this Article, three months after the date of deposit of the instrument of ratification of that State.

Article XXV

1. States Members of the United Nations, Members of the specialized agencies and of the International Atomic Energy Agency not represented at the eleventh session of the Diplomatic Conference on Maritime Law, may accede to this Convention.

2. The instruments of accession shall be deposited with the Belgian Government.

3. The Convention shall come into force in respect of the acceding State three months after the date of deposit of the instrument of accession of that State, but not before the date of entry into force of the Convention as established by Article XXIV.

Article XXVI

1. A conference for the purpose of revising this Convention shall be convened by the Belgian Government and the International Atomic Energy Agency after the Convention has been in force five years.

2. Such a conference shall also be convened by the Belgian Government and the International Atomic Energy Agency before the expiry of this term or thereafter, if one third of the Contracting States express a desire to that effect.

Article XXVII

1. Any Contracting State may denounce this Convention by notification to the Belgian Government at any time after the first revision Conference held in accordance with the provisions of Article XXVI 1.

2. This denunciation shall take effect one year after the date on which the notification has been received by the Belgian Government.

Article XXVIII

The Belgian Government shall notify the States represented at the eleventh session of the Diplomatic Conference on Maritime Law, and the States acceding to this Convention, of the following:

1. Signatures, ratifications and accessions received in accordance with Articles XXII, XXIII and XXV.
2. The date on which the Convention will come into force in accordance with Article XXIV.
3. Denunciations received in accordance with Article XXVII.

IN WITNESS WHEREOF, the undersigned Plenipotentiaries, whose credentials have been found in order, have signed this Convention.

DONE at Brussels, this twenty-fifth day of May, one thousand nine hundred and sixty-two, in the English, French, Russian and Spanish languages in a single copy, which shall remain deposited in the archives of the Belgian Government, which shall issue certified copies.

In the case of any disparity in the texts, the English and French versions shall be authentic.

Signatories and Parties

State	Date of Signature	Date of Ratification, Accession (A) or Succession (S)
Belgium	25 May 1962	
China, Republic of	25 May 1962	
Germany, Federal Republic	25 October 1974	
India	25 May 1962	
Indonesia	25 May 1962	
Ireland	25 May 1962	
Korea, Republic of	25 May 1962	
Lebanon	3 June 1975	3 June 1975
Liberia	25 May 1962	
Madagascar		13 July 1965 (A)
Malaysia	25 May 1962	
Monaco	25 May 1962	
Netherlands[1]	30 December 1968	20 March 1974
Panama	25 May 1962	
Philippines	25 May 1962	

[1] For the Kingdom in Europe, Surinam and Netherlands Antilles.

State	Date of Signature	Date of Ratification, Accession (A) or Succession (S)
Portugal	25 May 1962	31 July 1968
Syria		1 August 1974 (A)
United Arab Republic	25 May 1962	
Yugoslavia	25 May 1962	
Zaire		17 July 1967 (A)

Select Bibliography

Colliard, "La Convention de Bruxelles relative à la Responsabilité des Exploitants de Navires Nucléaires", 8 *AFDI* 41 (1962).

Jenks, "Liability for Ultra-hazardous Activities in International Law", 117 *RC* 99 (1966, I) at 137-43.

Hardy, "The Liability of Operators of Nuclear Ships", 12 *ICLQ* 778 (1963).

Könz, "The 1962 Brussels Convention on the Liability of Operators of Nuclear Ships", 57 *AJIL* 100 (1963).

Schuster, "Nuclear Ship Pollution: National and International Regulation and Liability", 5 *Env. Law* 203 (1975).

Simon & Hennebicq, "La Responsabilité des Exploitants de Navires Nucléaires. Convention de Bruxelles du 25 mai 1962", 39 *RDIDC* 633 (1962).

Szasz, "The Convention on the Liability of Operators of Nuclear Ships", 2 *J Mar. Law & Com.* 541 (1970-71).

Zaldivar, "Responsabilidad emergente de la explotacion de buques nucleares", *Jornadas sobra derecho de la navegacion,* Buenos Aires (1961).

IAEA, Report of a Panel of Legal Experts, *Liability of Operators of Nuclear Ships,* Vienna (1960).

3. VIENNA CONVENTION ON CIVIL LIABILITY FOR NUCLEAR DAMAGE
21 May 1963

Editorial Note

The Vienna Convention was negotiated under the auspices of the IAEA. Its provisions are generally to the same effect as those of the earlier Paris Convention, with the important difference that the Vienna Convention is potentially of worldwide geographical application. Its purpose is to establish minimum standards to provide protection under national law against damage resulting from certain peaceful uses of nuclear energy. Pursuant to Article II, the operator of a nuclear installation is liable for "nuclear damage" (as defined in Article I(1)(k)) upon proof that such damage was caused by a nuclear incident in the installation or, with certain limitations, in the course of carriage to or from the installation. The liability of the operator is absolute (Article IV(1)) although, as is the case under the Paris Convention, provision is made for certain defences and exceptions to liability (Article IV).

As general rules, actions must be brought within 10 years from the date of the nuclear incident (Article VI) and jurisdiction over actions lies only with the courts of the Contracting State within whose territory the nuclear incident occurred (Article XI). If an action is brought against a State itself, it may not, except in respect of measures of execution, invoke any jurisdictional immunities (Article XIV). Final judgments which are recognized (Article XII(1)) are enforceable in the territory of any of the Contracting States (Article XII(2)).

The Vienna Convention, like the Paris Convention, permits the installation State to limit the liability of the operator, but in no event to less than US $5 million for any one nuclear incident (Article V). Operators are required to maintain insurance or other financial security; however, if the security is inadequate to satisfy claims, Article VII provides that the installation State is required to meet any deficiencies up to the limit, if any, of the operator's liability as established under Article V. In contrast to the position under the Brussels Convention, no provision is made for further compensation beyond this limit by either the installation State or the Parties jointly.

The Optional Protocol establishes a dispute settlement mechanism. Unless some other form of settlement has been agreed upon by the Parties within 2 months of any dispute, the ICJ is given compulsory jurisdiction. The Optional Protocol is not in force. [1]

To date, the Vienna Convention has met with only limited acceptance. The harmonization of its provisions with those of the Paris Convention by way of a Joint Protocol is seen within the IAEA as a possible incentive to broaden adherence.

---

[1] It has been signed by the UK (11 November 1964) and ratified by the Philippines (15 November 1965).

Date of signature: 21 May 1963
Entry into force: 12 November 1977
Depositary: Director General of IAEA
Authentic languages: English, French, Russian and Spanish
Text reprinted from: 1063 *UNTS* 265
Also published in: 1963 *UN JYB* 148
Misc. 9 (1964), Cmnd. 2333

Text

VIENNA CONVENTION ON CIVIL LIABILITY FOR NUCLEAR DAMAGE

THE CONTRACTING PARTIES,

HAVING RECOGNIZED the desirability of establishing some minimum standards to provide financial protection against damage resulting from certain peaceful uses of nuclear energy,

BELIEVING that a convention on civil liability for nuclear damage would also contribute to the development of friendly relations among nations, irrespective of their differing constitutional and social systems,

HAVE DECIDED to conclude a convention for such purposes, and thereto have agreed as follows:

Article I

1. For the purposes of this Convention:
   (a) "Person" means any individual, partnership, any private or public body whether corporate or not, any international organization enjoying legal personality under the law of the Installation State, and any State or any of its constituent sub-divisions.
   (b) "National of a Contracting Party" includes a Contracting Party or any of its constituent sub-divisions, a partnership, or any private or public body whether corporate or not established within the territory of a Contracting Party.
   (c) "Operator", in relation to a nuclear installation, means the person designated or recognized by the Installation State as the operator of that installation.
   (d) "Installation State", in relation to a nuclear installation, means the Contracting Party within whose territory that installation is situated or, if it is not situated within the territory of any State, the

Contracting Party by which or under the authority of which the nuclear installation is operated.

(e) "Law of the competent court" means the law of the court having jurisdiction under this Convention, including any rules of such law relating to conflict of laws.

(f) "Nuclear fuel" means any material which is capable of producing energy by a self-sustaining chain process of nuclear fission.

(g) "Radioactive products or waste" means any radioactive material produced in, or any material made radioactive by exposure to the radiation incidental to, the production or utilization of nuclear fuel, but does not include radioisotopes which have reached the final stage of fabrication so as to be usable for any scientific, medical, agricultural, commercial or industrial purpose.

(h) "Nuclear materials" means:

　(i)　nuclear fuel, other than natural uranium and depleted uranium, capable of producing energy by a self-sustaining chain process of nuclear fission outside a nuclear reactor, either alone or in combination with some other material; and

　(ii)　radioactive products or waste.

(i) "Nuclear reactor" means any structure containing nuclear fuel in such an arrangement that a self-sustaining chain process of nuclear fission can occur therein without an additional source of neutrons.

(j) "Nuclear installation" means:

　(i)　any nuclear reactor other than one with which a means of sea or air transport is equipped for use as a source of power, whether for propulsion thereof or for any other purpose;

　(ii)　any factory using nuclear fuel for the production of nuclear material, or any factory for the processing of nuclear material, including any factory for the reprocessing of irradiated nuclear fuel; and

　(iii)　any facility where nuclear material is stored, other than storage incidental to the carriage of such material;

provided that the Installation State may determine that several nuclear installations of one operator which are located at the same site shall be considered as a single nuclear installation.

(k) "Nuclear damage" means:

　(i)　loss of life, any personal injury or any loss of, or damage to, property which arises out of or results from the radioactive properties or a combination of radioactive properties with toxic, explosive or other hazardous properties of nuclear fuel or radioactive products or waste in, or of nuclear material coming from, originating in, or sent to, a nuclear installation;

(ii) any other loss or damage so arising or resulting if and to the extent that the law of the competent court so provides; and

(iii) if the law of the Installation State so provides, loss of life, any personal injury or any loss of, or damage to, property which arises out of or results from other ionizing radiation emitted by any other source of radiation inside a nuclear installation.

(l) "Nuclear incident" means any occurrence or series of occurrences having the same origin which causes nuclear damage.

2. An Installation State may, if the small extent of the risks involved so warrants, exclude any small quantities of nuclear material from the application of this Convention, provided that:

(a) maximum limits for the exclusion of such quantities have been established by the Board of Governors of the International Atomic Energy Agency; and

(b) any exclusion by an Installation State is within such established limits.

The maximum limits shall be reviewed periodically by the Board of Governors.

Article II

1. The operator of a nuclear installation shall be liable for nuclear damage upon proof that such damage has been caused by a nuclear incident:

(a) in his nuclear installation; or

(b) involving nuclear material coming from or originating in his nuclear installation, and occurring:

(i) before liability with regard to nuclear incidents involving the nuclear material has been assumed, pursuant to the express terms of a contract in writing, by the operator of another nuclear installation;

(ii) in the absence of such express terms, before the operator of another nuclear installation has taken charge of the nuclear material; or

(iii) where the nuclear material is intended to be used in a nuclear reactor with which a means of transport is equipped for use as a source of power, whether for propulsion thereof or for any other purpose, before the person duly authorized to operate such reactor has taken charge of the nuclear material; but

(iv) where the nuclear material has been sent to a person within the territory of a non-Contracting State, before it has been unloaded from the means of transport by which it has arrived in the territory of that non-Contracting State;

(c) involving nuclear material sent to his nuclear installation, and occurring:

(i) after liability with regard to nuclear incidents involving the nuclear material has been assumed by him, pursuant to the express terms of a contract in writing, from the operator of another nuclear installation;

(ii) in the absence of such express terms, after he has taken charge of the nuclear material; or

(iii) after he has taken charge of the nuclear material from a person operating a nuclear reactor with which a means of transport is equipped for use as a source of power, whether for propulsion thereof or for any other purpose; but

(iv) where the nuclear material has, with the written consent of the operator, been sent from a person within the territory of a non-Contracting State, only after it has been loaded on the means of transport by which it is to be carried from the territory of that State;

provided that, if nuclear damage is caused by a nuclear incident occurring in a nuclear installation and involving nuclear material stored therein incidentally to the carriage of such material, the provisions of sub-paragraph (a) of this paragraph shall not apply where another operator or person is solely liable pursuant to the provisions of sub-paragraph (b) or (c) of this paragraph.

2. The Installation State may provide by legislation that, in accordance with such terms as may be specified therein, a carrier of nuclear material or a person handling radioactive waste may, at his request and with the consent of the operator concerned, be designated or recognized as operator in the place of that operator in respect of such nuclear material or radioactive waste respectively. In this case such carrier or such person shall be considered, for all the purposes of this Convention, as an operator of a nuclear installation situated within the territory of that State.

3. (a) Where nuclear damage engages the liability of more than one operator, the operators involved shall, in so far as the damage attributable to each operator is not reasonably separable, be jointly and severally liable.

(b) Where a nuclear incident occurs in the course of carriage of nuclear material, either in one and the same means of transport, or, in the case of storage incidental to the carriage, in one and the same nuclear installation, and causes nuclear damage which engages the liability of more than one operator, the total liability shall not exceed the highest amount applicable with respect to any one of them pursuant to Article V.

(c) In neither of the cases referred to in sub-paragraphs (a) and (b) of this paragraph shall the liability of any one operator exceed the amount applicable with respect to him pursuant to Article V.

4.   Subject to the provisions of paragraph 3 of this Article, where several nuclear installations of one and the same operator are involved in one nuclear incident, such operator shall be liable in respect of each nuclear installation involved up to the amount applicable with respect to him pursuant to Article V.

5.   Except as otherwise provided in this Convention, no person other than the operator shall be liable for nuclear damage. This, however, shall not affect the application of any international convention in the field of transport in force or open for signature, ratification or accession at the date on which this Convention is opened for signature.

6.   No person shall be liable for any loss or damage which is not nuclear damage pursuant to sub-paragraph (k) of paragraph 1 of Article I but which could have been included as such pursuant to sub-paragraph (k)(ii) of that paragraph.

7.   Direct action shall lie against the person furnishing financial security pursuant to Article VII, if the law of the competent court so provides.

Article III

The operator liable in accordance with this Convention shall provide the carrier with a certificate issued by or on behalf of the insurer or other financial guarantor furnishing the financial security required pursuant to Article VII. The certificate shall state the name and address of that operator and the amount, type and duration of the security, and these statements may not be disputed by the person by whom or on whose behalf the certificate was issued. The certificate shall also indicate the nuclear material in respect of which the security applies and shall include a statement by the competent public authority of the Installation State that the person named is an operator within the meaning of this Convention.

Article IV

1.   The liability of the operator for nuclear damage under this Convention shall be absolute.

2.   If the operator proves that the nuclear damage resulted wholly or partly either from the gross negligence of the person suffering the damage or from an act or omission of such person done with intent to cause damage, the competent court may, if its law so provides, relieve the operator wholly or

partly from his obligation to pay compensation in respect of the damage suffered by such person.

3.   (a) No liability under this Convention shall attach to an operator for nuclear damage caused by a nuclear incident directly due to an act of armed conflict, hostilities, civil war or insurrection.

(b) Except in so far as the law of the Installation State may provide to the contrary, the operator shall not be liable for nuclear damage caused by a nuclear incident directly due to a grave natural disaster of an exceptional character.

4.   Whenever both nuclear damage and damage other than nuclear damage have been caused by a nuclear incident or jointly by a nuclear incident and one or more other occurrences, such other damage shall, to the extent that it is not reasonably separable from the nuclear damage, be deemed, for the purposes of this Convention, to be nuclear damage caused by that nuclear incident. Where, however, damage is caused jointly by a nuclear incident covered by this Convention and by an emission of ionizing radiation not covered by it, nothing in this Convention shall limit or otherwise affect the liability, either as regards any person suffering nuclear damage or by way of recourse or contribution, of any person who may be held liable in connection with that emission of ionizing radiation.

5.   The operator shall not be liable under this Convention for nuclear damage:

(a) to the nuclear installation itself or to any property on the site of that installation which is used or to be used in connection with that installation; or

(b) to the means of transport upon which the nuclear material involved was at the time of the nuclear incident.

6.   Any Installation State may provide by legislation that sub-paragraph (b) of paragraph 5 of this Article shall not apply, provided that in no case shall the liability of the operator in respect of nuclear damage, other than nuclear damage to the means of transport, be reduced to less than US $5 million for any one nuclear incident.

7.   Nothing in this Convention shall affect:

(a) the liability of any individual for nuclear damage for which the operator, by virtue of paragraph 3 or 5 of this Article, is not liable under this Convention and which that individual caused by an act or omission done with intent to cause damage; or

(b) the liability outside this Convention of the operator for nuclear damage for which, by virtue of sub-paragraph (b) of paragraph 5 of this Article, he is not liable under this Convention.

Article V

1. The liability of the operator may be limited by the Installation State to not less than US $5 million for any one nuclear incident.

2. Any limits of liability which may be established pursuant to this Article shall not include any interest or costs awarded by a court in actions for compensation of nuclear damage.

3. The United States dollar referred to in this Convention is a unit of account equivalent to the value of the United States dollar in terms of gold on 29 April 1963, that is to say US $35 per one troy ounce of fine gold.

4. The sum mentioned in paragraph 6 of Article IV and in paragraph 1 of this Article may be converted into national currency in round figures.

Article VI

1. Rights of compensation under this Convention shall be extinguished if an action is not brought within ten years from the date of the nuclear incident. If, however, under the law of the Installation State the liability of the operator is covered by insurance or other financial security or by State funds for a period longer than ten years, the law of the competent court may provide that rights of compensation against the operator shall only be extinguished after a period which may be longer than ten years, but shall not be longer than the period for which his liability is so covered under the law of the Installation State. Such extension of the extinction period shall in no case affect rights of compensation under this Convention of any person who has brought an action for loss of life or personal injury against the operator before the expiry of the aforesaid period of ten years.

2. Where nuclear damage is caused by a nuclear incident involving nuclear material which at the time of the nuclear incident was stolen, lost, jettisoned or abandoned, the period established pursuant to paragraph 1 of this Article shall be computed from the date of that nuclear incident, but the period shall in no case exceed a period of twenty years from the date of the theft, loss, jettison or abandonment.

3. The law of the competent court may establish a period of extinction or prescription of not less than three years from the date on which the person suffering nuclear damage had knowledge or should have had knowledge of the damage and of the operator liable for the damage, provided that the period established pursuant to paragraphs 1 and 2 of this Article shall not be exceeded.

4. Unless the law of the competent court otherwise provides, any person who claims to have suffered nuclear damage and who has brought an action for compensation within the period applicable pursuant to this Article may amend his claim to take into account any aggravation of the damage, even after the expiry of that period, provided that final judgment has not been entered.

5.   Where jurisdiction is to be determined pursuant to sub-paragraph (b) of paragraph 3 of Article XI and a request has been made within the period applicable pursuant to this Article to any one of the Contracting Parties empowered so to determine, but the time remaining after such determination is less than six months, the period within which an action may be brought shall be six months, reckoned from the date of such determination.

Article VII
1.   The operator shall be required to maintain insurance or other financial security covering his liability for nuclear damage in such amount, of such type and in such terms as the Installation State shall specify. The Installation State shall ensure the payment of claims for compensation for nuclear damage which have been established against the operator by providing the necessary funds to the extent that the yield of insurance or other financial security is inadequate to satisfy such claims, but not in excess of the limit, if any, established pursuant to Article V.
2.   Nothing in paragraph 1 of this Article shall require a Contracting Party or any of its constituent sub-divisions, such as States or Republics, to maintain insurance or other financial security to cover their liability as operators.
3.   The funds provided by insurance, by other financial security or by the Installation State pursuant to paragraph 1 of this Article shall be exclusively available for compensation due under this Convention.
4.   No insurer or other financial guarantor shall suspend or cancel the insurance or other financial security provided pursuant to paragraph 1 of this Article without giving notice in writing of at least two months to the competent public authority or, in so far as such insurance or other financial security relates to the carriage of nuclear material, during the period of the carriage in question.

Article VIII
Subject to the provisions of this Convention, the nature, form and extent of the compensation, as well as the equitable distribution thereof, shall be governed by the law of the competent court.

Article IX
1.   Where provisions of national or public health insurance, social insurance, social security, workmen's compensation or occupational disease compensation systems include compensation for nuclear damage, rights of beneficiaries of such systems to obtain compensation under this Convention and rights of recourse by virtue of such systems against the operator liable shall be determined, subject to the provisions of this Convention, by the law of the

Contracting Party in which such systems have been established, or by the regulations of the intergovernmental organization which has established such systems.

2. (a) If a person who is a national of a Contracting Party, other than the operator, has paid compensation for nuclear damage under an international convention or under the law of a non-Contracting State, such person shall, up to the amount which he has paid, acquire by subrogation the rights under this Convention of the person so compensated. No rights shall be so acquired by any person to the extent that the operator has a right of recourse against such person under this Convention.

(b) Nothing in this Convention shall preclude an operator who has paid compensation for nuclear damage out of funds other than those provided pursuant to paragraph 1 of Article VII from recovering from the person providing financial security pursuant to that paragraph or from the Installation State, up to the amount he has paid, the sum which the person so compensated would have obtained under this Convention.

Article X

The operator shall have a right of recourse only:

(a) if this is expressly provided for by a contract in writing; or

(b) if the nuclear incident results from an act or omission done with intent to cause damage, against the individual who has acted or omitted to act with such intent.

Article XI

1. Except as otherwise provided in this Article, jurisdiction over actions under Article II shall lie only with the courts of the Contracting Party within whose territory the nuclear incident occurred.

2. Where the nuclear incident occurred outside the territory of any Contracting Party, or where the place of the nuclear incident cannot be determined with certainty, jurisdiction over such actions shall lie with the courts of the Installation State of the operator liable.

3. Where under paragraph 1 or 2 of this Article jurisdiction would lie with the courts of more than one Contracting Party, jurisdiction shall lie:

(a) if the nuclear incident occurred partly outside the territory of any Contracting Party, and partly within the territory of a single Contracting Party, with the courts of the latter; and

(b) in any other case, with the courts of that Contracting Party which is determined by agreement between the Contracting Parties whose courts would be competent under paragraph 1 or 2 of this Article.

Article XII

1.   A final judgment entered by a court having jurisdiction under Article XI shall be recognized within the territory of any other Contracting Party, except:

(a) where the judgment was obtained by fraud;

(b) where the party against whom the judgment was pronounced was not given a fair opportunity to present his case; or

(c) where the judgment is contrary to the public policy of the Contracting Party within the territory of which recognition is sought, or is not in accord with fundamental standards of justice.

2.   A final judgment which is recognized shall, upon being presented for enforcement in accordance with the formalities required by the law of the Contracting Party where enforcement is sought, be enforceable as if it were a judgment of a court of that Contracting Party.

3.   The merits of a claim on which the judgment has been given shall not be subject to further proceedings.

Article XIII

This Convention and the national law applicable thereunder shall be applied without any discrimination based upon nationality, domicile or residence.

Article XIV

Except in respect of measures of execution, jurisdictional immunities under rules of national or international law shall not be invoked in actions under this Convention before the courts competent pursuant to Article XI.

Article XV

The Contracting Parties shall take appropriate measures to ensure that compensation for nuclear damage, interest and costs awarded by a court in connection therewith, insurance and reinsurance premiums and funds provided by insurance, reinsurance or other financial security, or funds provided by the Installation State, pursuant to this Convention, shall be freely transferable into the currency of the Contracting Party within whose territory the damage is suffered, and of the Contracting Party within whose territory the claimant is habitually resident, and, as regards insurance or reinsurance premiums and payments, into the currencies specified in the insurance or reinsurance contract.

Article XVI

No person shall be entitled to recover compensation under this Convention to the extent that he has recovered compensation in respect of the same nuclear damage under another international convention on civil liability in the field of nuclear energy.

Article XVII

This Convention shall not, as between the parties to them, affect the application of any international agreements or international conventions on civil liability in the field of nuclear energy in force, or open for signature, ratification or accession at the date on which this Convention is opened for signature.

Article XVIII

This Convention shall not be construed as affecting the rights, if any, of a Contracting Party under the general rules of public international law in respect of nuclear damage.

Article XIX

1. Any Contracting Party entering into an agreement pursuant to sub-paragraph (b) of paragraph 3 of Article XI shall furnish without delay to the Director General of the International Atomic Energy Agency for information and dissemination to the other Contracting Parties a copy of such agreement.

2. The Contracting Parties shall furnish to the Director General for information and dissemination to the other Contracting Parties copies of their respective laws and regulations relating to matters covered by this Convention.

Article XX

Notwithstanding the termination of the application of this Convention to any Contracting Party, either by termination pursuant to Article XXV or by denunciation pursuant to Article XXVI, the provisions of this Convention shall continue to apply to any nuclear damage caused by a nuclear incident occurring before such termination.

Article XXI

This Convention shall be open for signature by the States represented at the International Conference on Civil Liability for Nuclear Damage held in Vienna from 29 April to 19 May 1963.

Article XXII

This Convention shall be ratified, and the instruments of ratification shall be deposited with the Director General of the International Atomic Energy Agency.

Article XXIII

This Convention shall come into force three months after the deposit of the fifth instrument of ratification, and, in respect of each State ratifying it thereafter, three months after the deposit of the instrument of ratification by that State.

Article XXIV

1. All States Members of the United Nations, or of any of the specialized agencies or of the International Atomic Energy Agency not represented at the International Conference on Civil Liability for Nuclear Damage, held in Vienna from 29 April to 19 May 1963, may accede to this Convention.

2. The instruments of accession shall be deposited with the Director General of the International Atomic Energy Agency.

3. This Convention shall come into force in respect of the acceding State three months after the date of deposit of the instrument of accession of that State but not before the date of the entry into force of this Convention pursuant to Article XXIII.

Article XXV

1. This Convention shall remain in force for a period of ten years from the date of its entry into force. Any Contracting Party may, by giving before the end of that period at least 12 months' notice to that effect to the Director General of the International Atomic Energy Agency, terminate the application of this Convention to itself at the end of that period of ten years.

2. This Convention shall, after that period of ten years, remain in force for a further period of five years for such Contracting Parties as have not terminated its application pursuant to paragraph 1 of this Article, and thereafter for successive periods of five years each for those Contracting Parties which have not terminated its application at the end of one of such periods, by giving, before the end of one of such periods, at least 12 months' notice to that effect to the Director General of the International Atomic Energy Agency.

Article XXVI

1. A conference shall be convened by the Director General of the International Atomic Energy Agency at any time after the expiry of a period of five years from the date of the entry into force of this Convention in order to consider the revision thereof, if one-third of the Contracting Parties express a desire to that effect.

2. Any Contracting Party may denounce this Convention by notification to the Director General of the International Atomic Energy Agency within a

period of twelve months following the first revision conference held pursuant to paragraph 1 of this Article.

3. Denunciation shall take effect one year after the date on which notification to that effect has been received by the Director General of the International Atomic Energy Agency.

Article XXVII

The Director General of the International Atomic Energy Agency shall notify the States invited to the International Conference on Civil Liability for Nuclear Damage held in Vienna from 29 April to 19 May 1963 and the States which have acceded to this Convention of the following:

(a) signatures and instruments of ratification and accession received pursuant to Articles XXI, XXII and XXIV;

(b) the date on which this Convention will come into force pursuant to Article XXIII;

(c) notifications of termination and denunciation received pursuant to Articles XXV and XXVI;

(d) requests for the convening of a revision conference pursuant to Article XXVI.

Article XXVIII

This Convention shall be registered by the Director General of the International Atomic Energy Agency in accordance with Article 102 of the Charter of the United Nations.

Article XXIX

The original of this Convention, of which the English, French, Russian and Spanish texts are equally authentic, shall be deposited with the Director General of the International Atomic Energy Agency, who shall issue certified copies.

IN WITNESS WHEREOF, the undersigned Plenipotentiaries, duly authorized thereto, have signed this Convention.

DONE in Vienna, this twenty-first day of May, one thousand nine hundred and sixty-three.

OPTIONAL PROTOCOL OF 21 MAY 1963
CONCERNING THE COMPULSORY SETTLEMENT OF DISPUTES

THE STATES PARTIES to the present Protocol and to the Vienna Convention on Civil Liability for Nuclear Damage hereinafter referred to as the "Convention", adopted by the International Conference held at Vienna from 29 April to 19 May 1963;

EXPRESSING their wish to resort in all matters concerning them in respect of any dispute arising out of the interpretation or application of the Convention to the compulsory jurisdiction of the International Court of Justice, unless some other form of settlement has been agreed upon by the parties within a reasonable period,

HAVE AGREED as follows:

Article I

Disputes arising out of the interpretation or application of the Convention shall lie within the compulsory jurisdiction of the International Court of Justice and may accordingly be brought before the Court by an application made by any party to a dispute being a Party to the present Protocol.

Article II

The parties to a dispute may agree, within a period of two months after one party has notified its opinion to the other that a dispute exists, to resort not to the International Court of Justice but to an arbitral tribunal. After the expiry of the said period, either party may bring the dispute before the Court by an application.

Article III

1. Within the same period of two months, the parties may agree to adopt a conciliation procedure before resorting to the International Court of Justice.

2. The conciliation commission shall make its recommendations within five months after its appointment. If its recommendations are not accepted by the parties to the dispute within two months after they have been delivered, either party may bring the dispute before the Court by an application.

Article IV

The present Protocol shall be open for signature by all States which may become Parties to the Convention.

Article V

The present Protocol is subject to ratification. The instruments of ratification shall be deposited with the Director General of the International Atomic Energy Agency.

Article VI

The present Protocol shall remain open for accession by all States which may become Parties to the Convention. The instruments of accession shall be deposited with the Director General of the International Atomic Energy Agency.

Article VII

1. The present Protocol shall enter into force on the same day as the Convention or on the thirtieth day following the date of deposit of the second instrument of ratification or accession to the Protocol with the Director General of the International Atomic Energy Agency, whichever date is the later.

2. For each State ratifying or acceding to the present Protocol after its entry into force in accordance with paragraph 1 of this Article, the Protocol shall enter into force on the thirtieth day after deposit by such State of its instrument of ratification or accession.

Article VIII

The Director General of the International Atomic Energy Agency shall inform all States which may become Parties to the Convention:

(a) of signatures to the present Protocol and of the deposit of instruments of ratification or accession, in accordance with Articles IV, V and VI;

(b) of the date on which the present Protocol will enter into force, in accordance with Article VII.

Article IX

The original of the present Protocol, of which the English, French, Russian and Spanish texts are equally authentic, shall be deposited with the Director General of the International Atomic Energy Agency who shall issue certified copies.

IN WITNESS WHEREOF the undersigned Plenipotentiaries, being duly authorized thereto by their respective Governments, have signed the present Protocol.

DONE in Vienna, this twenty-first day of May, one thousand nine hundred and sixty-three.

Signatories and Parties

State	Date of Signature	Date of Ratification, Accession (A) or Succession (S)
Argentina		25 April 1967
Bolivia		10 April 1968 (A)
Cameroon		6 March 1964 (A)
Colombia	21 May 1963	
Cuba		25 October 1965
Egypt		5 November 1965
Morocco	30 November 1984	
Niger		24 July 1979 (A)
Peru		26 August 1980 (A)
Philippines		15 November 1965 [2]
Spain	6 September 1963	
Trinidad & Tobago		31 January 1966 (A)
United Kingdom	11 November 1964	
Yugoslavia		12 August 1977 [3]

Select Bibliography

Jenks, "Liability for Ultra-hazardous Activities in International Law", 117 RC 99 (1966, I) at 128-33.

Lagorce, "Etude comparative des conventions OCDE et AIEA sur la responsabilité civile dans la domaine de l'énergie nucléaire", in Puget, *Aspects du Droit de l'Energie Atomique* (1965) p. 93.

IAEA, "Civil Liability for Nuclear Damage", Official Records, *Legal Series* No. 2, pp. 149 *et seq.* (1964) [*travaux préparatoires*].

IAEA, "Resolution of the Board of Governors concerning the establishment of maximum limits for exclusion of small quantities of nuclear material from the application of the Vienna Convention on civil liability for nuclear damage", *reprinted in*: Rüster *et al.*, *International Protection of the Environment*, Vol. XIII, p. 6642.

IAEA, Report of the Sixth Meeting of the Standing Committee on Civil Liability for Nuclear Damage, "The Question of International Liability For Damage Arising From A Nuclear Accident", *Doc.* GOV/2305, 19 May 1987.

---

[2] Implemented by Atomic Energy Regulatory and Liability Act No. 5207 of 1968.
[3] Implemented by Act on Liability for Nuclear Damage of 19 April 1978, 23 *NLB.*

4. NORDIC MUTUAL EMERGENCY ASSISTANCE AGREEMENT IN CONNECTION WITH RADIATION ACCIDENTS
17 October 1963, Vienna

Editorial Note

This Agreement was the first to establish a framework within which a State could request and use the assistance of another Contracting State in the event of a nuclear incident. It also provides an important role for the IAEA. It does not specify with precision the nature or type of assistance which may be requested; and it does not impose on States any obligation to provide assistance. The Agreement establishes the terms and conditions on which assistance could be given.

The requesting State assumes full responsibility for the assistance operations (Article I(1)). This includes responsibility to supervise assisting personnel, to meet the costs of the operation (Article III) and, subject to any special liability of the operator of the nuclear installation under applicable national legislation, responsibility to bear all associated risks and claims other than those arising in the territory of the assisting State (Article IV). The requesting State must also afford ''the necessary facilities, privileges and immunities with a view to securing the expeditious performance of functions under this Agreement'' (Article VI).

The role of the IAEA under Article II is to advise on the appropriate measures to be taken and the assistance required, to provide help in securing assistance from non-parties, and to co-ordinate the provision of assistance.

Date of signature: 17 October 1963
Entry into force: 19 June 1964
Depositary: IAEA
Authentic language: English
Text reprinted from: 525 *UNTS* 76
Also published in: *IAEA Doc.* INFCIRC/49

Text

NORDIC MUTUAL EMERGENCY ASSISTANCE AGREEMENT IN CONNECTION WITH RADIATION ACCIDENTS

THE CONTRACTING PARTIES, desiring to assist each other to the extent possible in the event of an incident involving damage from ionizing radiation, and desiring to establish in advance the terms upon which a Contracting State requesting assistance (hereinafter referred to as the "Requesting State") may use the assistance provided by another Contracting State or by the International Atomic Energy Agency (hereinafter referred to as the "Assisting Party"), have agreed as follows:

Article I
General terms of assistance

1. The Requesting State shall have full responsibility for the use of the assistance in conformity with this Agreement, and any personnel provided by the Assisting Party shall be subject to the direction and supervision of the Requesting State in the performance of their functions while within the territory of the Requesting State.

2. Equipment or materials shall remain the property of the Assisting Party, unless otherwise agreed, and shall be returned to it at its request.

3. The Requesting State shall employ the assistance exclusively for the purpose for which such assistance has been made available, and shall itself provide, to the extent of its capabilities, any local facilities and services required for the proper and effective administration of the assistance, and for the protection of personnel, equipment or materials.

4. The assistance shall not be used in such a way as to further any military purpose.

Article II
Special functions of the Agency

1. The International Atomic Energy Agency shall, at the request of and in consultation with the Requesting State:
    (a) Advise upon the measures to be taken and the assistance required.
    (b) Assist in securing from its Member States not parties to this Agreement such assistance as cannot readily be provided by the other Contracting Parties.
    (c) Co-ordinate the provision of assistance.

2. At any time after he has been notified by a Contracting State of the existence of an emergency within its territory, the Director General of the Agency may designate, in consultation with that State, an observer, who may enter its territory for the purpose of investigating the nature and extent of the emergency and reporting to him thereon. The Director General may, in addition, authorize such person to act as his representative.

Article III
Financial provisions

1. The Requesting State shall defray all expenses payable within its

territory in connection with the assistance, and shall pay to assisting personnel a reasonable subsistence allowance in local currency.

2. The Assisting Party shall defray such expenses relative to the assistance provided by it as are payable outside the Requesting State, including the following:

(a) Salaries of personnel.

(b) Purchase price, or fees due for the use, of equipment, facilities or materials.

(c) Cost of transport of personnel, equipment or materials outside the territory of the Requesting State, including subsistence allowances for personnel.

3. Unless otherwise agreed, the Requesting State shall reimburse the Assisting Party for any expense incurred pursuant to paragraph 2. Such reimbursement should correspond to the reasonable cost of the service, equipment, materials or facilities, or of the use thereof, to the Assisting Party at the time they were made available. Reimbursement shall be effected no later than sixty days after the Assisting Party has notified its claim to the Requesting State.

Article IV
Liability

1. The Requesting State shall bear all risks and claims resulting from, occurring in the course of or otherwise connected with, the assistance rendered on its territory and covered by this Agreement. In particular, the Requesting State shall be responsible for dealing with claims which might be brought by third parties against the Assisting Party or personnel. Except in respect of liability of individuals having caused the damage by wilful misconduct or by gross negligence, the Requesting State shall hold the Assisting Party or personnel harmless in case of any claims or liabilities in connection with the assistance.

2. The Requesting State shall compensate the Assisting Party for the death of, or temporary or permanent injury to, personnel, as well as for loss of, or damage to, non-perishable equipment or materials, caused within its territory in connection with the assistance.

3. The Assisting State shall bear all risks and claims in connection with damage or injury occurring in its own territory.

4. The Requesting and the Assisting States shall be released from their obligations under paragraphs 1-3 to the extent that the damage is covered by an operator of a nuclear installation who is liable for nuclear damage under the applicable national law.

5. The provisions of this Article shall not prejudice any recourse action under the applicable national law, except that recourse actions can be brought against assisting personnel only in respect of damage or injury which they have caused by wilful misconduct or gross negligence.

Article V
Designation of competent authorities
1. The competent authorities authorized by the Contracting Parties to receive requests for and to accept offers of assistance, and to accept communications relating thereto, are listed in the Annex[1] to this Agreement.
2. The Contracting Parties shall inform each other of any changes in respect of such competent authorities.

Article VI
Facilities, privileges and immunities
The Requesting State shall afford, in relation to the assistance, the necessary facilities, privileges and immunities with a view to securing the expeditious performance of functions under this Agreement. In relation to assistance provided by the International Atomic Energy Agency, the Requesting State shall apply the Agreement on the Privileges and Immunities of the Agency.

Article VII
Use of information
An Assisting Party shall not make any public statements concerning the incident, nor communicate any information obtained by it under this Agreement except with the consent of the Requesting State.

Article VIII
Special conditions
An Assisting Party or the Requesting State may attach special conditions to their request for, or offer or acceptance of, assistance. Such special conditions shall become binding as soon as they have been accepted by the other party or parties concerned.

Article IX
Settlement of disputes
Any dispute concerning the interpretation or application of this Agreement which is not settled by negotiation shall, at the request of any party to the

[1 The Annex is not reproduced here.]

dispute, be settled by arbitration, or, if the parties do not agree upon the constitution of an arbitral tribunal within three months after the request for arbitration was made, by the International Court of Justice.

Article X
Termination of assistance

1. The Requesting State may at any time in writing request the termination of the assistance provided under this Agreement.

2. An Assisting Party may, after having given written notice, terminate its assistance if:

(a) In its opinion such assistance is no longer needed by the Requesting State.

(b) Its domestic needs so require.

(c) The Requesting State fails to observe the terms of this Agreement.

3. Upon such request for, or notice of, termination the Requesting State and the Assisting Party shall consult together with a view to concluding any operations in progress at the time of such termination and facilitating withdrawal of the assistance.

Article XI
Entry into force

This Agreement shall enter into force upon:

(a) signature without reservation in respect of ratification or

(b) signature with reservation in respect of ratification, followed by ratification, on behalf of two States and the International Atomic Energy Agency.

Instruments of ratification shall be deposited with the Director General of the Agency.

Article XII
Withdrawal from Agreement

Any party may withdraw from this Agreement by written notice to that effect addressed to the other parties. Such withdrawal shall take effect twelve months after receipt of such notice. Withdrawal shall not, however, terminate the application of this Agreement in respect of any assistance commenced prior to the date on which withdrawal takes effect.

DONE in Vienna, this 17th day of October 1963 in a single copy in English, which shall be deposited in the archives of the International Atomic Energy Agency, whose Director General shall send a certified copy hereof to each Contracting State.

Parties

State	Date of Ratification or Signature (S)
Denmark	17 August 1964
Finland	16 June 1965
Norway	17 October 1963 (S)
Sweden	19 June 1964
IAEA	17 October 1963 (S)

There are a number of other similar Agreements, some of which are listed below:

(1) France-Federal Republic of Germany, Agreement on Mutual Assistance in the Event of Catastrophes and Grave Disasters, 3 February 1977, entered into force 1 December 1980;
reprinted in: Bundesgesetzblatt 1980, II, p. 1438;
also in: Journal officiel de la République française of 4 January 1981.

(2) Federal Republic of Germany-Luxembourg, Treaty on Mutual Assistance in the Event of Catastrophes and Grave Disasters, 2 March 1978;
reprinted in: Bundesgesetzblatt 1981, II, p. 447.

(3) Federal Republic of Germany-Switzerland, Agreement on Radiation Protection in Case of Emergency, 31 May 1978, entered into force 10 January 1979;
reprinted in: Bundesgesetzblatt 1980, II, p. 563;
also in: Sammlung der eidgenössischen Gesetze No. 9 of 13 March 1979;
and in: 22 NLB 51 (1978).

(4) Belgium-Federal Republic of Germany, Agreement on Mutual Emergency Assistance, 6 November 1980, entered into force 1 May 1984;
reprinted in: Bundesgesetzblatt 1982, II, p. 1006.

(5) Belgium-France, Agreement on Mutual Assistance in the Event of Catastrophes and Serious Disasters, 21 April 1981;
reprinted in: Moniteur Belge of 29 May 1984.

5. CONVENTION ON INTERNATIONAL LIABILITY FOR DAMAGE CAUSED BY SPACE OBJECTS
29 March 1972, Geneva

Editorial Note

This Convention establishes an inter-State liability and dispute-settlement regime for certain damage caused by space objects. It is based on a draft prepared by the UN General Assembly's Committee on Peaceful Uses of Outer Space. The Committee's brief was to elaborate on the rights and obligations pertaining to liability for damage caused by space objects as laid down in the 1967 *Treaty on Principles Governing the Activities of States in the Exploration and Use of Outer Space, Including the Moon and Other Celestial Bodies* (610 *UNTS* 205, 6 *ILM* 386) (the *travaux préparatoires* are available in UN Doc. A/AC.105/C.2/SR). The Convention was commended by the General Assembly to United Nations members on 29 November 1971 by UN General Assembly Resolution 2777 (XXVI), adopted by 93 votes to none, with 4 abstentions.

Subject only to the limited exceptions set out in Articles VI and VII a State which launches a space object (as defined by Article I(d)) is absolutely liable to pay compensation for all loss of life, personal injury or property damage caused by the object on the surface of the earth or to an aircraft in flight (Article II). The definition of damage does not appear to extend to environmental harm. Liability for all damage caused elsewhere, including damage to another space object, or to persons or property on board, is dependent on the existence of some fault attributable to the launching State (Article III). In some situations States may share joint and several liability for damage, notably where it is caused on the surface of a third State as a result of damage by one space object to another (Articles IV and V).

The Convention contains detailed provisions relating to the procedure and time-limits for presentation of claims for compensation by States which suffer damage or whose natural or judicial persons suffer damage (Articles VIII-XI). It also establishes the principles on which the measure of compensation is to be determined (Article XII). It is envisaged that compensation will be agreed upon through diplomatic channels but, given that this will not always be possible, a procedure for the establishment of a Claims Commission is included (Articles XIV-XX). No ceiling on liability is provided.

Article XXI provides that where a State is faced with a serious danger to its population as a result of damage to its territory by a space object, the Contracting States, and especially the launching State, are to "examine the possibility of rendering appropriate and rapid assistance". No obligation to render assistance is created.

Canadian claim for damage caused by Soviet Cosmos 954

On 24 January 1978 Cosmos 954, a nuclear-powered satellite launched by the USSR, disintegrated over Canada. Canadian authorities took immediate steps to locate, recover, remove and test the radioactive debris and to clean-up the affected areas. In doing so they incurred expenses which, they claimed, totalled Canadian $6,041,174.70.

Canada and the USSR were Parties to the 1972 Convention on Liability for Damage Caused by Space Objects and the incident was thus the first and only occasion to date for application of the Convention.

On 23 January 1979 Canada formally presented a claim to the USSR for compensation in the above-mentioned sum (see 18 *ILM* 899-908 (1979)). In its response the USSR confirmed its adherence to the Convention and noted that it would ''consider the question of such damage in strict accordance with the provisions'' of the Convention (18 *ILM* 923 (1979)).

Agreement on the amount of compensation was finally reached in 1981 without the establishment of a Claims Commission. By a Protocol dated 2 April 1981 the USSR agreed to pay, and Canada agreed to accept, Canadian $3,000,000 in final settlement of the claim.

Date of signature:	29 March 1972
Entry into force:	1 September 1972
Depositaries:	Governments of USSR, UK and USA
Authentic languages:	English, Russian, French, Spanish and Chinese
Text reprinted from:	961 *UNTS* 187
Also published in:	24 *UST* 2391 (1973), *TIAS* 7762
	UKTS 16 (1974), Cmnd. 5551

Text

CONVENTION ON INTERNATIONAL LIABILITY FOR DAMAGE CAUSED BY SPACE OBJECTS

THE STATES PARTIES TO THIS CONVENTION,

RECOGNIZING the common interest of all mankind in furthering the exploration and use of outer space for peaceful purposes,

RECALLING the Treaty on Principles Governing the Activities of States in the Exploration and Use of Outer Space, including the Moon and Other Celestial Bodies,

TAKING into consideration that, notwithstanding the precautionary measures to be taken by States and international intergovernmental organizations involved in the launching of space objects, damage may on occasion be caused by such objects,

RECOGNIZING the need to elaborate effective international rules and procedures concerning liability for damage caused by space objects and to ensure, in particular, the prompt payment under the terms of this Convention of a full and equitable measure of compensation to victims of such damage,

BELIEVING that the establishment of such rules and procedures will contribute to the strengthening of international cooperation in the field of the exploration and use of outer space for peaceful purposes,

HAVE AGREED on the following:

Article I

For the purposes of this Convention:
- (a) The term "damage" means loss of life, personal injury or other impairment of health; or loss of or damage to property of States or of persons, natural or judicial, or property of international intergovernmental organizations;
- (b) The term "launching" includes attempted launching;
- (c) The term "launching State" means:
  - (i) A State which launches or procures the launching of a space object;
  - (ii) A State from whose territory or facility a space object is launched;
- (d) The term "space object" includes component parts of a space object as well as its launch vehicle and parts thereof.

Article II

A launching State shall be absolutely liable to pay compensation for damage caused by its space objects on the surface of the earth or to aircraft in flight.

Article III

In the event of damage being caused elsewhere than on the surface of the earth to a space object of one launching State or to persons or property on board such a space object by a space object of another launching State, the latter shall be liable only if the damage is due to its fault or the fault of persons for whom it is responsible.

Article IV

1. In the event of damage being caused elsewhere than on the surface of the earth to a space object of one launching State or to persons or property on board such a space object by a space object of another launching State, and of damage thereby being caused to a third State or to its natural or judicial persons, the first two States shall be jointly and severally liable to the third State, to the extent indicated by the following:
  - (a) If the damage has been caused to the third State on the surface of the earth or to aircraft in flight, their liability to the third State shall be absolute;

(b) If the damage has been caused to a space object of the third State or to persons or property on board that space object elsewhere than on the surface of the earth, their liability to the third State shall be based on the fault of either of the first two States or on the fault of persons for whom either is responsible.

2.   In all cases of joint and several liability referred to in paragraph 1 of this article, the burden of compensation for the damage shall be apportioned between the first two States in accordance with the extent to which they were at fault; if the extent of the fault of each of these States cannot be established, the burden of compensation shall be apportioned equally between them. Such apportionment shall be without prejudice to the right of the third State to seek the entire compensation due under this Convention from any or all of the launching States which are jointly and severally liable.

Article V

1.   Whenever two or more States jointly launch a space object, they shall be jointly and severally liable for any damage caused.

2.   A launching State which has paid compensation for damage shall have the right to present a claim for indemnification to other participants in the joint launching. The participants in a joint launching may conclude agreements regarding the apportioning among themselves of the financial obligation in respect of which they are jointly and severally liable. Such agreements shall be without prejudice to the right of a State sustaining damage to seek the entire compensation due under this Convention from any or all of the launching States which are jointly and severally liable.

3.   A State from whose territory or facility a space object is launched shall be regarded as a participant in a joint launching.

Article VI

1.   Subject to the provisions of paragraph 2 of this article, exoneration from absolute liability shall be granted to the extent that a launching State establishes that the damage has resulted either wholly or partially from gross negligence or from an act or omission done with intent to cause damage on the part of a claimant State or of natural or judicial persons it represents.

2.   No exoneration whatever shall be granted in cases where the damage has resulted from activities conducted by a launching State which are not in conformity with international law including, in particular, the Charter of the United Nations and the Treaty on Principles Governing the Activities of States in the Exploration and Use of Outer Space, including the Moon and Other Celestial Bodies.

Article VII

The provisions of this Convention shall not apply to damage caused by a space object of a launching State to:

(a) Nationals of that launching State;

(b) Foreign nationals during such time as they are participating in the operation of that space object from the time of its launching or at any stage thereafter until its descent, or during such time as they are in the immediate vicinity of a planned launching or recovery area as the result of an invitation by that launching State.

Article VIII

1.   A State which suffers damage, or whose natural or judicial persons suffer damage, may present to a launching State a claim for compensation for such damage.

2.   If the State of nationality has not presented a claim, another State may, in respect of damage sustained in its territory by any natural or judicial person, present a claim to a launching State.

3.   If neither the State of nationality nor the State in whose territory the damage was sustained has presented a claim or notified its intention of presenting a claim, another State may, in respect of damage sustained by its permanent residents, present a claim to a launching State.

Article IX

A claim for compensation for damage shall be presented to a launching State through diplomatic channels. If a State does not maintain diplomatic relations with the launching State concerned, it may request another State to present its claim to that launching State or otherwise represent its interests under this Convention. It may also present its claim through the Secretary-General of the United Nations, provided the claimant State and the launching State are both Members of the United Nations.

Article X

1.   A claim for compensation for damage may be presented to a launching State not later than one year following the date of the occurrence of the damage or the identification of the launching State which is liable.

2.   If, however, a State does not know of the occurrence of the damage or has not been able to identify the launching State which is liable, it may present a claim within one year following the date on which it learned of the aforementioned facts; however, this period shall in no event exceed one year following the date on which the State could reasonably be expected to have learned of the facts through the exercise of due diligence.

3.   The time-limits specified in paragraphs 1 and 2 of this article shall apply even if the full extent of the damage may not be known. In this event, however, the claimant State shall be entitled to revise the claim and submit additional documentation after the expiration of such time-limits until one year after the full extent of the damage is known.

Article XI
1.   Presentation of a claim to a launching State for compensation for damage under this Convention shall not require the prior exhaustion of any local remedies which may be available to a claimant State or to natural or judicial persons it represents.
2.   Nothing in this Convention shall prevent a State, or natural or judicial persons it might represent, from pursuing a claim in the courts or administrative tribunals or agencies of a launching State. A State shall not, however, be entitled to present a claim under this Convention in respect of the same damage for which a claim is being pursued in the courts or administrative tribunals or agencies of a launching State or under another international agreement which is binding on the States concerned.

Article XII
The compensation which the launching State shall be liable to pay for damage under this Convention shall be determined in accordance with international law and the principles of justice and equity, in order to provide such reparation in respect of the damage as will restore the person, natural or judicial, State or international organization on whose behalf the claim is presented to the condition which would have existed if the damage had not occurred.

Article XIII
Unless the claimant State and the State from which compensation is due under this Convention agree on another form of compensation, the compensation shall be paid in the currency of the claimant State or, if that State so requests, in the currency of the State from which compensation is due.

Article XIV
If no settlement of a claim is arrived at through diplomatic negotiations as provided for in article IX, within one year from the date on which the claimant State notifies the launching State that it has submitted the documentation of its claim, the parties concerned shall establish a Claims Commission at the request of either party.

Article XV

1. The Claims Commission shall be composed of three members: one appointed by the claimant State, one appointed by the launching State and the third member, the Chairman, to be chosen by both parties jointly. Each party shall make its appointment within two months of the request for the establishment of the Claims Commission.

2. If no agreement is reached on the choice of the Chairman within four months of the request for the establishment of the Commission, either party may request the Secretary-General of the United Nations to appoint the Chairman within a further period of two months.

Article XVI

1. If one of the parties does not make its appointment within the stipulated period, the Chairman shall, at the request of the other party, constitute a single-member Claims Commission.

2. Any vacancy which may arise in the Commission for whatever reason shall be filled by the same procedure adopted for the original appointment.

3. The Commission shall determine its own procedure.

4. The Commission shall determine the place or places where it shall sit and all other administrative matters.

5. Except in the case of decisions and awards by a single-member Commission, all decisions and awards of the Commission shall be by majority vote.

Article XVII

No increase in the membership of the Claims Commission shall take place by reason of two or more claimant States or launching States being joined in any one proceeding before the Commission. The claimant States so joined shall collectively appoint one member of the Commission in the same manner and subject to the same conditions as would be the case for a single claimant State. When two or more launching States are so joined, they shall collectively appoint one member of the Commission in the same way. If the claimant States or the launching States do not make the appointment within the stipulated period, the Chairman shall constitute a single-member Commission.

Article XVIII

The Claims Commission shall decide the merits of the claim for compensation and determine the amount of compensation payable, if any.

Article XIX

1. The Claims Commission shall act in accordance with the provisions of article XII.

2.   The decision of the Commission shall be final and binding if the parties have so agreed; otherwise the Commission shall render a final and recommendatory award, which the parties shall consider in good faith. The Commission shall state the reasons for its decision or award.

3.   The Commission shall give its decision or award as promptly as possible and no later than one year from the date of its establishment, unless an extension of this period is found necessary by the Commission.

4.   The Commission shall make its decision or award public. It shall deliver a certified copy of its decision or award to each of the parties and to the Secretary-General of the United Nations.

Article XX

The expenses in regard to the Claims Commission shall be borne equally by the parties, unless otherwise decided by the Commission.

Article XXI

If the damage caused by a space object presents a large-scale danger to human life or seriously interferes with the living conditions of the population or the functioning of vital centres, the States Parties, and in particular the launching State, shall examine the possibility of rendering appropriate and rapid assistance to the State which has suffered the damage, when it so requests. However, nothing in this article shall affect the rights or obligations of the States Parties under this Convention.

Article XXII

1.   In this Convention, with the exception of articles XXIV to XXVII, references to States shall be deemed to apply to any international intergovernmental organization which conducts space activities if the organization declares its acceptance of the rights and obligations provided for in this Convention and if a majority of the States members of the organization are States Parties to this Convention and to the Treaty on Principles Governing the Activities of States in the Exploration and Use of Outer Space, including the Moon and Other Celestial Bodies.

2.   States members of any such organization which are States Parties to this Convention shall take all appropriate steps to ensure that the organization makes a declaration in accordance with the preceding paragraph.

3.   If an international intergovernmental organization is liable for damage by virtue of the provisions of this Convention, that organization and those of its members which are States Parties to this Convention shall be jointly and severally liable; provided, however, that:

(a) Any claim for compensation in respect of such damage shall be first presented to the organization;

(b) Only where the organization has not paid, within a period of six months, any sum agreed or determined to be due as compensation for such damage, may the claimant State invoke the liability of the members which are States Parties to this Convention for the payment of that sum.

4. Any claim, pursuant to the provisions of this Convention, for compensation in respect of damage caused to an organization which has made a declaration in accordance with paragraph 1 of this article shall be presented by a State member of the organization which is a State Party to this Convention.

Article XXIII

1. The provisions of this Convention shall not affect other international agreements in force in so far as relations between the States Parties to such agreements are concerned.

2. No provision of this Convention shall prevent States from concluding international agreements reaffirming, supplementing or extending its provisions.

Article XXIV

1. This Convention shall be open to all States for signature. Any State which does not sign this Convention before its entry into force in accordance with paragraph 3 of this article may accede to it at any time.

2. This Convention shall be subject to ratification by signatory States. Instruments of ratification and instruments of accession shall be deposited with the Governments of the United States of America, the United Kingdom of Great Britain and Northern Ireland and the Union of Soviet Socialist Republics, which are hereby designated the Depositary Governments.

3. This Convention shall enter into force on the deposit of the fifth instrument of ratification.

4. For States whose instruments of ratification or accession are deposited subsequent to the entry into force of this Convention, it shall enter into force on the date of the deposit of their instruments of ratification or accession.

5. The Depositary Governments shall promptly inform all signatory and acceding States of the date of each signature, the date of deposit of each instrument of ratification of and accession to this Convention, the date of its entry into force and other notices.

6. This Convention shall be registered by the Depositary Governments pursuant to Article 102 of the Charter of the United Nations.

Article XXV

Any State Party to this Convention may propose amendments to this Convention. Amendments shall enter into force for each State Party to the Convention accepting the amendments upon their acceptance by a majority of the States Parties to the Convention and thereafter for each remaining State Party to the Convention on the date of acceptance by it.

Article XXVI

Ten years after the entry into force of this Convention, the question of the review of this Convention shall be included in the provisional agenda of the United Nations General Assembly in order to consider, in the light of past application of the Convention, whether it requires revision. However, at any time after the Convention has been in force for five years, and at the request of one third of the States Parties to the Convention, and with the concurrence of the majority of the States Parties, a conference of the States Parties shall be convened to review this Convention.

Article XXVII

Any State Party to this Convention may give notice of its withdrawal from the Convention one year after its entry into force by written notification to the Depositary Governments. Such withdrawal shall take effect one year from the date of receipt of this notification.

Article XXVIII

This Convention, of which the English, Russian, French, Spanish and Chinese texts are equally authentic, shall be deposited in the archives of the Depositary Governments. Duly certified copies of this Convention shall be transmitted by the Depositary Governments to the Governments of the signatory and acceding States.

Signatories and Parties

State	Date of Signature	Date of Ratification, Accession (A) or Succession (S)
Algeria	20 April 1972	
Argentina	29 March 1972	14 November 1986
Australia		20 January 1975 (A)

State	Date of Signature	Date of Ratification, Accession (A) or Succession (S)
Austria [1]	30 May 1972	10 January 1980
Belgium	29 March 1972	13 August 1976
Benin	29 March 1972	25 April 1975
Botswana	29 March 1972	11 March 1974
Brazil	13 July 1972	9 March 1973
Bulgaria	29 March 1972	16 May 1975
Burundi	29 March 1972	
Byelorussian SSR	29 March 1972	27 December 1973
Cambodia	29 March 1972	
Canada [1]		20 February 1975 (A)
Central African Republic	27 April 1972	
Chile		1 December 1976 (A)
China, Republic of	29 March 1972	9 February 1973
Colombia	29 March 1972	
Costa Rica	29 March 1972	
Cuba		25 November 1982
Cyprus	28 April 1972	15 May 1973
Czechoslovakia	29 March 1972	8 September 1973
Denmark [1]	19 April 1972	1 April 1977
Dominican Republic	26 April 1972	23 February 1973
Ecuador	25 April 1972	17 August 1972
Egypt	19 May 1972	
El Salvador	29 March 1972	
European Space Agency		23 September 1976 (Acceptance)
Fiji		4 April 1973 (A)
Finland	29 March 1972	1 February 1977
France		31 December 1975 (A)
Gabon		5 February 1982 (A)
Gambia	2 June 1972	
German Democratic Republic	29 March 1972	30 August 1972
Germany, Federal Republic		18 December 1975 (A)
Ghana	29 March 1972	
Greece	12 April 1972	27 April 1977

[1] Declaration on ratification or accession that will recognize as binding, in relation to any other State accepting the same obligation, the decision of a Claims Commission concerning any dispute to which it may become a party under the Convention.

State	Date of Signature	Date of Ratification, Accession (A) or Succession (S)
Guatemala	29 March 1972	
Haiti	29 March 1972	
Honduras	29 March 1972	
Hungary	29 March 1972	27 December 1972
Iceland	29 March 1972	
India		9 July 1979 (A)
Iran	29 March 1972	13 February 1974
Iraq		4 October 1972 (A)
Ireland[1]	29 March 1972	29 June 1972
Israel		21 June 1977 (A)
Italy	29 March 1972	22 February 1983
Japan		20 June 1983 (A)
Jordan	25 May 1972	
Kenya		25 September 1975 (A)
Korea, Republic of[2]	29 March 1972	14 January 1980
Kuwait[3]	7 June 1972	30 October 1972
Laos	29 March 1972	20 March 1973
Lebanon	29 March 1972	
Liechtenstein		24 December 1979 (A)
Luxembourg	25 April 1972	18 October 1983
Mali	4 April 1972	9 June 1972
Malta		13 January 1978 (A)
Mexico	29 March 1972	8 April 1974
Mongolia	29 March 1972	5 September 1972
Morocco	29 March 1972	15 March 1973
Nepal	29 March 1972	
Netherlands[1]		17 February 1981 (A)
New Zealand[4]	19 June 1972	30 October 1974
Nicaragua	29 March 1972	
Niger	24 May 1972	1 September 1972
Norway	29 March 1972	
Oman	23 June 1972	
Pakistan	6 July 1972	10 April 1973
Panama	29 March 1972	5 June 1974

[2] Declaration on signature that signature does not in any way mean or imply recognition of any territory or regime which has not been recognized by the Government of the Republic of Korea.

[3] Declaration on ratification that ratification does not in any way imply recognition of Israel, nor does it oblige it to apply the provisions of the Convention in respect of Israel.

[4] Declaration on ratification that it will accept as binding decisions of any Claims Commission established in accordance with Article XIV of the Convention.

State	Date of Signature	Date of Ratification, Accession (A) or Succession (S)
Papua New Guinea		27 October 1980 (S) (with effect from 16 September 1975)
Peru	10 April 1972	
Philippines	22 August 1972	
Poland	29 March 1972	25 January 1973
Qatar		11 January 1974 (A)
Romania	29 March 1972	5 March 1980
Rwanda	29 March 1972	
Saudi Arabia		17 December 1975 (A)
Senegal	14 April 1972	26 March 1975
Seychelles		5 January 1978 (A)
Sierra Leone	14 July 1972	
Singapore	19 July 1972	19 August 1985
South Africa	29 March 1972	
Spain	29 March 1972	2 January 1980
Sri Lanka		9 April 1973 (A)
Sweden [1]		15 June 1976 (A)
Switzerland	29 March 1972	22 January 1974
Syria		6 February 1980 (A)
Tanzania	31 May 1972	
Togo	10 April 1972	26 April 1976
Trinidad & Tobago		8 February 1980 (A)
Tunisia	29 March 1972	18 May 1973
Ukrainian SSR	29 March 1972	16 October 1973
USSR [5]	29 March 1972	9 October 1973
United Kingdom [6]	29 March 1972	9 October 1973
USA	29 March 1972	9 October 1973
Venezuela	29 March 1972	1 August 1978
Yugoslavia		20 October 1975 (A)
Zaire	29 March 1972	
Zambia		28 August 1973 (A)

[5] Objection dated 5 August 1976 that the statement by the Federal Republic of Germany extending the Convention to Western sectors of Berlin could not be regarded as having juridical force.

[6] Declaration dated 17 April 1972 that if a regime is not recognized as the Government of a State, neither signature nor deposit of any instrument by it, nor notification of any of those acts, will bring about recognition of that regime by any other State.

Select Bibliography

Alexander, ''Measuring Damages under the Convention on International Liability for Damage Caused by Space Objects'', 6 *J of Space Law* 151 (1978).

Christol, ''International Liability for Damage Caused by Space Objects'', 74 *AJIL* 346 (1980).

Deleau, ''La Responsabilité pour Dommages Causés par les Objets Lancés dans l'Espace Extra-Atmosphérique'', 14 *AFDI* 746-55 (1968).

Foster, ''The Convention on International Liability for Damage Caused by Space Objects'', 10 *Can. Ybk Int'l Law* 137 (1972).

Galloway, ''United Nations Consideration of Nuclear Power for Satellites'', *Proc. 22nd Colloquium on the Law of Outer Space* 131 (1980).

On the Canadian Cosmos 954 Claim see:

De Bellis, ''La Caduta del Satellite Cosmos 954 e la Responsabilità dello Stato di Lancio'', 64 *Rivista di diritto internazionale* 845 (1981).

Galloway, ''Nuclear Powered Satellites: the USSR Cosmos 954 and the Canadian Claim, 12 *Akron L Rev* 401 (1979).

Matte, ''Cosmos 954: Coexistence pacifique et vide juridique'', 3 *Annals Air & Space L* 483 (1978).

Reis *et al.*, Articles on liability following the Cosmos accident, 6 *J of Space Law* 125-69 (1978).

Schwartz & Berlin, ''After the Fall: an Analysis of Canadian Legal Claims for Damage Caused by Cosmos 954'', 27 *McGill LJ* 676 (1982).

6.1   STOCKHOLM DECLARATION OF THE UNITED NATIONS CONFERENCE ON THE HUMAN ENVIRONMENT
16 June 1972

6.2   UN GENERAL ASSEMBLY RESOLUTION 2995 ON "COOPERATION BETWEEN STATES IN THE FIELD OF THE ENVIRONMENT" and RESOLUTION 2996 ON "INTERNATIONAL RESPONSIBILITY OF STATES IN REGARD TO THE ENVIRONMENT"
15 December 1972

Editorial Note

The UN Conference on the Human Environment was held at Stockholm from 5 to 16 June 1972. It was convened pursuant to UN General Assembly Resolution 2398 (XXIII) of 3 December 1968 (*Ybk UN* 1968 pp. 476-7), on a proposal from Sweden. Delegates from 113 States attended the Conference, representing most of the UN membership with the exception of the USSR, Cuba and a number of other socialist participants who refused to attend on the ground that the criteria for invitations to the Conference had effectively excluded certain States, notably the German Democratic Republic.

The Conference adopted a Declaration of Principles for the Preservation and Enhancement of the Human Environment and an Action Plan consisting of 109 Recommendations for environmental action at the international level (Report of the UN Conference on the Human Environment, *UN Doc.* A/CONF. 48/14 at 2-65 and Corr. 1 (1972)).

The Declaration of Principles is based on a draft Declaration prepared by the Preparatory Committee for the Conference (*UN Doc.* A/CONF.48/PC.17). It reflects the compromise that was eventually reached between, on the one hand, those delegates who believed it should serve principally to stimulate public awareness of, and concern over, environmental issues and, on the other hand, those delegates who insisted that it should provide specific guidelines for future governmental and intergovernmental action.

In the context of transfrontier radioactive pollution the most significant of the 26 Principles are Principles 21 and 22. Principle 21 affirms the responsibility of States to ensure that activities within their jurisdiction do not cause damage in another State or beyond national jurisdiction, such as in outer space or on the high seas. This responsibility is said to extend also to activities under a State's "control", such as those carried out by its nationals or by or on ships registered in its territory.

Principle 22 requires States to cooperate in developing international environmental law. It is a substantially weakened version of an earlier proposal to include a provision requiring States to pay compensation for all environmental damage caused by activities carried on within their territory. The earlier proposal failed because of concerns on the part of a number of delegates that it would have implied acceptance of a no-fault or 'strict' standard of liability in relation to environmental harm. These delegates made clear that in their view liability to pay compensation would only exist where there had been negligence attributable to the State concerned (*UN Doc.* A/CONF.48/PC.12 Annex 1 at 15 (1971)). The relevance of fault in this connection remains controversial.

The draft Declaration prepared by the Preparatory Committee also contained a third relevant principle, "Principle 20". This provided:

Relevant information must be supplied by States on activities or developments within their jurisdiction or under their control whenever they believe, or have reason to believe, that such information is needed to avoid the risk of significant adverse effects on the environment in areas beyond their national jurisdiction (*UN Doc.* A/CONF.48/4 Annex para. 20 at 4 (1972)).

This Principle was not agreed at the Conference following the objections of a number of developing States, which maintained that the obligation to consult might be abused by developed States to impede development projects.

The Report of the Conference was considered by the UN General Assembly at its 27th session. On 15 December 1972 eleven resolutions concerning the environment were passed. Resolution 2994 (XXVII) (*Ybk UN* 1972 p. 330) notes with satisfaction the Conference Report. Resolution 2995 (XXVII) (*Ybk UN* 1972 pp. 330-1) was a partial revival of the Preparatory Committee's "Principle 20". It provides that technical information on proposed works should be supplied to other States where there is a risk of significant transboundary environmental harm, but that this information should be received in good faith and not used to delay or impede development of natural resources. Resolution 2996 (XXVII) (*Ybk UN* 1972 p. 331) affirms that Resolution 2995 is not to be construed as limiting principles 21 and 22 of the Stockholm Declaration. Resolutions 2997 to 3004 (XXVII) (*Ybk UN* 1972 pp. 331-7) concern institutional and financial arrangements for international environmental cooperation, and in particular the establishment of the UN Environmental Programme, to be based at Nairobi, Kenya.

Text reprinted from:	*UN Doc.* A/CONF.48/14, 16 June 1972
Also published in:	11 *ILM* 1416 (1972)
	Ybk UN 1972 at 319

Text

STOCKHOLM DECLARATION OF THE UNITED NATIONS CONFERENCE ON THE HUMAN ENVIRONMENT

THE UNITED NATIONS CONFERENCE ON THE HUMAN ENVIRONMENT,
HAVING MET at Stockholm from 5 to 16 June 1972,
HAVING CONSIDERED the need for a common outlook and for common principles to inspire and guide the peoples of the world in the preservation and enhancement of the human environment,

I

PROCLAIMS THAT:

1. Man is both creature and moulder of his environment, which gives him physical sustenance and affords him the opportunity for intellectual, moral, social and spiritual growth. In the long and tortuous evolution of the human race on this planet a stage has been reached when, through the rapid acceleration of science and technology, man has acquired the power to transform his environment in countless ways and on an unprecedented scale. Both aspects of man's environment, the natural and the man-made, are essential to his well-being and to the enjoyment of basic human rights—even the right to life itself.

2. The protection and improvement of the human environment is a major issue which affects the well-being of peoples and economic development throughout the world; it is the urgent desire of the peoples of the whole world and the duty of all Governments.

3. Man has constantly to sum up experience and go on discovering, inventing, creating and advancing. In our time, man's capability to transform his surroundings, if used wisely, can bring to all peoples the benefits of development and the opportunity to enhance the quality of life. Wrongly or heedlessly applied, the same power can do incalculable harm to human beings and the human environment. We see around us growing evidence of man-made harm in many regions of the earth: dangerous levels of pollution in water, air, earth and living beings; major and undesirable disturbances to the ecological balance of the biosphere; destruction and depletion of irreplaceable resources; and gross deficiencies harmful to the physical, mental and social health of man, in the man-made environment, particularly in the living and working environment.

4. In the developing countries most of the environmental problems are caused by under-development. Millions continue to live far below the minimum levels required for a decent human existence, deprived of adequate

food and clothing, shelter and education, health and sanitation. Therefore, the developing countries must direct their efforts to development, bearing in mind their priorities and the need to safeguard and improve the environment. For the same purpose, the industrialized countries should make efforts to reduce the gap between themselves and the developing countries. In the industrialized countries, environmental problems are generally related to industrialization and technological development.

5.   The natural growth of population continuously presents problems on the preservation of the environment, and adequate policies and measures should be adopted, as appropriate, to face these problems. Of all things in the world, people are the most precious. It is the people that propel social progress, create social wealth, develop science and technology and, through their hard work, continuously transform the human environment. Along with social progress and the advance of production, science and technology, the capability of man to improve the environment increases with each passing day.

6.   A point has been reached in history when we must shape our actions throughout the world with a more prudent care for their environmental consequences. Through ignorance or indifference we can do massive and irreversible harm to the earthly environment on which our life and well-being depend. Conversely, through fuller knowledge and wiser action, we can achieve for ourselves and our posterity a better life in an environment more in keeping with human needs and hopes. There are broad vistas for the enhancement of environmental quality and the creation of a good life. What is needed is an enthusiastic but calm state of mind and intense but orderly work. For the purpose of attaining freedom in the world of nature, man must use knowledge to build, in collaboration with nature, a better environment. To defend and improve the human environment for present and future generations has become an imperative goal for mankind—a goal to be pursued together with, and in harmony with, the established and fundamental goals of peace and of world-wide economic and social development.

7.   To achieve this environmental goal will demand the acceptance of responsibility by citizens and communities and by enterprises and institutions at every level, all sharing equitably in common efforts. Individuals in all walks of life as well as organizations in many fields, by their values and the sum of their actions, will shape the world environment of the future. Local and national governments will bear the greatest burden for large-scale environmental policy and action within their jurisdictions. International co-operation is also needed in order to raise resources to support the developing countries in carrying out their responsibilities in this field. A growing class of environmental problems, because they are regional or global in extent or because they affect the common international realm, will require extensive co-

operation among nations and action by international organizations in the common interest. The Conference calls upon Governments and peoples to exert common efforts for the preservation and improvement of the human environment, for the benefit of all the people and for their posterity.

II
Principles

STATES THE COMMON CONVICTION THAT:

Principle 1

Man has the fundamental right to freedom, equality and adequate conditions of life, in an environment of a quality that permits a life of dignity and well-being, and he bears a solemn responsibility to protect and improve the environment for present and future generations. In this respect, policies promoting or perpetuating apartheid, racial segregation, discrimination, colonial and other forms of oppression and foreign domination stand condemned and must be eliminated.

Principle 2

The natural resources of the earth including the air, water, land, flora and fauna and especially representative samples of natural ecosystems must be safeguarded for the benefit of present and future generations through careful planning or management, as appropriate.

Principle 3

The capacity of the earth to produce vital renewable resources must be maintained and, wherever practicable, restored or improved.

Principle 4

Man has a special responsibility to safeguard and wisely manage the heritage of wildlife and its habitat which are now gravely imperilled by a combination of adverse factors. Nature conservation including wildlife must therefore receive importance in planning for economic development.

Principle 5

The non-renewable resources of the earth must be employed in such a way as to guard against the danger of their future exhaustion and to ensure that benefits from such employment are shared by all mankind.

Principle 6

The discharge of toxic substances or of other substances and the release of heat, in such quantities or concentrations as to exceed the capacity of the environment to render them harmless, must be halted in order to ensure that serious or irreversible damage is not inflicted upon ecosystems. The just struggle of the peoples of all countries against pollution should be supported.

Principle 7

States shall take all possible steps to prevent pollution of the seas by substances that are liable to create hazards to human health, to harm living resources and marine life, to damage amenities or to interfere with other legitimate uses of the sea.

Principle 8

Economic and social development is essential for ensuring a favourable living and working environment for man and for creating conditions on earth that are necessary for the improvement of the quality of life.

Principle 9

Environmental deficiencies generated by the conditions of underdevelopment and natural disasters pose grave problems and can best be remedied by accelerated development through the transfer of substantial quantities of financial and technological assistance as a supplement to the domestic effort of the developing countries and such timely assistance as may be required.

Principle 10

For the developing countries, stability of prices and adequate earnings for primary commodities and raw material are essential to environmental management since economic factors as well as ecological processes must be taken into account.

Principle 11

The environmental policies of all States should enhance and not adversely affect the present or future development potential of developing countries, nor should they hamper the attainment of better living conditions for all, and appropriate steps should be taken by States and international organizations with a view to reaching agreement on meeting the possible national and international economic consequences resulting from the application of environmental measures.

Principle 12

Resources should be made available to preserve and improve the environment, taking into account the circumstances and particular requirements of developing countries and any costs which may emanate from their incorporating environmental safeguards into their development planning and the need for making available to them, upon their request, additional international technical and financial assistance for this purpose.

Principle 13

In order to achieve a more rational management of resources and thus to improve the environment, States should adopt an integrated and co-ordinated approach to their development planning so as to ensure that development is compatible with the need to protect and improve the human environment for the benefit of their population.

Principle 14

Rational planning constitutes an essential tool for reconciling any conflict between the needs of development and the need to protect and improve the environment.

Principle 15

Planning must be applied to human settlements and urbanization with a view to avoiding adverse effects on the environment and obtaining maximum social, economic and environmental benefits for all. In this respect projects which are designed for colonialist and racist domination must be abandoned.

Principle 16

Demographic policies, which are without prejudice to basic human rights and which are deemed appropriate by Governments concerned, should be applied in those regions where the rate of population growth or excessive population concentrations are likely to have adverse effects on the environment or development, or where low population density may prevent improvement of the human environment and impede development.

Principle 17

Appropriate national institutions must be entrusted with the task of planning, managing or controlling the environmental resources of States with the view to enhancing environmental quality.

Principle 18

Science and technology, as part of their contribution to economic and social development, must be applied to the identification, avoidance and control of environmental risks and the solution of environmental problems and for the common good of mankind.

Principle 19

Education in environmental matters, for the younger generation as well as adults, giving due consideration to the underprivileged, is essential in order to broaden the basis for an enlightened opinion and responsible conduct by individuals, enterprises and communities in protecting and improving the environment in its full human dimension. It is also essential that mass media of communications avoid contributing to the deterioration of the environment, but, on the contrary, disseminate information of an educational nature, on the need to protect and improve the environment in order to enable man to develop in every respect.

Principle 20

Scientific research and development in the context of environmental problems, both national and multinational, must be promoted in all countries, especially the developing countries. In this connection, the free flow of up-to-date scientific information and transfer of experience must be supported and assisted, to facilitate the solution of environmental problems; environmental technologies should be made available to developing countries on terms which would encourage their wide dissemination without constituting an economic burden on the developing countries.

Principle 21

States have, in accordance with the Charter of the United Nations and the principles of international law, the sovereign right to exploit their own resources pursuant to their own environmental policies, and the responsibility to ensure that activities within their jurisdiction or control do not cause damage to the environment of other States or of areas beyond the limits of national jurisdiction.

Principle 22

States shall co-operate to develop further the international law regarding liability and compensation for the victims of pollution and other environmental damage caused by activities within the jurisdiction or control of such States to areas beyond their jurisdiction.

Principle 23

Without prejudice to such criteria as may be agreed upon by the international community, or to standards which will have to be determined nationally, it will be essential in all cases to consider the systems of values prevailing in each country, and the extent of the applicability of standards which are valid for the most advanced countries but which may be inappropriate and of unwarranted social cost for the developing countries.

Principle 24

International matters concerning the protection and improvement of the environment should be handled in a co-operative spirit by all countries, big or small, on an equal footing. Co-operation through multilateral or bilateral arrangements or other appropriate means is essential to effectively control, prevent, reduce and eliminate adverse environmental effects resulting from activities conducted in all spheres, in such a way that due account is taken of the sovereignty and interests of all States.

Principle 25

States shall ensure that international organizations play a co-ordinated, efficient and dynamic role for the protection and improvement of the environment.

Principle 26

Man and his environment must be spared the effects of nuclear weapons and all other means of mass destruction. States must strive to reach prompt agreement, in the relevant international organs, on the elimination and complete destruction of such weapons.

UN GENERAL ASSEMBLY RESOLUTION 2995 (XXVII) ON "CO-OPERATION BETWEEN STATES IN THE FIELD OF THE ENVIRONMENT"

Text reprinted from: 27 *UN GAOR* (Supp. No. 30) 42

THE GENERAL ASSEMBLY,

HAVING CONSIDERED principle 20 as contained in the draft text of a preamble and principles of the declaration on the human environment, referred to it for consideration by the United Nations Conference on the Human Environment,

RECALLING its resolution 2849(XXVI) of 20 December 1971 entitled "Development and environment",

BEARING IN MIND that, in exercising their sovereignty over their natural resources, States must seek, through effective bilateral and multilateral co-operation or through regional machinery, to preserve and improve the environment,

1. EMPHASIZES that in the exploration, exploitation and development of their natural resources, States must not produce significant harmful effects in zones situated outside their national jurisdiction;

2.   RECOGNIZES that co-operation between States in the field of the environment, including co-operation towards the implementation of principles 21 and 22 of the Declaration of the United Nations Conference on the Human Environment, will be effectively achieved if official and public knowledge is provided of the technical data relating to the work to be carried out by States within their national jurisdiction, with a view to avoiding significant harm that may occur in the environment of the adjacent area;

3.   FURTHER RECOGNIZES that the technical data referred to in paragraph 2 above will be given and received in the best spirit of co-operation and good-neighbourliness, without this being construed as enabling each State to delay or impede the programmes and projects of exploration, exploitation and development of the natural resources of the States in whose territories such programmes and projects are carried out.

UN GENERAL ASSEMBLY RESOLUTION 2996 (XXVII) ON "INTERNATIONAL RESPONSIBILITY OF STATES IN REGARD TO THE ENVIRONMENT"

Text reprinted from: 27 *UN GAOR* (Supp. No. 30) 42

THE GENERAL ASSEMBLY,

RECALLING principles 21 and 22 of the Declaration of the United Nations Conference on the Human Environment concerning the international responsibility of States in regard to the environment,

BEARING IN MIND that those principles lay down the basic rules governing this matter,

DECLARES that no resolution adopted at the twenty-seventh session of the General Assembly can affect principles 21 and 22 of the Declaration of the United Nations Conference on the Human Environment.

Select Bibliography

(The preparatory documents relating to the Stockholm Conference may be found in the series *UN Doc.* A/CONF.48.)

Report of the UN Conference on the Human Environment, Stockholm 5-16 June 1972, *UN Doc.* A/CONF.48/14/Rev.1.

Kennett, "The Stockholm Conference on the Human Environment", 48 *Int. Affairs* 33 (1972).

Kiss, "Dix Ans après Stockholm, une Décennie de Droit international de l'Environnement", 28 *AFDI* 784 (1982).

Sohn, "The Stockholm Declaration on the Human Environment", 14 *Harv. Int'l LJ* 423 (1973).

"Post Stockholm: Influencing National Environmental Law and Practice Through International Law and Policy", 66 *Proc. ASIL* 1 (1972).

"Ten Years After Stockholm: International Environmental Law", 77 *Proc. ASIL* 411 (1983).

7. NORDIC CONVENTION ON THE PROTECTION OF THE ENVIRONMENT
19 February 1974, Stockholm

Editorial Note

The Nordic Convention is in many respects unique in establishing a comprehensive regime for the protection of the environment. In particular it allows any person who is affected or may be affected by a nuisance caused by "environmentally harmful activities" in another Contracting State to bring before the appropriate court or Administrative Authority ("examining authority") of that State the permissibility of such activities, the question of measures to prevent damage, and compensation (Article 3). The Convention also provides for the appointment of a supervisory authority in each State to be entrusted with the task of safeguarding general environmental interests (Article 4). For this purpose the supervisory authority is given certain rights in other States, including the right to institute proceedings regarding "environmentally harmful activities" (Article 4) and the power to publish in local newspapers or elsewhere communications with examining authorities (Article 7). Article 10 provides for the possibility of on-site inspections where necessary to determine damage.

Date of signature:	19 February 1974
Entry into force:	5 October 1976
Depositary:	Swedish Ministry of Foreign Affairs
Authentic languages:	Danish, Finnish, Norwegian and Swedish
Text reprinted from:	1092 *UNTS* 279
Also published in:	13 *ILM* 591 (1974)

Text

NORDIC CONVENTION ON THE PROTECTION OF THE ENVIRONMENT

The Governments of Denmark, Finland, Norway and Sweden, Convinced of the urgent need to protect and improve the environment, Have Agreed as follows:

Article 1
For the purpose of this Convention, environmentally harmful activities shall mean the discharge from the soil or from buildings or installations of solid or

liquid waste, gases or any other substance into water-courses, lakes or the sea and the use of land, the seabed, buildings or installations in any other way which entails, or may entail environmental nuisance by water pollution or any other effect on water conditions, sand drift, air pollution, noise, vibration, changes in temperature, ionizing radiation, light etc.

The Convention shall not apply insofar as environmentally harmful activities are regulated by a special agreement between two or more of the Contracting States.

Article 2

In considering the permissibility of environmentally harmful activities, the nuisance which such activities entail or may entail in another Contracting State shall be equated with a nuisance in the State where the activities are carried out.

Article 3

Any person who is affected or may be affected by a nuisance caused by environmentally harmful activities in another Contracting State shall have the right to bring before the appropriate Court or Administrative Authority of that State the question of the permissibility of such activities, including the question of measures to prevent damage, and to appeal against the decision of the Court or the Administrative Authority to the same extent and on the same terms as a legal entity of the State in which the activities are being carried out.

The provisions of the first paragraph of this Article shall be equally applicable in the case of proceedings concerning compensation for damage caused by environmentally harmful activities. The question of compensation shall not be judged by rules which are less favourable to the injured party than the rules of compensation of the State in which the activities are being carried out.

Article 4

Each State shall appoint a special authority (supervisory authority) to be entrusted with the task of safeguarding general environmental interests insofar as regards nuisances arising out of environmentally harmful activities in another Contracting State. For the purpose of safeguarding such interests, the supervisory authority shall have the right to institute proceedings before or be heard by the competent Court or Administrative Authority of another Contracting State regarding the permissibility of the environmentally harmful activities, if an authority or other representative of general environmental interests in that State can institute proceedings or be heard in matters of this kind, as well as the right to appeal against the decision of the Court or the Administrative Authority in accordance with the procedures and rules of appeal applicable to such cases in the State concerned.

Article 5

If the Court or the Administrative Authority examining the permissibility of environmentally harmful activities (examining authority) finds that the activities entail or may entail nuisance of significance in another Contracting State, the examining authority shall, if proclamation or publication is required in cases of that nature, send as soon as possible a copy of the documents of the case to the supervisory authority of the other State, and afford it the opportunity of giving its opinion. Notification of the date and place of a meeting or inspection shall, where appropriate, be given well in advance to the supervisory authority which, moreover, shall be kept informed of any developments that may be of interest to it.

Article 6

Upon the request of the supervisory authority, the examining authority shall, insofar as compatible with the procedural rules of the State in which the activities are being carried out, require the applicant for a permit to carry out environmentally harmful activities to submit such additional particulars, drawings and technical specifications as the examining authority deems necessary for evaluating the effects in the other State.

Article 7

The supervisory authority, if it finds it necessary on account of public or private interests, shall publish communications from the examining authority in the local newspaper or in some other suitable manner. The supervisory authority shall also institute such investigations of the effects in its own State as it deems necessary.

Article 8

Each State shall defray the cost of the activities of its supervisory authority.

Article 9

If, in a particular case, the supervisory authority has informed the appropriate Court or Administrative Authority of the State in which the activities are being carried out that in the case concerned the duties of the supervisory authority shall be discharged by another authority, the provisions of this Convention relating to supervisory activities shall, where appropriate, apply to that authority.

Article 10

If necessary for determining the damage caused in another State by environmentally harmful activities, the supervisory authority of that other State shall upon request of the examining authority of the State in which the activities are being carried out make arrangements for on-site inspection. The examining authority or an expert appointed by it may be present at such an inspection.

Where necessary, more detailed instructions concerning inspections such as those referred to in the preceding paragraph shall be drawn up in consultation between the countries concerned.

Article 11

Where the permissibility of environmentally harmful activities which entail or may entail considerable nuisance in another Contracting State is being examined by the Government or by the appropriate Minister or Ministry of the State in which the activities are being carried out, consultations shall take place between the States concerned if the Government of the former State so requests.

Article 12

In cases such as those referred to in Article 11, the Government of each State concerned may demand that an opinion be given by a Commission which, unless otherwise agreed, shall consist of a chairman from another Contracting State to be appointed jointly by the parties and three members from each of the States concerned. Where such a Commission has been appointed, the case cannot be decided upon until the Commission has given its opinion.

Each State shall remunerate the members it has appointed. Fees or other remuneration of the Chairman as well as any other costs incidental to the activities of the Commission which are not manifestly the responsibility of one or the other State, shall be equally shared by the States concerned.

Article 13

This Convention shall also apply to the continental shelf areas of the Contracting States.

Article 14

This Convention shall enter into force six months from the date on which all the Contracting States have notified the Swedish Ministry for Foreign Affairs that the constitutional measures necessary for the entry into force of the Convention have been implemented. The Swedish Ministry for Foreign Affairs shall notify the other Contracting States of the receipt of such communications.

Article 15

Actions or cases relevant to this Convention, which are pending before a Court or an Administrative Authority on the date when this Convention enters into force, shall be dealt with and judged according to provisions previously in force.

Article 16

Any Contracting State wishing to denounce this Convention shall give notice of its intention in writing to the Swedish Government, which shall forthwith inform the other Contracting States of the denunciation and of the date on which notice was received.

The denunciation shall take effect twelve months from the date on which the Swedish Government received such notification or on such later date as may be indicated in the notice of denunciation.

This Convention shall be deposited with the Swedish Ministry for Foreign Affairs, which shall send certified copies thereof to the Government of each Contracting State.

IN WITNESS WHEREOF the undersigned, representatives of the Contracting States, being duly authorized thereto by their respective Governments, have signed this Convention.

DONE at Stockholm, this 19th day of February 1974 in a single copy in the Danish, Finnish, Norwegian and Swedish languages, all texts being equally authoritative.

Protocol

In connection with the signing today of the Nordic Environmental Protection Convention the duly authorized signatory agreed that the following comments on its application shall be appended to the Convention.

In the application of *Article 1* discharge from the soil, or from buildings or installations of solid or liquid waste, gases or other substances into watercourses, lakes or the sea shall be regarded as environmentally harmful activities only if the discharge entails or may entail a nuisance to the surroundings.

The right established in *Article 3* for anyone who suffers injury as a result of environmentally harmful activities in a neighbouring State to institute proceedings for compensation before a court or administrative authority of that State shall, in principle, be regarded as including the right to demand the purchase of his real property.

Article 5 shall be regarded as applying also to applications for permits where such applications are referred to certain authorities and organizations for their opinion but not in conjunction with proclamation or publication procedures. The Contracting States shall require officials of the supervisory authority to observe *professional secrecy* as regards trade secrets, operational devices or business conditions of which they have become cognizant in dealing with cases concerning environmentally harmful activities in another State.

Select Bibliography

Broms, "The Nordic Convention on the Protection of the Environment", in Flinterman *et al.* (eds.), *Transboundary Air Pollution* (1986), p. 141.

Bunge, "Transboundary Co-operation between France and the Federal Republic of Germany", in Flinterman *et al., op. cit.*, p. 181.

Fleischer, "Nordisk Miljovernkonvensjon", *TFR* 1976: 83.

Kiss, "La Convention nordique sur l'Environnement", 20 *AFDI* 808 (1974).

Phillips, "Nordic Co-operation for the Protection of the Environment Against Air Pollution and the Possibility of Transboundary Private Litigation", in Flinterman *et al., op. cit.*, p. 153.

Sommer, "Transboundary Co-operation between Poland and its Neighbouring States", in Flinterman *et al., op. cit.*, p. 205.

Vukas, "Transboundary Co-operation between Yugoslavia and its Neighbouring States", in Flinterman *et al., op. cit.*, p. 199.

8. OECD, COUNCIL RECOMMENDATION ON PRINCIPLES CONCERNING TRANSFRONTIER POLLUTION
14 November 1974

Editorial Note

The Annex to the 1974 Council Recommendation establishes guiding principles for the members of the OECD for harmonizing environmental policies in relation to pollution originating in one country and having effects within others. The essence of these principles lies in the role they give to private persons in the prevention of transfrontier pollution and the establishment of a regime of access without discrimination on the grounds of nationality to the courts of polluting States.

Title B, which sets out a number of factors to be taken into account in defining a concerted long-term policy for the protection of the environment in affected zones, calls on countries to take "all appropriate measures to prevent and control transfrontier pollution". Countries should be guided by the Principle of Non-Discrimination in the application of their legal and statutory provisions (Title C) and grant Equal Right of Access to the judicial and administrative authorities in the country from which the pollution originates (Title D). The important role of information in the creation of a regime for the protection of the environment from transfrontier pollution is recognized by Title E and the establishment of early warning systems and contingency plans for assistance is recommended (Title F).

Text reprinted from: *OECD Doc.* C(74)224 of 21 November 1974

Text

OECD, COUNCIL RECOMMENDATION ON PRINCIPLES CONCERNING TRANSFRONTIER POLLUTION

THE COUNCIL,

HAVING REGARD to Article 5(b) of the Convention on the Organisation for Economic Co-operation and Development of 14th December, 1960;

CONSIDERING that the protection and improvement of the environment are common objectives of Member countries;

CONSIDERING that the common interests of countries concerned by transfrontier pollution should induce them to co-operate more closely in a spirit of international solidarity and to initiate concerted action for preventing and controlling transfrontier pollution;

HAVING REGARD to the Recommendations of the United Nations Conference on the Human Environment held in Stockholm in June 1972 and in particular those Principles of the Declaration on the Human Environment which are relevant to transfrontier pollution;

ON THE PROPOSAL of the Environment Committee;

I. RECOMMENDS that, without prejudice to future developments in international law and international co-operation in relation to transfrontier pollution, Member countries should be guided in their environmental policy by the principles concerning transfrontier pollution contained in this Recommendation and its Annex, which is an integral part of this Recommendation.

II. INSTRUCTS the Environment Committee to prepare without delay, taking account of the work undertaken by other international organisations, a programme of work designed to elaborate further these principles and to facilitate their practical implementation.

III. RECOMMENDS Member countries to co-operate in developing international law applicable to transfrontier pollution.

IV. INSTRUCTS the Environment Committee, within the framework of its mandate, to examine or investigate further, as the case may be, the issues related to the Principles of the Stockholm Declaration regarding responsibility and liability, taking into account the work undertaken by other international organisations, to submit a first report to the Council on its work by 1st March, 1976 and to seek to formulate as soon as possible Draft Recommendations.

V. INSTRUCTS the Environment Committee to investigate further the issues concerning equal right of hearing, to formulate as soon as possible Draft Recommendations and to report to the Council on its work by 1st July, 1975.

Annex

Some principles concerning transfrontier pollution

Title A—Introduction

This Annex sets forth some principles designed to facilitate the development of harmonized environmental policies with a view to solving transfrontier pollution problems. Their implementation should be based on a fair balance of rights and obligations among countries concerned by transfrontier pollution.

These principles should subsequently be supplemented and developed in the light of work undertaken by the OECD or other appropriate international organisations.

For the purpose of these principles, pollution means the introduction by man, directly or indirectly, of substances or energy into the environment resulting in deleterious effects of such a nature as to endanger human health, harm living resources and ecosystems, and impair or interfere with amenities and other legitimate uses of the environment.

Unless otherwise specified, these principles deal with pollution originating in one country and having effects within other countries.

Title B[1]—International solidarity

1.   Countries should define a concerted long-term policy for the protection and improvement of the environment in zones liable to be affected by transfrontier pollution.

Without prejudice to their rights and obligations under international law and in accordance with their responsibility under Principle 21 of the Stockholm Declaration, countries should seek, as far as possible, an equitable balance of their rights and obligations as regards the zones concerned by transfrontier pollution.

In implementing this concerted policy, countries should among other things:

(a) take account of:
—levels of existing pollution and the present quality of the environment concerned;
—the nature and quantities of pollutants;
—the assimilative capacity of the environment, as established by mutual agreement by the countries concerned, taking into account the particular characteristics and use of the affected zone;
—activities at the source of pollution and activities and uses sensitive to such pollution;
—the situation, prospective use and development of the zones concerned from a socio-economic standpoint;
(b) define:
—environmental quality objectives and corresponding protective measures;
(c) promote:
—guidelines for a land-use planning policy consistent with the requirements both of environmental protection and socio-economic development;

---

[1] The Delegate for Spain reserved his position on Title B.

(d) draw up and maintain up to date:
   (i) lists of particularly dangerous substances regarding which efforts should be made to eliminate polluting discharges, if necessary by stages, and
   (ii) lists of substances regarding which polluting discharges should be subject to very strict control.

2.   Pending the definition of such concerted long-term policies countries should, individually and jointly, take all appropriate measures to prevent and control transfrontier pollution, and harmonize as far as possible their relevant policies.

3.   Countries should endeavour to prevent any increase in transfrontier pollution, including that stemming from new or additional substances and activities, and to reduce, and as far as possible eliminate any transfrontier pollution existing between them within time limits to be specified.

Title C—Principle of non-discrimination

4.   Countries should initially base their action on the principle of non-discrimination, whereby:
   (a) polluters causing transfrontier pollution should be subject to legal or statutory provisions no less severe than those which would apply for any equivalent pollution occurring within their country, under comparable conditions and in comparable zones, taking into account, when appropriate, the special nature and environmental needs of the zone affected;
   (b) in particular, without prejudice to quality objectives or standards applying to transfrontier pollution mutually agreed upon by the countries concerned, the levels of transfrontier pollution entering into the zones liable to be affected by such pollution should not exceed those considered acceptable under comparable conditions and in comparable zones inside the country in which it originates, taking into account, when appropriate, the special state of the environment in the affected country;
   (c) any country whenever it applies the Polluter-Pays Principle should apply it to all polluters within this country without making any difference according to whether pollution affects this country or another country;
   (d) persons affected by transfrontier pollution should be granted no less favourable treatment than persons affected by a similar pollution in the country from which such transfrontier pollution originates.

Title D[2]*—Principle of equal right of hearing*

5. Countries should make every effort to introduce, where not already in existence, a system affording equal right of hearing, according to which:

(a) whenever a project, a new activity or a course of conduct may create a significant risk of transfrontier pollution and is investigated by public authorities, those who may be affected by such pollution should have the same rights of standing in judicial or administrative proceedings in the country where it originates as those of that country;

(b) whenever transfrontier pollution gives rise to damage in a country, those who are affected by such pollution should have the same rights of standing in judicial or administrative proceedings in the country where such pollution originates as those of that country, and they should be extended procedural rights equivalent to the rights extended to those of that country.

Title E[3]*—Principle of information and consultation*

6. Prior to the initiation in a country of works or undertakings which might create a significant risk of transfrontier pollution, this country should provide early information to other countries which are or may be affected. It should provide these countries with relevant information and data, the transmission of which is not prohibited by legislative provisions or prescriptions or applicable international conventions, and should invite their comments.

7. Countries should enter into consultation on an existing or foreseeable transfrontier pollution problem at the request of a country which is or may be directly affected and should diligently pursue such consultations on this particular problem over a reasonable period of time.

8. Countries should refrain from carrying out projects or activities which might create a significant risk of transfrontier pollution without first informing the countries which are or may be affected and, except in cases of extreme urgency, providing a reasonable amount of time in the light of circumstances for diligent consultation. Such consultations held in the best spirit of co-operation and good neighbourliness should not enable a country to unreasonably delay or to impede the activities or projects on which consultations are taking place.

[2] The Delegate for Spain reserved his position on Title D.
[3] The Delegate for Spain reserved his position on Title E.

Title F—Warning systems and incidents

9.   Countries should promptly warn other potentially affected countries of any situation which may cause any sudden increase in the level of pollution in areas outside the country of origin of pollution, and take all appropriate steps to reduce the effects of any such sudden increase.

10.   Countries should assist each other, wherever necessary, in order to prevent incidents which may result in transfrontier pollution, and to minimise, and if possible eliminate, the effects of such incidents, and should develop contingency plans to this end.

Title G—Exchange of scientific information, monitoring measures and research

11.   Countries concerned should exchange all relevant scientific information and data on transfrontier pollution, when not prohibited by legislative provisions or prescriptions or by applicable international conventions. They should develop and adopt pollution measurement methods providing results which are compatible.

12.   They should, when appropriate, co-operate in scientific and technical research programmes inter alia for identifying the origin and pathways of transfrontier pollution, any damage caused and the best methods of pollution prevention and control, and should share all information and data thus obtained.

They should, where necessary, consider setting up jointly, in zones affected by transfrontier pollution, a permanent monitoring system or network for assessing the levels of pollution and the effectiveness of measures taken by them to reduce pollution.

Title H—Institutions

13.   Countries concerned by a particular problem of transfrontier pollution should consider the advantages of co-operation, by setting up international commissions or other bodies, or by strengthening existing institutions, in order to deal more effectively with particular aspects of such problems.

Such institutions could be authorised to collect any data needed for a proper evaluation of the problem and its causes, and make to the countries concerned practical proposals for concerted efforts to combat transfrontier pollution. With the consent of the States concerned, they could also carry out any necessary additional investigations into the origin and degree of pollution, review the effectiveness of any pollution prevention and control measures which have been taken, and publish reports of their findings.

Title I—Disputes

14. Should negotiations and other means of diplomatically settling disputes concerning transfrontier pollution fail, countries should have the opportunity to submit such a dispute to a procedure of legal settlement which is prompt, effective and binding.

Title J—International Agreements

15. Countries should endeavour to conclude, where necessary, bilateral or multilateral agreements for the abatement of transfrontier pollution in accordance with the above principles, to bring promptly into force any agreements which may already have been signed.

16. When negotiating new bilateral or multilateral agreements countries should, while taking into account the principles set out above, strive for the application of efficient pollution prevention and control measures in accordance with the Polluter-Pays Principle.

Such agreements could, inter alia, include provisions for practical procedures promoting the prompt and equitable compensation of persons affected by transfrontier pollution, and could also contain procedures facilitating the provision of information and consultation.

Select Bibliography

Dupuy, ''La recommandation C/74 224 de l'OCDE concernant des principes relatifs à la pollution transfrontière'', 1 *Revue Juridique de l'Environnement* 25 (1977).

McCaffrey, ''The OECD Principles concerning Transfrontier Pollution: a Commentary'', 1 *Env. Policy & Law* 2 (1975).

Seidl-Hohenveldern, ''Transfrontier Pollution and Recommendation C(74)224 of the Council of the OECD'', in *Melanges in memoriam Garcia-Arias,* Revista Temis, Saragossa, 1973-74, pp. 273-85.

Stein, ''The OECD Guiding Principles on Transfrontier Pollution'', 6 *Ga. J Int'l & Comp. L* 245 (1976).

9. OECD, COUNCIL RECOMMENDATION FOR THE IMPLEMENTATION OF A REGIME OF EQUAL RIGHT OF ACCESS AND NON-DISCRIMINATION IN RELATION TO TRANSFRONTIER POLLUTION
17 May 1977

Editorial Note

The 1977 OECD Recommendation, which is supplemental to the 1974 OECD Recommendation (No. 8 above), establishes guiding principles for the promotion of individual rights in the event of pollution damage. It recognizes that private rights may be protected by the establishment of a regime of equal right of access to, and non-discrimination before, the courts of a polluting country.

In particular it is recommended that the country of origin of the pollution should ensure that any person suffering damage as a result of transfrontier pollution should receive at least equivalent treatment to that afforded in the country of origin. This is to include the right of standing in all administrative and judicial procedures in the country of origin to prevent, abate, or obtain compensation for, pollution (Title B(4)). The role of environmental protection groups and public authorities in exposed countries is also recognized: it is recommended that such bodies should be granted the same right of standing (Title B(6)).

Text reprinted from: *OECD Doc.* C(77)28 of 23 May 1977

Text

OECD, COUNCIL RECOMMENDATION FOR THE IMPLEMENTATION OF A REGIME OF EQUAL RIGHT OF ACCESS AND NON-DISCRIMINATION IN RELATION TO TRANSFRONTIER POLLUTION

THE COUNCIL,

HAVING REGARD to Article 5(b) of the Convention on the Organisation for Economic Co-operation and Development of 14th December, 1960;

HAVING REGARD to the Declaration on the Human Environment adopted in Stockholm in June 1972 and in particular Principles 21, 22, 23 and 24 of that Declaration;

HAVING REGARD to the Recommendations of the Council of 14th November, 1974, on Principles concerning Transfrontier Pollution and of

11th May, 1976, on Equal Right of Access in relation to Transfrontier Pollution (C(74)224 and C(76)55(Final)) and without prejudice to such Recommendations;

CONSIDERING that the protection and improvement of the environment are common objectives of Member countries;

CONSCIOUS that pollution originating in the area within the national jurisdiction of a State may have effects on the environment outside this jurisdiction;

CONSIDERING that the implementation of a regime of equal right of access and non-discrimination among Member countries should lead to improved protection of the environment without prejudice to other channels available for the solution of transfrontier pollution problems;

ON THE PROPOSAL of the Environment Committee:

RECOMMENDS that Member countries, in regard to each other, take into account the principles concerning transfrontier pollution set forth in the Annex to this Recommendation, which is an integral part of it, in their domestic legislation, possibly on the basis of reciprocity, notably regarding individual rights, and in bilateral or multilateral international agreements.

Annex

Introduction

This Annex sets out a number of principles intended to promote the implementation between Member countries of a regime of equal right of access and non-discrimination in matters of transfrontier pollution, while maintaining a fair balance of rights and obligations between Countries concerned by such pollution.

These principles do not prejudice any more favourable measures for the protection of the environment and of persons whose property, rights or interests are or could be affected by pollution the origin of which is situated within the area under the jurisdiction of a Member country.

For the purposes of this Recommendation:

(a) "Pollution" means any introduction by man, directly or indirectly, of substance or energy into the environment resulting in deleterious effects of such a nature as to endanger human health, harm living resources and eco-systems, impair amenities or interfere with other legitimate uses of the environment.

(b) "Domestic pollution" means any intentional or unintentional pollution, the physical origin of which is situated wholly within the area under the national jurisdiction of one Country and which has effects within that area only.

(c) "Transfrontier pollution" means any intentional or unintentional pollution whose physical origin is subject to, and situated wholly or in part within the area under, the national jurisdiction of one Country and which has effects in the area under the national jurisdiction of another Country.

(d) "Country" means any Member country which participates in this Recommendation.

(e) "Country of origin" means any Country within which, and subject to the jurisdiction of which, transfrontier pollution originates or could originate in connection with activities carried on or contemplated in that Country.

(f) "Exposed Country" means any Country affected by transfrontier pollution or exposed to a significant risk of transfrontier pollution.

(g) "Countries concerned" means any Country of origin of transfrontier pollution and any Country exposed to such pollution.

(h) "Regions concerned by transfrontier pollution" means any region of origin of transfrontier pollution in the Country of origin and any regions of the Country of origin and of any exposed Country where such pollution produces or might produce its effects.

(i) "Person" means any natural or legal person, either private or public.

(j) "Regime of environmental protection" means any set of statutory and administrative measures related to the protection of the environment, including those concerning the property, rights or interests of persons.

A. *Principles to facilitate the solution at inter-state level of transfrontier pollution problems*

1. When preparing and giving effect to their policies affecting the environment, Countries should, consistent with their obligations and rights as regards the protection of the environment, take fully into consideration the effects of such policies on the environment of exposed Countries so as to protect such environment against transfrontier pollution.

2. With a view to improved protection of the environment, Countries should attempt by common agreement to:

(a) Make their environmental policies mutually compatible, particularly those bearing on regions concerned by transfrontier pollution;

(b) Bring closer together quality objectives and environmental standards adopted by Countries, apply them systematically to cases of transfrontier pollution and, where necessary, improve those already in force;

(c) Work out additional rules of conduct of States to be applied in matters of transfrontier pollution.

3. (a) Pending the implementation of the objectives laid down in paragraph 2, and without prejudice to more favourable measures taken in accordance with paragraphs 1 and 2 above, each Country should ensure that its regime of environmental protection does not discriminate between pollution originating from it which affects or is likely to affect the area under its national jurisdiction and pollution originating from it which affects or is likely to affect an exposed Country;

(b) Thus, transfrontier pollution problems should be treated by the Country of origin in an equivalent way to similar domestic pollution problems occurring under comparable conditions in the Country of origin;

(c) In the event of difficulties arising between Countries concerned because the situations resulting from transfrontier pollution and domestic pollution are manifestly not comparable, for example as a result of unco-ordinated land use policies in regions concerned by transfrontier pollution, those countries should strive to arrive at a mutually agreed arrangement which ensures to the largest extent possible the application of the principle referred to in sub-paragraph (a) of this paragraph

B. *Legal protection of persons*

4. (a) Countries of origin should ensure that any person who has suffered transfrontier pollution damage or is exposed to a significant risk of transfrontier pollution, shall at least receive equivalent treatment to that afforded in the Country of origin in cases of domestic pollution and in comparable circumstances, to persons of equivalent condition or status;

(b) From a procedural standpoint, this treatment includes the right to take part in, or have resort to, all administrative and judicial procedures existing within the Country of origin, in order to prevent domestic pollution, to have it abated and/or to obtain compensation for the damage caused.

5. Where in spite of the existence of a liability ceiling instituted by an international agreement, there exists in a Country a system of additional compensation financed or administered by the public authorities, then such Country should not be required in the absence of reciprocal arrangements to

grant entitlement to such additional compensation to victims of transfrontier pollution, but it should in advance inform the exposed Countries of the particular situation.

6. (a) Where the domestic law of Countries permits private non profit legal persons that are resident within their own territories, such as environmental defence associations, to commence proceedings to safeguard environmental interests which it is their aim to protect, those Countries should grant the same right for comparable matters to similar legal persons resident in exposed Countries, provided that the latter satisfy the conditions laid down for the former in the Country of origin;

    (b) When some of the conditions concerning matters of form laid down in the Country of origin cannot reasonably be imposed on legal persons resident in an exposed Country, these latter should be entitled to commence proceedings in the Country of origin if they satisfy comparable conditions.

7. When the law of a Country of origin permits a public authority to participate in administrative or judicial proceedings in order to safeguard general environmental interests, the Country of origin should consider, if its legal system allows it, providing, by means of international agreement if it deems it necessary, competent public authorities of exposed Countries with access to such proceedings.

C. *Exchange of information and consultation*

8. (a) The Country of origin, on its own initiative or at the request of an exposed Country, should communicate to the latter appropriate information concerning it in matters of transfrontier pollution or significant risk of such pollution and enter into consultations with it.[1]

    (b) In order to enable a Country of origin to implement adequately those principles set out in Title A of this Recommendation, each exposed Country should, on its own initiative or at the request of the Country of origin, supply appropriate information of mutual concern.

    (c) Each Country should designate one or more authorities entitled to receive directly information communicated under sub-paragraphs (a) and (b) of this paragraph.

9. (a) Countries of origin should take any appropriate measures to provide persons exposed to a significant risk of transfrontier pollution with

---

[1] The Delegate for Spain reserved his position on the last six words of paragraph 8(a).

sufficient information to enable them to exercise in a timely manner the rights referred to in this Recommendation. As far as possible, such information should be equivalent to that provided in the Country of origin in cases of comparable domestic pollution.

(b) Exposed Countries should designate one or more authorities which will have the duty to receive and the responsibility to disseminate such information within limits of time compatible with the exercise of existing procedures in the Country of origin.

10.   Countries should encourage and facilitate regular contacts between representatives designated by them at regional and/or local levels in order to examine such transfrontier pollution matters as may arise.

Select Bibliography

Handl, "The Principle of 'Equitable Use' as applied to Internationally Shared Natural Resources: its Role in Resolving Potential International Disputes over Transfrontier Pollution", 14 *Revue belge de droit int.* 40 (1978-79).

Seidl-Hohenveldern, "Alternative Approaches to Transfrontier Environmental Injuries", 2 *Env. Policy & Law* 6 (1976).

Van Hoogstraten, Dupuy & Smets, "Equal Right of Access: Transfrontier Pollution", 2 *Env. Policy & Law* 77 (1976).

Willheim, "Private Remedies for Transfrontier Environmental Damage: a critique of OECD's Doctrine of Equal Right of Access", 7 *Australian Ybk Int'l L* 174 (1976-77).

OECD, *Non-Discrimination in Matters of Transfrontier Pollution* (1978).

10. GENEVA CONVENTION ON LONG-RANGE TRANSBOUNDARY AIR POLLUTION
13 November 1979

Editorial Note

The Geneva Convention was negotiated within the UN Economic Commission for Europe on the initiative of the Scandinavian countries which had long been concerned about the problem of acid precipitation. The definition of ''air pollution'' in Article 1(a) is clearly wide enough to bring radioactive fallout within the scope of the Convention. This was the first multilateral Convention relating to the protection of the environment which involved almost all nations of Eastern and Western Europe, and its parties include the USA and the USSR. It was also the first to deal specifically with the problem of long-range transboundary air pollution where it is not possible to distinguish the contribution of individual emission sources (Article 1(b)). The politically varied and regionally comprehensive adherence to the Convention might be a result of the ''soft'' nature of the obligations it establishes. In particular it is clear from a solitary footnote that the question of State liability for damage from transboundary air pollution is beyond its scope. Article 2, which sets out the general obligation to limit, reduce and prevent air pollution, is hedged with qualifications. The ''best available technology'' requirement in Article 6 is limited to that ''which is economically feasible''.

The Convention obliges States to exchange information, consult and undertake research. Article 8 sets out in detail the type of information to be exchanged. Article 5 imposes an obligation to consult ''upon request'' the Parties to the consultation being, on the one hand, States ''which are actually affected by or exposed to a significant risk of long-range transboundary air pollution'' and, on the other hand, States ''within which and subject to whose jurisdiction a significant contribution to long-range transboundary air pollution originates, or could originate''. While provision is made in Article 7 for multilateral research and development the form this is to take is unclear.

Article 9 provides for the further development of the ''Co-operative programme for the monitoring and evaluation of the long-range transmission of air pollutants in Europe'' (''EMEP''). EMEP has established stations to monitor the flows of sulphur dioxide across national borders. Until 1984 it was financed by UNEP and by voluntary contributions from governments. UNEP's financing ceased at the end of 1984 and as a result several of the Parties to the 1979 Convention adopted a Protocol on the Long-Term Financing of EMEP. This Protocol, signed in Geneva on 28 September 1984, provides that financing is to consist of mandatory contributions made on an annual basis by all Parties to the Protocol which are in the geographical scope of EMEP. A scale of contributions is contained in an Annex to the Protocol. In addition, voluntary contributions may be made by the Parties or Signatories to the Protocol, even if their territory lies outside EMEP's geographical scope (Protocol to the 1979 Convention on

Long-Term Financing of the Co-operative Programme for Monitoring and Evaluation of the Long-Range Transmission of Air Pollutants in Europe (EMEP), 28 September 1984, Geneva, reprinted in 24 *ILM* 485 (1985)).

Date of signature:	13 November 1979
Entry into force:	16 March 1983
Depositary:	Secretary General of the UN
Authentic languages:	English, French and Russian
Text reprinted from:	*UN Doc.* ECE/HLM.1/R.1
Also published in:	*Misc.* 10 (1980), Cmnd. 7885
	18 *ILM* 1442 (1979)
UN Registration:	21623

Text

GENEVA CONVENTION ON LONG-RANGE TRANSBOUNDARY AIR POLLUTION

THE PARTIES TO THE PRESENT CONVENTION

DETERMINED to promote relations and co-operation in the field of environmental protection,

AWARE of the significance of the activities of the United Nations Economic Commission for Europe in strengthening such relations and co-operation, particularly in the field of air pollution including long-range transport of air pollutants,

RECOGNIZING the contribution of the Economic Commission for Europe to the multilateral implementation of the pertinent provisions of the Final Act of the Conference on Security and Co-operation in Europe,

COGNIZANT of the references in the chapter on environment of the Final Act of the Conference on Security and Co-operation in Europe calling for co-operation to control air pollution and its effects, including long-range transport of air pollutants, and to the development through international co-operation of an extensive programme for the monitoring and evaluation of long-range transport of air pollutants, starting with sulphur dioxide and with possible extension to other pollutants,

CONSIDERING the pertinent provisions of the Declaration of the United Nations Conference on the Human Environment, and in particular principle 21, which expresses the common conviction that States have, in accordance with the Charter of the United Nations and the principles of international law, the sovereign right to exploit their own resources pursuant to their own environmental policies, and the responsibility to ensure that activities within their jurisdiction or control do not cause damage to the environment of other States or of areas beyond the limits of national jurisdiction,

RECOGNIZING the existence of possible adverse effects, in the short and long term, of air pollution including transboundary air pollution,

CONCERNED that a rise in the level of emissions of air pollutants within a region as forecast may increase such adverse effects,

RECOGNIZING the need to study the implications of the long-range transport of air pollutants and the need to seek solutions for the problems identified,

AFFIRMING their willingness to reinforce active international co-operation to develop appropriate national policies and by means of exchange of information, consultation, research and monitoring, to co-ordinate national action for combating air pollution including long-range transboundary air pollution,

HAVE AGREED as follows:

Definitions
Article 1
For the purposes of the present Convention:
  (a) ''air pollution'' means the introduction by man, directly or indirectly, of substances or energy into the air resulting in deleterious effects of such a nature as to endanger human health, harm living resources and ecosystems and material property and impair or interfere with amenities and other legitimate uses of the environment, and ''air pollutants'' shall be construed accordingly;
  (b) ''long-range transboundary air pollution'' means air pollution whose physical origin is situated wholly or in part within the area under the national jurisdiction of one State and which has adverse effects in the area under the jurisdiction of another State at such a distance that it is not generally possible to distinguish the contribution of individual emission sources or groups of sources.

Fundamental principles
Article 2
The Contracting Parties, taking due account of the facts and problems involved, are determined to protect man and his environment against air pollution and shall endeavour to limit and, as far as possible, gradually reduce and prevent air pollution including long-range transboundary air pollution.

Article 3

The Contracting Parties, within the framework of the present Convention, shall by means of exchanges of information, consultation, research and monitoring, develop without undue delay policies and strategies which shall serve as a means of combating the discharge of air pollutants, taking into account efforts already made at national and international levels.

Article 4

The Contracting Parties shall exchange information on and review their policies, scientific activities and technical measures aimed at combating, as far as possible, the discharge of air pollutants which may have adverse effects, thereby contributing to the reduction of air pollution including long-range transboundary air pollution.

Article 5

Consultations shall be held, upon request, at an early stage between, on the one hand, Contracting Parties which are actually affected by or exposed to a significant risk of long-range transboundary air pollution and, on the other hand, Contracting Parties within which and subject to whose jurisdiction a significant contribution to long-range transboundary air pollution originates, or could originate, in connexion with activities carried on or contemplated therein.

Air quality management
Article 6

Taking into account articles 2 to 5, the ongoing research, exchange of information and monitoring and the results thereof, the cost and effectiveness of local and other remedies and, in order to combat air pollution, in particular that originating from new or rebuilt installations, each Contracting Party undertakes to develop the best policies and strategies including air quality management systems and, as part of them, control measures compatible with balanced development, in particular by using the best available technology which is economically feasible and low- and non-waste technology.

Research and development
Article 7

The Contracting Parties, as appropriate to their needs, shall initiate and co-operate in the conduct of research into and/or development of:

 (a) existing and proposed technologies for reducing emissions of sulphur compounds and other major air pollutants, including technical and economic feasibility, and environmental consequences;

(b) instrumentation and other techniques for monitoring and measuring emission rates and ambient concentrations of air pollutants;

(c) improved models for a better understanding of the transmission of long-range transboundary air pollutants;

(d) the effects of sulphur compounds and other major air pollutants on human health and the environment, including agriculture, forestry, materials, aquatic and other natural ecosystems and visibility, with a view to establishing a scientific basis for dose/effect relationships designed to protect the environment;

(e) the economic, social and environmental assessment of alternative measures for attaining environmental objectives including the reduction of long-range transboundary air pollution;

(f) education and training programmes related to the environmental aspects of pollution by sulphur compounds and other major air pollutants.

Exchange of information
Article 8

The Contracting Parties, within the framework of the Executive Body referred to in article 10 and bilaterally, shall, in their common interests, exchange available information on:

(a) data on emissions at periods of time to be agreed upon, of agreed air pollutants, starting with sulphur dioxide, coming from grid-units of agreed size; or on the fluxes of agreed air pollutants, starting with sulphur dioxide, across national borders, at distances and at periods of time to be agreed upon;

(b) major changes in national policies and in general industrial development, and their potential impact, which would be likely to cause significant changes in long-range transboundary air pollution;

(c) control technologies for reducing air pollution relevant to long-range transboundary air pollution;

(d) the projected cost of the emission control of sulphur compounds and other major air pollutants on a national scale;

(e) meteorological and physico-chemical data relating to the processes during transmission;

(f) physico-chemical and biological data relating to the effects of long-range transboundary air pollution and the extent of the damage[1] which these data indicate can be attributed to long-range transboundary air pollution;

[1] The present Convention does not contain a rule on State liability as to damage.

(g) national, subregional and regional policies and strategies for the control of sulphur compounds and other major air pollutants.

Implementation and further development of the co-operative programme for the monitoring and evaluation of the long-range transmission of air pollutants in Europe
Article 9
The Contracting Parties stress the need for the implementation of the existing "Co-operative programme for the monitoring and evaluation of the long-range transmission of air pollutants in Europe" (hereinafter referred to as EMEP) and, with regard to the further development of this programme, agree to emphasize:

(a) the desirability of Contracting Parties joining in and fully implementing EMEP which, as a first step, is based on the monitoring of sulphur dioxide and related substances;

(b) the need to use comparable or standardized procedures for monitoring whenever possible;

(c) the desirability of basing the monitoring programme on the framework of both national and international programmes. The establishment of monitoring stations and the collection of data shall be carried out under the national jurisdiction of the country in which the monitoring stations are located;

(d) the desirability of establishing a framework for a co-operative environmental monitoring programme, based on and taking into account present and future national, subregional, regional and other international programmes;

(e) the need to exchange data on emissions at periods of time to be agreed upon, of agreed air pollutants, starting with sulphur dioxide, coming from grid-units of agreed size; or on the fluxes of agreed air pollutants, starting with sulphur dioxide, across national borders, at distances and at periods of time to be agreed upon. The method, including the model, used to determine the fluxes, as well as the method, including the model, used to determine the transmission of air pollutants based on the emissions per grid-unit, shall be made available and periodically reviewed, in order to improve the methods and the models;

(f) their willingness to continue the exchange and periodic updating of national data on total emissions of agreed air pollutants, starting with sulphur dioxide;

(g) the need to provide meteorological and physico-chemical data relating to processes during transmission;

(h) the need to monitor chemical components in other media such as water, soil and vegetation, as well as a similar monitoring programme to record effects on health and environment;

(i) the desirability of extending the national EMEP networks to make them operational for control and surveillance purposes.

Executive body
Article 10

1. The representatives of the Contracting Parties shall, within the framework of the Senior Advisers to ECE Governments on Environmental Problems, constitute the Executive Body of the present Convention, and shall meet at least annually in that capacity.

2. The Executive Body shall:

(a) review the implementation of the present Convention;

(b) establish, as appropriate, working groups to consider matters related to the implementation and development of the present Convention and to this end to prepare appropriate studies and other documentation and to submit recommendations to be considered by the Executive Body;

(c) fulfil such other functions as may be appropriate under the provisions of the present Convention.

3. The Executive Body shall utilize the Steering Body for the EMEP to play an integral part in the operation of the present Convention, in particular with regard to data collection and scientific co-operation.

4. The Executive Body, in discharging its functions, shall, when it deems appropriate, also make use of information from other relevant international organizations.

Secretariat
Article 11

The Executive Secretary of the Economic Commission for Europe shall carry out, for the Executive Body, the following secretariat functions:

(a) to convene and prepare the meetings of the Executive Body;

(b) to transmit to the Contracting Parties reports and other information received in accordance with the provisions of the present Convention;

(c) to discharge the functions assigned by the Executive Body.

Amendments to the Convention
Article 12

1. Any Contracting Party may propose amendments to the present Convention.

2. The text of proposed amendments shall be submitted in writing to the Executive Secretary of the Economic Commission for Europe, who shall communicate them to all Contracting Parties. The Executive Body shall discuss proposed amendments at its next annual meeting provided that such proposals have been circulated by the Executive Secretary of the Economic Commission for Europe to the Contracting Parties at least ninety days in advance.

3. An amendment to the present Convention shall be adopted by consensus of the representatives of the Contracting Parties, and shall enter into force for the Contracting Parties which have accepted it on the ninetieth day after the date on which two-thirds of the Contracting Parties have deposited their instruments of acceptance with the depositary. Thereafter, the amendment shall enter into force for any other Contracting Party on the ninetieth day after the date on which that Contracting Party deposits its instrument of acceptance of the amendment.

Settlement of disputes
Article 13
If a dispute arises between two or more Contracting Parties to the present Convention as to the interpretation or application of the Convention, they shall seek a solution by negotiation or by any other method of dispute settlement acceptable to the parties to the dispute.

Signature
Article 14
1. The present Convention shall be open for signature at the United Nations Office at Geneva from 13 to 16 November 1979 on the occasion of the High-level Meeting within the framework of the Economic Commission for Europe on the Protection of the Environment, by the member States of the Economic Commission for Europe as well as States having consultative status with the Economic Commission for Europe, pursuant to paragraph 8 of Economic and Social Council resolution 36 (IV) of 28 March 1947, and by regional economic integration organizations, constituted by sovereign States members of the Economic Commission for Europe, which have competence in respect of the negotiation, conclusion and application of international agreements in matters covered by the present Convention.

2. In matters within their competence, such regional economic integration organizations shall, on their own behalf, exercise the rights and fulfil the responsibilities which the present Convention attributes to their member States. In such cases, the member States of these organizations shall not be entitled to exercise such rights individually.

Ratification, acceptance, approval and accession
Article 15

1. The present Convention shall be subject to ratification, acceptance or approval.

2. The present Convention shall be open for accession as from 17 November 1979 by the States and organizations referred to in article 14, paragraph 1.

3. The instruments of ratification, acceptance, approval or accession shall be deposited with the Secretary-General of the United Nations, who will perform the functions of the depositary.

Entry into force
Article 16

1. The present Convention shall enter into force on the ninetieth day after the date of deposit of the twenty-fourth instrument of ratification, acceptance, approval or accession.

2. For each Contracting Party which ratifies, accepts or approves the present Convention or accedes thereto after the deposit of the twenty-fourth instrument of ratification, acceptance, approval or accession, the Convention shall enter into force on the ninetieth day after the date of deposit by such Contracting Party of its instrument of ratification, acceptance, approval or accession.

Withdrawal
Article 17

At any time after five years from the date on which the present Convention has come into force with respect to a Contracting Party, that Contracting Party may withdraw from the Convention by giving written notification to the depositary. Any such withdrawal shall take effect on the ninetieth day after the date of its receipt by the depositary.

Authentic texts
Article 18

The original of the present Convention, of which the English, French and Russian texts are equally authentic, shall be deposited with the Secretary-General of the United Nations.

IN WITNESS WHEREOF the undersigned, being duly authorized thereto, have signed the present Convention.

DONE at Geneva, this thirteenth day of November, one thousand nine hundred and seventy-nine.

Signatories and Parties

State	Date of Signature	Date of Ratification, Acceptance (AA) or Accession (A)
Austria	13 November 1979	16 December 1982
Belgium	13 November 1979	15 July 1982
Bulgaria	14 November 1979	9 June 1981
Byelorussian SSR	14 November 1979	13 June 1980
Canada	13 November 1979	15 December 1981
Czechoslovakia	13 November 1979	23 December 1983
Denmark	14 November 1979	18 June 1982
European Economic Community	14 November 1979	15 July 1982 (A)
Finland	13 November 1979	15 April 1981
France	13 November 1979	3 November 1981 (A)
German Democratic Republic	13 November 1979	7 June 1982
Germany, Federal Republic	13 November 1979	15 July 1982 [2]
Greece	14 November 1979	30 August 1983
Holy See	14 November 1979	
Hungary	13 November 1979	22 September 1980
Iceland	13 November 1979	5 May 1983
Ireland	13 November 1979	15 July 1982
Italy	14 November 1979	15 July 1982
Liechtenstein	14 November 1979	22 November 1983
Luxembourg	13 November 1979	15 July 1982
Netherlands	13 November 1979	15 July 1982 [3]
Norway	13 November 1979	13 February 1981
Poland	13 November 1979	19 July 1985
Portugal	14 November 1979	29 September 1980

[2] Declaration that "the Convention shall also apply to Berlin (West) with effect from the date on which it enters into force for the Federal Republic of Germany".

In this regard the Secretary-General of the UN has received communications from the USSR (20 April 1983 and 2 December 1985), the German Democratic Republic (28 July 1983), France, United Kingdom and United States (27 April 1984, 18 October 1985 and 28 July 1986) and Federal Republic of Germany (13 June 1984) on the application of the Convention to West Berlin and on the interpretation of the Quadripartite Agreement of 3 September 1971.

[3] For the Kingdom in Europe.

State	Date of Signature	Date of Ratification, Acceptance (AA) or Accession (A)
Romania	14 November 1979[4]	
San Marino	14 November 1979	
Spain	14 November 1979	15 June 1982
Sweden	13 November 1979	12 February 1981
Switzerland	13 November 1979	6 May 1983
Turkey	13 November 1979	18 April 1983
Ukrainian SSR	14 November 1979	5 June 1980
USSR	13 November 1979	22 May 1980
United Kingdom	13 November 1979	15 July 1982[5]
USA	13 November 1979	30 November 1981 (AA)
Yugoslavia	13 November 1979	18 March 1987

Select Bibliography

Demidecki-Demidowicz, "Implementation of the Convention on Long-range Transboundary Air Pollution", 13 *Env. Policy & Law* 48 (1984).

Dupuy & Smets, "Pollution transfrontalière—Information et Consultation", 7 *Env. Policy & Law* 3 (1981).

Gündling, "Multilateral Co-operation of States under the ECE Convention on Long-range Transboundary Air Pollution", in Flinterman *et al.* (eds.), *Transboundary Air Pollution* (1986), pp. 19-31.

Kiss, "La Coopération pan-Européenne dans la Domaine de la Protection de l'Environnement", 19 *AFDI* 717 at 721-5 (1979).

Kiss, "La Convention sur la Pollution Atmosphérique Transfrontière à Longue Distance", *Revue Juridique de l'Environnement* (1981), p. 30.

Rosencranz, "The ECE Convention of 1979 on Long-range Transboundary Air Pollution", 75 *AJIL* 975 (1981).

Tollan, "The Convention on Long-range Transboundary Air Pollution", 19 *J of World Trade Law* 615 (1985).

Wetstone & Rosencranz, "Transboundary Air Pollution: the Search for an International Response", 8 *Harv. Env. Law Review* 89 at 93 (1984).

---

[4] Romania interprets article 14 of this Convention, concerning the participation of regional economic integration organizations constituted by States members of the Economic Commission for Europe, to mean that it refers exclusively to international organizations to which States members have transferred their competence in respect of the signature, conclusion and application on their behalf of international agreements and in respect of the exercise of their rights and responsibilities in the field of transboundary pollution.

[5] Including the Bailiwick of Jersey, the Bailiwick of Guernsey, the Isle of Man, Gibraltar, the United Kingdom Sovereign Base Areas of Akrotiri and Dhekelia in the Island of Cyprus.

11. AGREEMENT BETWEEN PORTUGAL AND SPAIN ON CO-OPERATION IN MATTERS AFFECTING THE SAFETY OF NUCLEAR INSTALLATIONS IN THE VICINITY OF THE FRONTIER
31 March 1980, Lisbon

Editorial Note

This bilateral Agreement obliges each State to notify the other of applications for licences for the siting, construction or operation of nuclear installations in the vicinity of the frontier (Article 2). Notification must be accompanied by certain additional information, and comments and observations by the neighbouring country must be taken into account before the licence is issued (Article 3). Each State must set up the necessary systems to detect any signs of danger from radioactivity, and each must inform the other in cases where such danger could have repercussions in the other country (Article 5).

Date of signature: 31 March 1980
Entry into force: 13 July 1981
Authentic languages: Portuguese and Spanish
Text reprinted from: Text provided by OECD (unofficial translation)
UN Registration: 20356

Text

AGREEMENT BETWEEN PORTUGAL AND SPAIN ON CO-OPERATION IN MATTERS AFFECTING THE SAFETY OF NUCLEAR INSTALLATIONS IN THE VICINITY OF THE FRONTIER

The Governments of Spain and Portugal, wishing to extend existing co-operation between their two countries in the field of nuclear energy to other areas of common concern such as questions affecting the safety of nuclear installations in the vicinity of frontiers and the exchange of information on nuclear safety and the radiological protection of installations liable to affect the territories of both countries, have agreed as follows:

Article 1
For the purposes of the present Agreement the following definitions shall apply:

(a) Nuclear installations means:

Reactors, except those forming part of a means of transport; plant for the preparation and manufacture of nuclear substances; plant for the separation of isotopes from nuclear fuel; plant for the processing of irradiated nuclear fuel; installations for the storage of nuclear substances, except for storage of such substances for the purposes of transport, unless such installations are considered as being of negligible importance so far as nuclear safety and radiological protection in the neighbouring country is concerned, or at least where the constructor country considers this to be so.

(b) Nuclear installations in the vicinity of the frontier means:

Installations sited less than 30 km from the frontier between the two countries or any other distance defined at international level and accepted by the two parties.

(c) Competent authorities means:

The authorities specifically empowered in each of the two countries to grant licences for the siting, construction and operation of nuclear installations.

Article 2

The competent authorities of the constructor country shall notify the neighbouring country of applications for licences for the siting, construction or operation of nuclear installations in the vicinity of the frontier which are submitted to them, such notification being without prejudice to the relations existing between the applicant and the competent authorities of the constructor country.

Article 3

The competent authorities of the constructor country shall give notification, accompanied by documentation relating to the nuclear safety and radiological protection of the installation for which a licence is requested, at such time as to enable any comments and observations by the neighbouring country to be taken into account by the competent authorities of the constructor country before reaching the decision in question. The competent authorities of the neighbouring country shall for their part examine the documentation received without delay.

Article 4

The competent authorities of the neighbouring country shall at the appropriate time provide such information necessary for an assessment of the site, construction and operation of the installation as may be requested by the constructor country in connection with both the licence application and during the operation of the installation. The costs incurred by the neighbouring country in providing such information shall be reimbursed by the constructor country on the basis of the same criteria as those applied within its own territory.

Article 5

The competent authorities of the two countries agree to set up on their respective territories the systems necessary to detect any signs of danger from radioactivity and mutually to inform each other in cases where such danger could have repercussions in the other country.

Article 6

If the competent authorities of one country have valid reasons for complaint in regard to matters of radiological safety or protection, negotiations shall immediately be commenced between such competent authorities and the competent authorities of the neighbouring country.

The competent authorities of the two countries shall endeavour to conclude such negotiations in the shortest possible time.

Article 7

The competent authorities of the two countries agree to comply with restrictions imposed by either party concerning the secrecy of information or documents supplied relating to equipment, technical processes, operating conditions and commercial relations.

Article 8

The Governments of the two countries shall take the necessary steps to establish exceptional procedures for the crossing of the frontier, in case of emergency, by duly accredited officials.

Article 9

Independently of the above provisions, the competent authorities of the constructor country shall keep the competent authorities of the neighbouring country informed of significant incidents affecting other nuclear installations which might affect its territory.

Article 10

Civil liability for nuclear damage shall be governed by the provisions of the conventions on civil liability in the field of nuclear energy which are currently in force and have been ratified by both countries.

Article 11

To ensure the implementation of the present Agreement, a Permanent Technical Commission shall be set up, composed of an equal number, not exceeding 8, of specialists nominated by the competent authorities of the two countries.

The Permanent Technical Commission shall meet alternatively in Lisbon and Madrid at least once in every year and where a valid reason exists extraordinary meetings may be held on the initiative of one of the two countries in a place to be decided by common agreement.

Article 12

The present Agreement shall come into force on the day when the instruments of ratification are exchanged.

Article 13

The present Agreement shall remain in force for a period of ten years which shall be tacitly extended for subsequent periods of five years unless one of the countries gives the other one year's notice in advance of its intention to consider the Agreement as terminated.

Article 14

The present Agreement may be terminated by one of the two parties but such termination shall not be effective until one year after its notification.

IN WITNESS WHEREOF the duly authorised representatives of the Spanish and Portuguese Governments have signed the present Agreement.

DONE at Lisbon on 31st March 1980, in two copies, one in Spanish and the other in Portuguese, both texts being equally valid.

Select Bibliography

Bothe, "International Siting in Border Areas and National Environmental Politics", in OECD, *Transfrontier Pollution and the Role of States* (Paris, 1981), p. 79.

Bothe, Prieur & Ress (eds.), *Rechtsfragen Grenzüberschreitender Umweltbelastungen* (1984) (esp. p. 243 *et seq.*).

Commission of the European Communities, *Authorisation Procedure for the Construction and Operation of Nuclear Installations within the EC Member States, including Supervision and Control* (1978).

Dupuy & Smets, "Co-operation in Frontier Regions", 5 *Env. Policy & Law* 175 (1979).

Handl, "Hazardous Activities in Frontier Areas: International Legal Restraints on Significant and Nuclear Risk Creation", in *OECD Doc.* ENV/TFe/78.14 at 3, 6-7 (1978).

Handl, "An International Legal Perspective on the Conduct of Abnormally Dangerous Activities in Frontier Areas: the Case of Nuclear Plant Siting", 7 *Ecology LQ* 1 (1978).

Moser, "Licensing Nuclear Power Stations near National Borders", 1973 *Nuclear Inter Jura* 195.

Wildhaber, "Die Öldestillerieanlage Sennwald und das Völkerrecht der grenzüberschreitenden Luftverschmutzung", 97 *ASDI* 107 (1975).

A number of other similar agreements have been concluded. They include:

(1) Belgium-France, Convention on Radiological Protection relating to the Installations at the Ardennes Nuclear Power Station, 23 September 1966; *reprinted in:* 988 *UNTS* 288.

(2) France-FRG-Switzerland, Exchange of Notes concerning Tripartite Commission for Neighbourhood Problems in Border Areas (Upper Rhine Region), 22 October 1975; *reprinted in: Official Gazette* of 6 January 1977 (see 19 *NLB* 34).

(3) Guidelines for Nordic Co-operation concerning Nuclear Installations in the Border Areas between Denmark, Finland, Norway and Sweden in respect of Nuclear Safety Conditions, entered into force 15 November 1976; *reprinted in:* 19 *NLB* 38-40 (1977).

(4) Denmark-Federal Republic of Germany, Agreement Regulating the Exchange of Information on the Construction of Nuclear Installations along the Border, 4 July 1977; *reprinted in:* 17 *ILM* 274 (1978).

(5) Federal Republic of Germany-Netherlands, Memorandum on Exchange of Information and Consultation on Nuclear Installations in Border Areas, 27 September 1977; *reprinted in:* 27 *Rüster* 275; *also noted in:* 22 *NLB* 35 (1978).

(6) Federal Republic of Germany-Switzerland, Agreement on Mutual Information on Construction and Operation of Nuclear Installations in Border Areas, 10 August 1982; *reprinted in: Bundesgesetzblatt* 1983, II, p. 734.

(7) Austria-Czechoslovakia, Agreement on Questions of Common Interest in Relation to Nuclear Facilities, 18 November 1982, entered into force 1 June 1984; *reprinted in: Bundesgesetzblatt* No. 208/1984.

12. INTERNATIONAL LAW ASSOCIATION, MONTREAL RULES OF INTERNATIONAL LAW APPLICABLE TO TRANSFRONTIER POLLUTION
4 September 1982

Editorial Note

This Resolution was adopted by the 1982 Conference of the International Law Association, following extensive deliberations by the ILA's Committee on Legal Aspects of the Conservation of the Environment. Its purpose is to set out the rules of customary international law with regard to transfrontier pollution.

The definition of "transfrontier pollution" contained in the Resolution is modelled on that in the UN Environmental Commission for Europe's Convention on Long-range Transboundary Air Pollution (see above, No. 10), but differs from it in that it extends to pollution of all media and is not limited to pollution of the air.

As understood by the ILA, customary international law imposes on States a number of strict duties to protect other States from pollution damage. These include duties to prevent, abate and limit transfrontier pollution so as to avoid substantial injury to other States; duties to give notice to, and consult with, other potentially affected States concerning activities which might entail a significant risk of transfrontier pollution; and duties to provide appropriate information to affected and potentially affected States in the event of a pollution emergency.

Where so-called "highly dangerous substances" are concerned, States are said to be under an absolute duty to prevent their being discharged into the environment of another State. The Commentary in the Committee's Report makes clear that these would include radioactive substances.

Two draft Articles dealing with shared natural resources and the need for equitable utilization thereof were not adopted by the Conference. These matters were already the subject of a number of other instruments, including (with regard to international watercourses) the ILA's own Helsinki Rules on the Uses of International Rivers (see *Report of the Fifty-second Conference, Helsinki, 1966,* p. 477), and were not thought appropriate for inclusion in the present Montreal Rules.

Reprinted from: ILA, *Report of the Sixtieth Conference, Montreal, 1982* (London, 1983), p. 1.

Text

ILA, MONTREAL RULES OF INTERNATIONAL LAW APPLICABLE TO TRANSFRONTIER POLLUTION

The 60th Conference of the International Law Association held in Montreal, 29th August—4th September 1982:

HAVING RECEIVED AND CONSIDERED the Report of the Committee on Legal Aspects of the Conservation of the Environment;

APPROVES the Statement of The Rules of International Law Applicable to Transfrontier Pollution recommended in the Committee's report as follows:

Article 1 (Applicability)

The following rules of international law concerning transfrontier pollution are applicable except as may be otherwise provided by convention, agreement or binding custom among the States concerned.

Article 2 (Definition)

(1) "Pollution" means any introduction by man, directly or indirectly, of substance or energy into the environment resulting in deleterious effects of such a nature as to endanger human health, harm living resources, ecosystems and material property and impair amenities or interfere with other legitimate uses of the environment.

(2) "Transfrontier pollution" means pollution of which the physical origin is wholly or in part situated within the territory of one State and which has deleterious effects in the territory of another State.

Article 3 (Prevention and abatement)

(1) Without prejudice to the operation of the rules relating to the reasonable and equitable utilisation of shared national resources States are in their legitimate activities under an obligation to prevent, abate and control transfrontier pollution to such an extent that no substantial injury is caused in the territory of another State.

(2) Furthermore States shall limit new and increased transfrontier pollution to the lowest level that may be reached by measures practicable and reasonable under the circumstances.

(3) States should endeavour to reduce existing transfrontier pollution, below the requirements of paragraph 1 of this Article, to the lowest level that may be reached by measures practicable and reasonable under the circumstances.

Article 4 (Highly dangerous substances)

Notwithstanding the provisions in Article 3 States shall refrain from causing transfrontier pollution by discharging into the environment substances generally considered as being highly dangerous to human health. If such substances are already being discharged, States shall eliminate the polluting discharge within a reasonable time.

Article 5 (Prior notice)

(1) States planning to carry out activities which might entail a significant risk of transfrontier pollution shall give early notice to States likely to be affected. In particular they shall on their own initiative or upon request of the potentially affected States, communicate such pertinent information as will permit the recipient to make an assessment of the probable effects of the planned activities.

(2) In order to appraise whether a planned activity implies a significant risk of transfrontier pollution, States should make environmental assessment before carrying out such activities.

Article 6 (Consultations)

Upon request of a potentially affected State, the State furnishing the information shall enter into consultations on transfrontier pollution problems connected with the planned activities and pursue such consultations in good faith and over a reasonable period of time.

Article 7 (Emergency situations)

When as a result of an emergency situation or of other circumstances activities already carried out in the territory of a State cause or might cause a sudden increase in the existing level of transfrontier pollution the State of origin is under a duty:

(a) to promptly warn the affected or potentially affected States;
(b) to provide them with such pertinent information as will enable them to minimize the transfrontier pollution damage;
(c) to inform them of the steps taken to abate the cause of the increased transfrontier pollution level.

RECOMMENDS that these Rules be designated the "Montreal Rules of International Law Applicable to Transfrontier Pollution";

REQUESTS the Secretary General of the Association to transmit the Report to the Secretary General of the United Nations for submission to the International Law Commission.

Select Bibliography

ILA, Committee on Legal Aspects of the Conservation of the Environment, Reports; in *Report of the 58th Conference, 1978*, p. 383; *Report of the 59th Conference, 1980*, p. 529; and *Report of the 60th Conference, 1982*, p. 157.

ILA, Committee on Legal Aspects of Long Distance Air Pollution, First (Preliminary) Report, *Report of the 61st Conference, 1984*, p. 377.

13. INTERNATIONAL LAW COMMISSION, SPECIAL RAPPORTEUR'S SCHEMATIC OUTLINE ANNEXED TO FOURTH REPORT ON INTERNATIONAL LIABILITY FOR INJURIOUS CONSEQUENCES ARISING OUT OF ACTS NOT PROHIBITED BY INTERNATIONAL LAW

July 1983

Editorial Note

In 1978, the ILC began its work on the topic of "International Liability for Injurious Consequences Arising Out of Acts Not Prohibited by International Law". The topic emanated directly from the Commission's prior study on State Responsibility, but that study was limited to the consequences of internationally wrongful acts as it was thought that a joint examination of the two subjects could only make both of them more difficult to grasp.

The first Special Rapporteur on International Liability, Mr Robert Q. Quentin-Baxter, produced five reports between 1979 and his death in 1984. The second Special Rapporteur, Mr Julio Barboza, has produced two reports. Quentin-Baxter based his work on the fundamental principle reflected in the maxim *sic utere tuo ut alienum non laedas:* the duty to exercise one's own rights in ways that do not harm the interests of other subjects of law. His most significant contribution to the topic is the Schematic Outline which was submitted in his Third Report and resubmitted, as reproduced, with proposed changes as an Annex to his Fourth Report. The Schematic Outline contains what Quentin-Baxter considered to be compound primary obligations covering the whole field of preventing, minimizing and providing reparation for the occurrence of physical transboundary harm.

The scope of the topic is established in Section 1; although no indication is given there of the kind of risk that is included, the second Special Rapporteur is of the view that what was presumably meant were activities that had a higher-than-normal likelihood of causing substantial injuries within the territory of another State or in localities under its control.

The essential principle is found in Section 5, Article 3: "an innocent victim should not be left to bear his loss or injury". Four duties are imposed upon States. The first "requires measures of prevention that as far as possible avoid a risk of loss or injury". The second requires the "acting State" (later referred to as the "source State") to provide "all relevant and available information" of certain harmful or potentially harmful activity. A limited exception is available "for reasons of national or industrial security" and provision is made for a fact-finding machinery. A breach of the duty to inform does not in itself give rise to any right of action (s. 2, Art. 8) but it does allow the affected State "a liberal recourse to inferences of fact and circumstantial evidence".

The third duty arises in the circumstances specified in Section 3, Article 1 and consists of a "duty to enter into negotiations . . . . with a view to determining whether a regime is necessary and what form it should take". The negotiations are to be governed by the principles, factors and matters set out in Sections 5, 6 and 7 respectively. As is the case with the duty to inform, a breach of the duty to negotiate does not in itself give rise to any right of action (s. 3, Art. 4). Finally, there is the duty to make reparation for loss or injury. In the absence of an agreement between the source and affected States, the reparation due is to be ascertained in accordance with the "shared expectations of the States concerned and the principles set out in Section 5". The concept of "shared expectations" is defined in Section 4, Article 4 and account is also to be taken of the reasonableness of the conduct of the Parties.

The second Special Rapporteur has recently published a critical analysis of the Schematic Outline. He has suggested that the 'no right of action' provisions in Section 2, Article 8 and Section 3, Article 4 be deleted. Much of the analysis is devoted to a discussion of Section 4 of the Schematic Outline which has been the most controversial work both in the ILC and in the Sixth Committee ("Legal") of the General Assembly. Accordingly, the work of the ILC on this topic must be considered as still being very much in the formative stage. The chief difficulty has been to achieve a balance between the interests of the source State in using its territory as it sees fit for activities not prohibited by international law, and the interests of other States in ensuring that such activities do not cause unreasonable harm to their territory. The Schematic Outline is, in the words of the second Special Rapporteur, "the most important raw material for this topic".

Text reprinted from: *Ybk ILC,* 1983, Vol. II (Part One) p. 233

Text

ILC, SPECIAL RAPPORTEUR'S SCHEMATIC OUTLINE ANNEXED TO FOURTH REPORT ON INTERNATIONAL LIABILITY FOR INJURIOUS CONSEQUENCES ARISING OUT OF ACTS NOT PROHIBITED BY INTERNATIONAL LAW

Section 1

1. *Scope*

Activities within the territory or control of a State which give rise or may give rise to loss or injury to persons or things within the territory or control of another State.

2. *Definition*

    (a) "Acting State" and "affected State" have meanings corresponding to the terms of the provision describing the scope.

(b) "Activity" includes any human activity.

(c) "Loss or injury" means any loss or injury, whether to the property of a State, or to any person or thing within the territory or control of a State.

(d) "Territory or control" includes, in relation to places not within the territory of the acting State,

    (i) any activity which takes place within the substantial control of that State; and

    (ii) any activity conducted on ships or aircraft of the acting State, or by nationals of the acting State, and not within the territory or control of any other State, otherwise than by reason of the presence within that territory of a ship in course of innocent passage, or of an aircraft in authorized overflight.

3. Saving

Nothing contained in these articles shall affect any right or obligation arising independently of these articles.

Section 2

1. When an activity taking place within its territory or control gives or may give rise to loss or injury to persons or things within the territory or control of another State, the acting State has a duty to provide the affected State with all relevant and available information, including a specific indication of the kinds and degrees of loss or injury that it considers to be foreseeable, and the remedial measures it proposes.

2. When a State has reason to believe that persons or things within its territory or control are being or may be subjected to loss or injury by an activity taking place within the territory or control of another State, the affected State may so inform the acting State, giving as far as its means of knowledge will permit, a specific indication of the kinds and degrees of loss or injury that it considers to be foreseeable; and the acting State has thereupon a duty to provide all relevant and available information, including a specific indication of the kinds and degrees of loss or injury that it considers to be foreseeable, and the remedial measures it proposes.

3. If, for reasons of national or industrial security, the acting State considers it necessary to withhold any relevant information that would otherwise be available, it must inform the affected State that information is being withheld. In any case, reasons of national or industrial security cannot justify failure to give an affected State a clear indication of the kinds and degrees of loss or injury to which persons and things within the territory or control of that affected State are being or may be subjected; and the affected State is not

obliged to rely upon assurances which it has no sufficient means of knowledge to verify.

4.   If not satisfied that the measures being taken in relation to the loss or injury foreseen are sufficient to safeguard persons and things within its territory or control, the affected State may propose to the acting State that fact-finding be undertaken.

5.   The acting State may itself propose that fact-finding be undertaken; and, when such a proposal is made by the affected State, the acting State has a duty to co-operate in good faith to reach agreement with the affected State upon the arrangements for and terms of reference of the inquiry, and upon the establishment of the fact-finding machinery. Both States shall furnish the inquiry with all relevant and available information.

6.   Unless the States concerned otherwise agree,
   (a) there should be joint fact-finding machinery, with reliance upon experts, to gather relevant information, assess its implications and, to the extent possible, recommend solutions;
   (b) the report should be advisory, not binding the States concerned.

7.   The acting State and the affected State shall contribute to the costs of the fact-finding machinery on an equitable basis.

8.   Failure to take any step required by the rules contained in this section shall not in itself give rise to any right of action. Nevertheless, unless it is otherwise agreed, the acting State has a continuing duty to keep under review the activity that gives or may give rise to loss or injury; to take whatever remedial measures it considers necessary and feasible to safeguard the interests of the affected State; and, as far as possible, to provide information to the affected State about the action it is taking.

Section 3

1.   If (a) it does not prove possible within a reasonable time either to agree upon the establishment and terms of reference of fact-finding machinery or for the fact-finding machinery to complete its terms of reference; or (b) any State concerned is not satisfied with the findings, or believes that other matters should be taken into consideration; or, (c) the report of the fact-finding machinery so recommends, the States concerned have a duty to enter into negotiations at the request of any one of them with a view to determining whether a regime is necessary and what form it should take.

2.   Unless the States concerned otherwise agree, the negotiations shall apply the principles set out in section 5; shall also take into account, as far as applicable, any relevant factor, including those set out in section 6, and may be guided by reference to any of the matters set out in section 7.

3. Any agreement concluded pursuant to the negotiations shall, in accordance with its terms, satisfy the rights and obligations of the States parties under the present articles; and may also stipulate the extent to which these rights and obligations replace any other rights and obligations of the parties.

4. Failure to take any step required by the rules contained in this section shall not in itself give rise to any right of action. Nevertheless, unless it is otherwise agreed, the acting State has a continuing duty to keep under review the activity that gives or may give rise to loss or injury; to take or continue whatever remedial measures it considers necessary and feasible to safeguard the interests of the affected State; and, as far as possible, to provide information to the affected State about the action it is taking.

Section 4

1. If any activity does give rise to loss or injury, and the rights and obligations of the acting and affected States under the present articles in respect of any such loss or injury have not been specified in an agreement between those States, those rights and obligations shall be determined in accordance with the provisions of this section. The States concerned shall negotiate in good faith to achieve this purpose.

2. Reparation shall be made by the acting State to the affected State in respect of any such loss or injury, unless it is established that the making of reparation for a loss or injury of that kind or character is not in accordance with the shared expectations of those States.

3. The reparation due to the affected State under the preceding article shall be ascertained in accordance with the shared expectations of the States concerned and the principles set out in section 5; and account shall be taken of the reasonableness of the conduct of the parties, having regard to the record of any exchanges or negotiations between them and to the remedial measures taken by the acting State to safeguard the interests of the affected State. Account may also be taken of any relevant factors, including those set out in section 6 and guidance may be obtained by reference to any of the matters set out in section 7.

4. In the two preceding articles, "shared expectations" include shared expectations which

(a) have been expressed in correspondence or other exchanges between the States concerned or, in so far as there are no such expressions,

(b) can be implied from common legislative or other standards or patterns of conduct normally observed by the States concerned, or in any regional or other grouping to which they both belong, or in the international community.

Section 5

1. The aim and purpose of the present articles is to ensure to acting States as much freedom of choice, in relation to activities within their territory or control, as is compatible with adequate protection of the interests of affected States.

2. Adequate protection requires measures of prevention that as far as possible avoid a risk of loss or injury and, in so far as that is not possible, measures of reparation; but the standards of adequate protection should be determined with due regard to the importance of the activity and its economic viability.

3. In so far as may be consistent with the preceding articles, an innocent victim should not be left to bear his loss or injury; the costs of adequate protection should be distributed with due regard to the distribution of the benefits of the activity; and standards of protection should take into account the means at the disposal of the acting State and the standards applied in the affected State and in regional and international practice.

4. To the extent that an acting State has not made available to an affected State information that is more accessible to the acting State concerning the nature and effects of an activity, and the means of verifying and assessing that information, the affected State shall be allowed a liberal recourse to inferences of fact and circumstantial evidence in order to establish whether the activity does or may give rise to loss or injury.

Section 6

Factors which may be relevant to balancing of interests include:

1. The degree of probability of loss or injury (i.e. how likely is it to happen?);

2. The seriousness of loss or injury (i.e. an assessment of quantum and degree of severity in terms of the consequences);

3. The probable cumulative effect of losses or injuries of the kind in question—in terms of conditions of life and security of the affected State, and more generally—if reliance is placed upon measures to ensure the provision of reparation rather than prevention (i.e. the acceptable mix between prevention and reparation);

4. The existence of means to prevent loss or injury, having regard to the highest known state of the art of carrying on the activity;

5. The feasibility of carrying on the activity by alternative means or in alternative places;

6. The importance of the activity to the acting State (i.e. how necessary is it to continue or undertake the activity, taking account of economic, social, security or other interests?);

7.   The economic viability of the activity considered in relation to the cost of possible means of protection;

8.   The availability of alternative activities;

9.   The physical and technical capacities of the acting State (considered, for example, in relation to its ability to take measures of prevention or make reparation or to undertake alternative activities);

10.   The way in which existing standards of protection compare with:
   (a) the standards applied by the affected State; and
   (b) the standards applied in regional and international practice;

11.   The extent to which the acting State:
   (a) has effective control over the activity; and
   (b) obtains a real benefit from the activity;

12.   The extent to which the affected State shares in the benefits of the activity;

13.   The extent to which the adverse effects arise from or affect the use of a shared resource;

14.   The extent to which the affected State is prepared to contribute to the cost of preventing or making reparation of loss or injury, or of maximizing its benefits from the activity;

15.   The extent to which the interests of:
   (a) the affected State, and
   (b) the acting State are compatible with the interests of the general
      community;

16.   The extent to which assistance to the acting State is available from third States or from international organizations;

17.   The applicability of relevant principles and rules of international law.

Section 7

Matters which may be relevant in negotiations concerning prevention and reparation include:

I. *Fact-finding and prevention*

1.   The identification of adverse effects and of material and non-material loss or injury to which they may give rise;

2.   The establishment of procedural means for managing the activity and monitoring its effects;

3.   The establishment of requirements concerning the structure and operation of the activity;

4.   The taking of measures to assist the affected State in minimizing loss or injury.

II. *Compensation as a means of reparation*

    1. A decision as to where primary and residual liability should lie, and whether the liability of some actors should be channelled through others;

    2. A decision as to whether liability should be unlimited or limited;

    3. The choice of a forum in which to determine the existence of liability and the amounts of compensation payable;

    4. The establishment of procedures for the presentation of claims;

    5. The identification of compensable loss or injury;

    6. The test of the measure of compensation for loss or injury;

    7. The establishment of forms and modalities for the payment of compensation awarded;

    8. Consideration of the circumstances which might increase or diminish liability or provide an exoneration from it.

III. *Authorities competent to make decisions concerning fact-finding, prevention and compensation*

At different phases of the negotiations, the States concerned may find it helpful to place in the hands of their national authorities or courts, international organizations or specially constituted commissions, the responsibility for making recommendations or taking decisions as to the matters referred to under headings I and II.

Section 8

Settlement of disputes (taking due account of recently concluded multilateral treaties that provide for such measures).

Select Bibliography

Akehurst, "International Liability for Injurious Consequences arising out of Acts not Prohibited by International Law", 16 *NYIL* 3 (1985).

Handl, "Liability as an Obligation Established by a Primary Rule of International Law, Some Basic Reflections on the International Law Commission's work", 16 *NYIL* 64 (1985).

Magraw, "Transboundary Harm: the International Law Commission's Study of International Liability", 80 *AJIL* 305 (1986).

McCaffrey, "An Update on the Contribution of the International Law Commission to International Environmental Law", 15 *Env. Law* 667 (1985).

Pinto, "Reflections on International Liability for Injurious Consequences arising out of Acts not Prohibited by International Law", 16 *NYIL* 17 (1985).

ILC Reports:

(a) Preliminary Report on International Liability for Injurious Consequences arising out of Acts not Prohibited by International Law: *UN Doc.* A/CN.4/334 and Adds. 1-2 (1980); *Ybk ILC,* 1980, Vol. II (Part One), p. 247.

(b) Second Report on International Liability for Injurious Consequences arising out of Acts not Prohibited by International Law: *UN Doc.* A/CN.4/346 and Adds. 1-2 (1981); *Ybk ILC,* 1981, Vol. II (Part One), p. 103.

(c) Third Report on International Liability for Injurious Consequences arising out of Acts not Prohibited by International Law: *UN Doc.* A/CN.4/360 and Corr. 1 (1982); *Ybk ILC,* 1982, Vol. II (Part One), p. 51.

(d) Fourth Report on International Liability for Injurious Consequences arising out of Acts not Prohibited by International Law: *UN Doc.* A/CN.4/373 and Corr. 1 (1983); *Ybk ILC,* 1983, Vol. II (Part One), p. 201.

(e) Fifth Report on International Liability for Injurious Consequences arising out of Acts not Prohibited by International Law: *UN Doc.* A/CN.4/383 and Add. 1 (1984); *Ybk ILC,* 1984, Vol. II (Part One), p. 155.

(f) Preliminary Report (Barboza) *UN Doc.* A/CN.4/394 and Add. 1 (1985).

(g) First Report on International Liability for Injurious Consequences arising out of Acts not Prohibited by International Law: *UN Doc.* A/CN.4/402 (1986).

14. EXCHANGE OF NOTES BETWEEN THE GOVERNMENT OF THE UNITED KINGDOM AND THE GOVERNMENT OF THE FRENCH REPUBLIC CONCERNING EXCHANGES OF INFORMATION IN THE EVENT OF EMERGENCIES OCCURRING IN ONE OF THE TWO STATES WHICH COULD HAVE RADIOLOGICAL CONSEQUENCES FOR THE OTHER STATE
18 July 1983

Editorial Note

This is one of many bilateral information agreements which have been concluded in recent years. Under the Agreement, France and the United Kingdom agree to provide each other with information enabling the risk to be assessed in the event of a civil emergency which could have radiological consequences for the other State. The information is to be communicated through reciprocal warning centres, capable of receiving and transmitting twenty-four hours per day. It should be noted that the Agreement only applies to emergencies arising out of civil activities.

Date of signature: 18 July 1983
Entry into force: 18 July 1983
Text reprinted from: 60 *UKTS* (1983), Cmnd. 9041

Text

EXCHANGE OF NOTES BETWEEN THE GOVERNMENT OF THE UNITED KINGDOM AND THE GOVERNMENT OF THE FRENCH REPUBLIC CONCERNING EXCHANGES OF INFORMATION IN THE EVENT OF EMERGENCIES OCCURRING IN ONE OF THE TWO STATES WHICH COULD HAVE RADIOLOGICAL CONSEQUENCES FOR THE OTHER STATE

No. 1

The Ambassador of the French Republic at London to the Minister of State for Foreign and Commonwealth Affairs

Ambassade de France
Londres, le 18 juillet 1983

No. 697

Monsieur le Ministre,

A la suite des entretiens qui se sont déroulés entre des représentants du Gouvernement de la République française et du Gouvernement du Royaume-Uni de Grande-Bretagne et d'Irlande du Nord, j'ai l'honneur, de vous proposer, d'ordre de mon Gouvernement, les mesures suivantes, au sujet des échanges d'information en cas de situation d'urgence survenant dans l'un des deux Etats et pouvant avoir des conséquences radiologiques pour l'autre Etat:

(1) Chaque Etat Partie informe sans retard l'autre Partie de toute situation d'urgence survenant sur son territoire du fait d'activités civiles, qui pourrait avoir des conséquences radiologiques susceptibles d'affecter l'autre Etat.

(2) Les Parties mettent en place et maintiennent en service un système approprié d'information mutuelle.

(3) En particulier, des centres d'alerte réciproque (ci-après dénommés centres d'alerte principaux) sont mis en place par le Gouvernement français au Ministère de l'Interieur et par le Gouvernement britannique au H.M. Nuclear Installations Inspectorate of the Health and Safety Executive (pour la transmission des alertes vers la France) ainsi qu'au Department of the Environment (pour la réception des alertes de France).

En tant que de besoin, d'autres centres d'alerte réciproque pourront être mis en place à l'échelon regional.

(4) Les Parties veillent à maintenir des liaisons appropriées entre les centres d'alerte. Chaque Partie notifiera par la voie diplomatique à l'autre Partie, et son centre d'alerte principal signalera directement au centre d'alerte principal de l'autre Partie, les modifications intéressant ses centres d'alerte qui pourraient empêcher qu'une information convenable soit transmise rapidement au centre d'alerte principal de l'autre Partie.

(5) Le système d'information mutuelle, établi en application du paragraphe (2) ci-dessus, doit être en mesure de recevoir et de transmettre vingt-quatre heures sur vingt-quatre les éventuelles informations dont il disposerait sur les situations d'urgence visées au paragraphe (1) ci-dessus.

(6) Les réseaux de transmission entre les centres d'alerte principaux du Gouvernement du Royaume-Uni et le centre d'alerte principal du Gouvernement de la République française visés au paragraphe (3) ci-dessus, seront éprouvés périodiquement et, dans tous les cas, au moins une fois par an.

(7) L'utilisation des réseaux de transmission, visés au paragraphe (6) ci-dessus, obéit à des procédures permettant d'exclure les informations erronées.

(8)   Les informations sur les situations d'urgence, visées au paragraphe (1) ci-dessus, doivent comporter toutes les données disponibles permettant d'évaluer le risque et notamment:

(a) la date, l'heure et le lieu de l'événement

(b) la nature et la cause de l'événement

(c) les caractéristiques de l'émission éventuelle (nature, forme physique et chimique ainsi que, dans la mesure du possible, quantité de substances radioactives émises); l'évolution prévisible de l'émission dans le temps; la nature du milieu de transfert (air et/ou eau); les données météorologiques et hydrologiques permettant de prévoir la dispersion des matières radioactives dans l'environnement.

(9)   Les informations relatives au situations d'urgence visées au paragraphe (1) ci-dessus doivent être complétées par la transmission des données disponibles sur les mesures prises ou envisagées pour y répondre par l'Etat où s'est produite une telle situation.

(10)   Les informations concernant l'évolution, dans les deux pays, de la situation créée par la situation d'urgence, notamment la fin de celle-ci, feront l'objet de transmissions complémentaires.

(11)   Lorsque se produit une situation d'urgence au sens du paragraphe (1), et après accord entre les autorités visées au paragraphe (3) ci-dessus, chaque Partie peut envoyer en mission une personne habilitée à recueillir directement auprès des autorités compétentes du pays où a eu lieu la situation d'urgence, tout renseignement susceptible d'éclairer son Gouvernement sur les conséquences que ladite situation d'urgence pourrait avoir dans son pays. Les autorités du pays où a eu lieu la situation d'urgence assureront les contacts que les deux Parties estimeraient utiles au bon déroulement de la mission.

(12)   La procédure d'information, établie par les paragraphes précédents, s'applique également à tout événement non couvert par les dispositions du paragraphe (1), ci-dessus, survenant dans l'un des deux Etats et pouvant avoir des conséquences radiologiques dans l'autre Etat.

(13)   Aucune information sur les données relevant du secret militaire ne fera l'objet d'une communication en vertu des présentes propositions.

(14)   La compétence des autorités nationales, chargées de l'exécution des présentes propositions, est régie par le droit interne respectif de chaque Etat.

(15)   Aux fin de l'application des paragraphes précédents l'expression Royaume-Uni de Grande-Bretagne et d'Irlande du Nord inclut les Iles Anglo-Normandes et l'Ile de Man, et le terme Etat sera ainsi interprété.

Les paragraphes précédents ne s'appliquent pas aux DOM-TOM de la France.

Au cas où les dispositions précédentes, dont le texte en langue française et le texte en langue anglaise feront également foi, recueilleraient l'accord du

Gouvernement du Royaume-Uni de Grande-Bretagne et d'Irlande du Nord, j'ai l'honneur de vous proposer que la présente lettre constitue, avec votre réponse, un accord entre nos deux Gouvernements, relatif aux échanges d'informations en cas de situation d'urgence pouvant avoir des conséquences radiologiques, qui prendra effet à la date de la réponse de Votre Excellence et demeurera en vigueur tant qu'une Partie n'aura pas notifié par écrit à l'autre Partie son intention de le dénoncer; dans ce cas, le présent accord prendra fin six moins après la date de cette notification.

Veuillez agréer, Monsieur le Ministre, l'assurance de ma haute considération.

E. De Margerie

No. 2

The Minister of State for Foreign and Commonwealth Affairs to the Ambassador of the French Republic at London

Foreign and Commonwealth Office
London
18 July 1983

Your Excellency

I have the honour to acknowledge the receipt of Your Excellency's Note number 697 of today's date, which in translation reads as follows:

Following discussions which have taken place between representatives of the Government of the United Kingdom of Great Britain and Northern Ireland and the Government of the French Republic, I have the honour, by order of my Government, to propose to you the following measures concerning exchanges of information in the event of emergencies occurring in one of the two States which could have radiological consequences for the other State:

(1) Each State-Party shall inform the other without delay of any emergency which occurs in its State as a result of civil activities which may have radiological consequences liable to affect the other State.

(2) The Parties shall establish and maintain an appropriate reciprocal information system.

(3)   In particular, reciprocal warning centres (hereinafter referred to as 'principal warning centres') shall be set up by the French Government at the Ministère de l'Intérieur and by the United Kingdom Government at HM Nuclear Installations Inspectorate of the Health and Safety Executive (for transmission of warnings to France) and the Department of the Environment (for the reception of warnings from France). Further reciprocal warning centres may be set up at regional level as required.

(4)   The Parties shall ensure that appropriate communications links are maintained between the warning centres. Each Party shall notify the other Party through the diplomatic channel, and its principal warning centre shall directly notify the principal warning centre of the other Party, of modifications affecting its warning centres which could prevent the rapid transmission of appropriate information to the principal warning centre of the other Party.

(5)   The reciprocal information system established pursuant to paragraph (2) above shall be capable of receiving and transmitting twenty-four hours a day any available information relating to an emergency referred to in paragraph (1) above.

(6)   The communications networks between the principal warning centres of the Government of the United Kingdom and the principal warning centre of the Government of the French Republic, referred to in paragraph (3) above, shall be tested periodically and, in any event, at least once a year.

(7)   The operation of the communications networks referred to in paragraph (6) above shall have procedures designed to eliminate false information.

(8)   Information on emergencies referred to in paragraph (1) above shall include all available data enabling the risk to be assessed including in particular:
(a) the date, time and place of the occurrence;
(b) the nature and cause of the occurrence; and
(c) the particular characteristics of any emission (type, physical and chemical form and, as far as possible, the quantity of radioactive substances emitted); the ways in which the emission can be expected to develop with the passage of time; the nature of the transfer medium (air and /or water); and meteorological and hydrological data which will make it possible to forecast the dispersion of the radioactive material in the environment.

(9)   Information relating to emergencies referred to in paragraph (1) above shall be supplemented by the transmission of available data on measures taken or envisaged by the State in which an emergency has occurred, in order to respond to it.

(10)   Information concerning the development in both States of the situation created by the emergency, in particular the end of the emergency, shall be subject of additional communications.

(11)   When an emergency arises within the meaning of paragraph (1) above, and after agreement has been reached between the authorities referred to in paragraph (3) above, each Party may send an authorised person to obtain directly from the competent authorities of the State in which the emergency occurred, information likely to enable his Government to assess the consequences which that emergency might have in its State. The authorities of the State in which the emergency arose will ensure the contacts which both Parties deem useful for the smooth progress of the mission.

(12)   The information procedure set out in the preceding paragraphs shall also apply to any incident not covered by the provisions of paragraph (1) above, which occurs in one of the two States and could have radiological consequences in the other State.

(13)   No information relating to military secrets shall be the subject of a communication under the terms of these proposals.

(14)   The competence of the national authorities responsible for implementing these proposals shall be governed by the respective national law of each State.

(15)   The preceding paragraphs shall apply as if references to the United Kingdom of Great Britain and Northern Ireland included the Channel Islands and the Isle of Man, and the term 'State' shall be construed accordingly. The preceding paragraphs shall not apply to the French Départements d'Outre-Mer and Territoires d'Outre-Mer.

If the foregoing proposals, the texts of which in the English and French languages are equally authoritative, are acceptable to the Government of the United Kingdom of Great Britain and Northern Ireland, I have the honour to suggest that this Note, together with your reply in that sense, shall constitute an Agreement between our two Governments which shall enter into force on the date of Your Excellency's reply and continue to be in force until six months after one Party has given written notice of termination to the other Party.

In reply, I have the honour to inform Your Excellency that the foregoing proposals are acceptable to the Government of the United Kingdom of Great Britain and Northern Ireland who therefore agree that your Note, together with this reply, shall constitute an Agreement between our two Governments which shall enter into force on today's date and continue in force until six months after one Party has given written notice of termination to the other Party.

I avail myself of this opportunity to renew to Your Excellency the assurance of my highest consideration.

Richard Luce

Select Bibliography

Collins, Emmerson & Phuong, "Information Exchange and Mutual Emergency Assistance", 28 *IAEA Bulletin* (No. 3) 16 (1986).
Constantin, "L'information et la Consultation Préalables des Etats Tiers susceptibles d'être affectés par une Pollution Transfrontière", 20 *Rev. Roum. d'Et. Internat.* 145 (1986).
Salo, "Information exchange after Chernobyl", 28 *IAEA Bulletin* (No. 3) 18 (1986).

A number of other such agreements have been concluded. They include:

(1) Switzerland-Federal Republic of Germany, Agreement on Radiation Protection in Case of Emergency, 31 May 1978, entered into force 10 January 1979; *reprinted in: Swiss Official Gazette (Sammlung der eidgenössischen Gesetze)* No. 9 of 13 March 1979; *also in:* 22 *NLB* 51 (1978).

(2) France-Switzerland, Agreement on Exchange of Information in Case of Radiation Emergency, 18 October 1979, entered into force 13 December 1979; *reprinted in: Journal officiel de la République française* of 21 and 22 April 1980 by Decree No. 80-279 of 16 April 1980.

(3) France-Federal Republic of Germany, Supplementary Agreement on Mutual Information in the Event of Radiological Incidents, 28 January 1981, entered into force 6 August 1981; *reprinted in: Bundesgesetzblatt* 1981, II, p. 885.

(4) Luxembourg-France, Agreement on Exchange of Information in Case of Radiological Emergencies, 11 April 1983, entered into force 27 April 1984; *reprinted in: Journal officiel de la République française* of 20 October 1984 by Decree No. 84-930 of 17 October 1984.

(5) Argentina-Brazil, Protocol of Co-operation concerning Prompt Notification and Mutual Assistance in the Event of Nuclear Accidents and Radiological Emergencies, 29 July 1986; *noted in:* 38 *NLB* 51 (1986).

15. IAEA, GUIDELINES FOR MUTUAL EMERGENCY ASSISTANCE ARRANGEMENTS IN CONNECTION WITH A NUCLEAR ACCIDENT OR RADIOLOGICAL EMERGENCY
January 1984

Editorial Note

These Guidelines were drawn up by a group of experts convened by the Director General of the IAEA with the authorization of the Board of Governors of the IAEA. Their purpose was two-fold: first, to serve as a model to be used by States for the negotiation of bilateral or regional treaties; second, to be readily agreed between a requesting and an assisting State at the time of a nuclear emergency.

The Guidelines contain provisions regarding the overall control and responsibility for the assistance, reimbursement of the assisting State's costs, protection of that State from liability for injury, loss or damage, and the privileges and immunities of its personnel. They also cover the identification and communication to other States of competent authorities and points of contact, the circumstances under which the assisting State can make public statements, disclosure of confidential information and the free movement of property brought into the requesting State. The Technical Annex[1] sets out the nature and degree of assistance which could be provided in different areas according to the particular emergency situation and the capabilities of requesting and assisting States, in the early, intermediate and late phases of an accident.

Text reprinted from: *IAEA Doc.* INFCIRC/310

Text

IAEA, GUIDELINES FOR MUTUAL EMERGENCY ASSISTANCE ARRANGEMENTS IN CONNECTION WITH A NUCLEAR ACCIDENT OR RADIOLOGICAL EMERGENCY

1. *Introduction*
1.1 The provisions relating to emergency assistance in the event of a nuclear accident or radiological emergency presented herein are recommended as guidelines for use by States for the negotiation of bilateral or regional agreements. These provisions could also be readily agreed to by a special

---

[1] The Technical Annex is not reproduced here.

agreement between a requesting and assisting State at the time of a nuclear accident or radiological emergency.

1.2   The provisions herein do not affect legal or other arrangements that either exist or may be entered, unless expressly agreed otherwise by the parties concerned.

1.3   Nothing herein derogates from the right of States to enter into different arrangements or to vary in any respect the provisions herein.

1.4   No State is required to request or accept, or offer or provide assistance by reason merely of acceptance or use of the provisions herein.

2. Direction and control of assistance

2.1   Within the territory of the requesting State, overall control of and responsibility for the assistance should rest with the requesting State. In particular:

  (a) the assistance should be subject to the general direction and supervision of the requesting State within its territory;

  (b) the assisting party should designate a person in charge of the personnel and equipment provided by it and should direct such personnel and the use of such equipment in cooperation with the competent authorities of the requesting State. That person should retain immediate authority and operational control over such an assistance team.

2.2   Unless the parties agree otherwise, the assistance should be used exclusively for the purpose for which it was requested.

3. Points of contact and competent authorities

3.1   States should identify and make known to each other (directly or through the International Atomic Energy Agency) and to the International Atomic Energy Agency their competent authorities and points of contact having primary responsibility for coordinating response operations in the event of a nuclear accident or radiological emergency.

3.2   The points of contact identified pursuant to the preceding paragraph should be those authorized by the States concerned to make and receive requests for, and to accept, offers of assistance, and to receive and transmit communications relating thereto. If the appropriate channels for subsequent communications are different than the initial points of contact, a State should so specify. If appropriate, a working language should be designated.

3.3   Competent authorities of a potential requesting State and assisting party should establish, in planning for response to any nuclear accident or radiological emergency, a joint contingency plan for such an occurrence, which should be updated as necessary. These authorities should consult periodically on the potential implementation of the provisions contained herein.

4. Public statements and information provided in confidence

4.1 The assisting party and its personnel should not release information to the public on the assistance provided in connection with a nuclear accident or radiological emergency without coordination with the authorities of the requesting State.

4.2 If an assisting party needs to make a public statement or report, for example, to its legislative body, concerning its assistance, the assisting party should to the extent practicable coordinate in advance with the requesting State on the content of the statement or report.

4.3 Information provided in confidence in connection with the assistance—such as commercial, proprietary, diplomatic or physical protection information—should be protected from disclosure by the recipient of the information to the maximum extent possible and should not be misused. However, this does not preclude appropriate regulatory use of such information.

5. Reimbursement for costs

5.1 Without prejudice to any responsibility third States or parties may have, the requesting State is responsible to, and should reimburse, any assisting party for its costs, unless otherwise agreed between them.

5.2 The costs of the assisting party include costs incurred for the services rendered by persons or entities acting on its behalf and all the expenses of the assisting party in connection with the assistance.

5.3 Reimbursement should correspond to the reasonable costs incurred, which could cover services (including salaries), subsistence, travel and transport, insurance (including insurance of personnel and property of the assisting party), equipment, materials or facilities provided, or the use thereof, and other documented expenses. The assisting party may waive reimbursement for certain costs, for example, costs within its territory and salaries of its government personnel.

6. Liability

6.1 An assisting party should be protected from liability that might arise out of the assistance rendered on the territory of the requesting State.

6.2 In particular, an assisting party and entities and personnel acting on its behalf should not be liable for damage or injury to or loss of life of any person, damage to or loss of any property, or damage to the environment, where caused by the nuclear accident or radiological emergency, or by any actions taken in rendering assistance that has been requested.

6.3   The requesting State should assume all responsibility for defending against claims that might be brought by third parties against the assisting party or entities or personnel acting on its behalf and should hold the assisting party and such entities and personnel harmless in the case of any claim or liability in connection with the nuclear accident, the radiological emergency or the assistance.

6.4   The above paragraphs should not affect liability under any applicable conventions or national law of any State and should not prevent compensation or indemnity under any such conventions or national law.

7. Facilities, privileges and immunities

7.1   The requesting State should afford personnel of an assisting party and personnel acting on its behalf the necessary privileges, immunities and facilities for the expeditious performance of their assistance functions.

7.2   The requesting State should itself provide, to the extent of its capabilities, any local facilities and services for the proper and effective administration of the assistance.

7.3   The requesting State should ensure the protection and security of personnel of the assisting party and entities acting on its behalf, and their documents and official and personal property.

7.4   Each State should facilitate the movement through its national territory of personnel and equipment involved in a nuclear accident or radiological emergency assistance as well as persons in need of medical treatment as a result of the accident or emergency.

8. Property and equipment

8.1   The requesting State should permit and facilitate the entry, free of duty, of property to be brought into the territory of the requesting State for the purpose of the assistance.

8.2   The requesting State should ensure the immunity from taxation, duties or other charges and from seizure or requisition of the property brought into the territory of the requesting State by the assisting party or entities or personnel acting on its behalf for the purpose of the assistance.

8.3   The requesting State should permit and facilitate the re-export of such property, free of duty.

8.4   If the assisting party so requests, the requesting State should, to the extent that it is able to do so, arrange for the requisite decontamination of recoverable equipment before its re-export.

9. Termination of assistance

9.1   The requesting State or assisting party may at any time, after appropriate consultations and after having given written notice, request the termination of the assistance.

9.2   Upon such request for termination of the assistance, the requesting State and the assisting party should consult with a view to concluding any operations in progress and facilitating withdrawal of the assistance.

10. Settlement of disputes

10.1   In the event of a dispute between two or more parties concerning any of the matters dealt with herein, such parties should consult with a view to the settlement of the dispute by negotiation or by any other peaceful means of settling disputes acceptable to all parties to the dispute.

10.2   Any dispute of this character which cannot be settled in the foregoing manner should, at the request of any party to the dispute, be submitted to arbitration for decision.

Select Bibliography

IAEA, "Mutual Emergency Assistance for Radiation Accidents", *IAEA-TECDOC*-237 (1980).

IAEA, "Planning for Off-Site Response to Radiation Accidents in Nuclear Facilities", *Safety Series* No. 55 (1981).

IAEA, "Preparedness of Public Authorities for Emergencies at Nuclear Power Plants", *Safety Series* No. 50-SG-G6 (1982).

IAEA, "Preparedness of the Operating Organization (Licencee) for Emergencies at Nuclear Power Plants", *Safety Series* No. 50-SG-06 (1982).

IAEA, "Emergency Response Planning for Transport Accidents Involving Radioactive Materials", *IAEA-TECDOC*-262 (1982) and Supplement, *IAEA TECDOC*-284 (1984).

ILO, "Radiation Protection of Workers", *ILO Code of Practice* (1987).

WHO, "Nuclear power: Accidental Releases—Principles of Public Health Action", *WHO Regional Publication, European Series* No. 16 (1984).

16. IAEA, GUIDELINES ON REPORTABLE EVENTS, INTEGRATED PLANNING AND INFORMATION EXCHANGE IN A TRANSBOUNDARY RELEASE OF RADIOACTIVE MATERIALS
January 1985

Editorial Note

These Guidelines, prepared by a group of experts under the auspices of the IAEA, are intended to assist States wishing to coordinate in advance their response to a radiological emergency, as well as serving as a model in the event of such an emergency. They constitute a further step in the development of an integrated and general regime of cooperation.

The Guidelines establish the criteria relevant to thresholds for reportable events and to intervention levels for the introduction of protective measures. They also set out the framework for the organization of information exchange at the time of an emergency, the nature of the information to be exchanged, and the various considerations on which integrated planning for such an emergency should be based.

Text reprinted from: *IAEA Doc.* INFCIRC/321

Text

IAEA, GUIDELINES ON REPORTABLE EVENTS, INTEGRATED PLANNING AND INFORMATION EXCHANGE IN A TRANSBOUNDARY RELEASE OF RADIOACTIVE MATERIALS

I. *Introduction*
1.1   The Report of the Group of Experts that met in June 1982 to study the most appropriate means of responding to the need for mutual assistance in connection with nuclear accidents stated, inter alia, that:

A nuclear accident in border areas could have serious radiological effects in the territories of neighbouring countries. Especially, in cases where the neighbouring country has no nuclear installation of its own, its capability to deal with the situation would be limited

and

In cases where serious accidents at nuclear power plants may have significant radiological impact in other States, special planning considerations need to be recognized and resolved. Issues such as establishing a threshold of reportable events, integrated planning and information exchange need prior arrangements.

1.2 The aforementioned Group of Experts agreed that ''there should be provisions for specification by participating States of the appropriate initial points of contact and, if different, of the appropriate channels for subsequent communications. There should also be provisions for advance notification of competent national authorities''. It is recognized that such provisions will entail a willingness among Member States to come to arrangements for protection of man and his environment, along the lines of the IAEA Guidelines for Mutual Emergency Assistance Arrangements in Connection with a Nuclear Accident or Radiological Emergency.

1.3 The Expert Group convened in May 1984 assumed that in emergency response planning use will be made of the relevant IAEA documents.

1.4 The Expert Group also took note of the activities of the IAEA with respect to intervention levels. It concluded that for those notifications where the threshold for reporting is based upon a categorization of emergency conditions (see paragraph 3.3), such notifications will normally have been initiated in advance of any need to introduce protective measures due to exceeding the intervention levels. The introduction of measures for the protection of individual members of the public, based upon these intervention levels, is not, however, the only threshold for the initiation of transboundary notifications.

II. *Formal arrangements*

2.1 Neighbouring States may wish to consider entering into bilateral or multilateral arrangements setting out their mutual willingness to co-operate and co-ordinate their response to any emergency which might involve a transboundary radiological release. The purpose of such arrangements is to facilitate the exchange of information, integrated planning and notification of an emergency among neighbouring States.

2.2 Such arrangements should identify the authorities responsible for advance emergency response planning and for action during an emergency. They should specify the type of information and the ways in which this information can be most speedily exchanged. Definitions of basic terms and concepts, the designation of liaison officers, an agreed language or code to be used in case of an emergency and plans concerning information to the public should also be included.

2.3   There should be provisions to compare the means and methods to be used for calculating radiological consequences. The basis for any preplanned protective measures and for their implementation should be indicated.

2.4   The potential for cross-border movement of evacuees and emergency response personnel and equipment should be taken into account.

III. *Reportable events*

3.1   The Expert Group was of the opinion that in formal arrangements among States an event should be considered to be reportable if there is the potential for, or actual occurrence of, a release of radioactive material which might transcend or has transcended an international boundary and which could be of radiological safety significance. The event might require the implementation of measures to protect the public.

3.2   The Expert Group recommended that in establishing a threshold for reportable events a spectrum of accidents should be taken into account instead of a single reference accident.

3.3   For the purpose of practical reporting, the Expert Group assumed that the operating organization of a nuclear facility has an emergency plan that categorizes emergency conditions. In cases where the off-site authorities are alerted according to this plan and where the Emergency Planning Zones would extend beyond the boundary with a neighbouring State, the competent national authorities of that State should be notified forthwith of the situation.

3.4   It was recognized that States may wish to include other events in their notification arrangements which do not fall within the categories referred to in paragraph 3.3.

3.5   It is recommended that intervention levels for the introduction of protective measures such as sheltering and evacuation be set in advance by the competent national authorities. It will remain for these authorities in the neighbouring States to decide on the actual level of radiological impact at which actions are to be taken, taking into account prevailing circumstances. The Expert Group was of the opinion that the implementation of actions resulting from such notifications should not normally lead to protective measures being introduced in the neighbouring State at an earlier stage, or being more stringent, than in the State in which the accident has occurred or is occurring.

IV. *Information exchange*

4.1   *Purpose*

4.1.1   The timely exchange of adequate information between the competent national authorities of the State in which the nuclear facility is situated and those in the neighbouring State(s) should allow adequate protection of the public which could be affected by the consequences of an emergency transcending international boundaries.

4.1.2 The information to be communicated will comprise data related to the site, the facility, the emergency response plan and the response to an emergency.

4.2 Organization of Information Exchange

4.2.1 Procedures for Communication

The States concerned should identify and make known to each other their competent national authorities and points of contact for the exchange of technical information and emergency response planning information. Points of contact should be identified as having primary responsibility for issuing or receiving notification of a potential or actual emergency. Procedures for verification of the notification received should be established.

4.2.2 Means of Communication

Reliable and diverse means of communication should be identified and the points of contact should be available on a 24-hour basis. If appropriate points of contact for subsequent communications are different from those for the initial notification, they should be specified. There may be several communication links, for example, to update information on the event, to exchange information on consequence assessment and information to be released to the public, and to offer or request assistance.

4.2.3 Identification and Testing of Communication Links

Lists should be prepared and exchanged with the names, telephone numbers (or means of contact on a 24-hour basis) and addresses of all points of contact and alternates. This information should be checked at regular intervals and updated immediately following any change. The channels of communication for initial notification and subsequent communications should be tested frequently.

4.2.4 Language Problems

In many cases national borders may also correspond to language borders. To avoid, in such cases, misunderstandings and time delays in information exchange in case of an emergency, practical solutions should be agreed during the advance emergency response planning stage.

4.3 Information to be Exchanged

4.3.1 Information needed for advance emergency response planning may include data such as:

—Characteristics of the facility and its possible radiological impact;

—Relevant regulations, plans and procedures on environmental protection and radiation protection in case of an emergency;

—Site-dependent characteristics influencing the dispersion of radioactive releases (e.g. topographical, hydrological, meteorological data);

—Technical information on monitoring equipment, sampling techniques, interpretation of measurements and other issues which may affect the assessment of the situation in case of an off-site emergency;

—Demographic and other relevant information for the Emergency Planning Zones.

4.3.2   Information needed in the event of an off-site emergency should contain all available facts of importance for assessing the situation, such as:

—Identification of the facility involved;

—The nature of the accident, the time at which it occurred and its possible development;

—The characteristics of the release;

—Information on meteorological and hydrological conditions, necessary for forecasting the dispersion and dilution of the release;

—Off-site protective measures taken or recommended;

—Results of environmental monitoring;

—Information on the development and termination of the emergency.

4.3.3   Both the advance emergency response planning and the emergency response data should be updated as necessary.

4.3.4   The confidentiality of any information provided in accordance with paragraphs 4.3.1 and 4.3.2 should be preserved.

4.4   *Liaison Groups*

4.4.1   To facilitate information exchange at the advance emergency response planning stage, the competent national authorities of the States involved in transboundary emergency response planning should meet periodically.

4.4.2   Consideration should be given to allow the competent national authorities of the States involved at the emergency response stage to exchange liaison groups.

4.5   *Public Information*

4.5.1   Dissemination of information to the public is an important responsibility of the appropriate authorities in each State. Particular arrangements ensuring the necessary co-ordination across international borders should be established.

4.5.2   Special attention should be given to the consistency of the guidance given to the public in the States involved.

4.5.3   It is important that notification of an emergency and broadcast of initial and subsequent information be made simultaneously, as far as possible, in the States involved.

V. *Integrated planning*

5.1 *Purpose*

The purpose of integrated planning is to provide for a co-ordinated response involving all the authorities and organizations having responsibilities in the event of an emergency requiring a transboundary response.

5.2 *Transboundary Considerations Related to Emergency Response Planning*

The competent national authorities of the States concerned should be consulted in the preparation of the relevant parts of the emergency response plans dealing with transboundary considerations.

5.3 *Some Considerations for Integrated Planning*

5.3.1 Range of Off-Site Consequences

The range (type and extent) of off-site consequences needs to be considered in procedures established by the competent national authorities of neighbouring States.

5.3.2 Updating Plans and Procedures

Following the establishment of emergency response plans and procedures, provisions should be made for their joint review and updating on a regular basis.

5.3.3 Testing of Emergency Preparedness

The integrated plan should be tested by exercises. Any deficiencies in the plan or in the emergency response as revealed by these exercises should be mutually corrected.

5.3.4 Consistency in Monitoring and the Interpretation of Measurements

5.3.4.1 Consistency in both the measurements made to quantify the radiological hazard and their interpretation is highly desirable.

5.3.4.2 As a part of the advanced emergency response planning, it would be advantageous for involved States to exchange information on such aspects as sampling techniques and the types, characteristics and quantities of their radiological monitoring equipment, and to participate in intercomparison exercises. Similarly, it is considered desirable to compare the methods used for interpretation of radiological measurements.

5.3.4.3 During an emergency, direct contact between the emergency monitoring team controllers could minimize any difficulty in interpretation of measurements.

5.3.5 Compatibility of Protective Measures

Consideration should be given to the actions to be taken on both sides of an international border arising from an emergency. It would be of mutual benefit to harmonize the degree of protection for affected populations and the environment by the adoption of compatible standards for protective measures.

5.3.6   Emergency Monitoring Teams

Particularly during the early and intermediate phases of an emergency, the prompt movement of emergency monitoring teams (possibly including those of the nuclear facility operator) across borders may be essential to obtain the necessary information on which to base response actions. The competent national authorities of the States involved should be aware of any limitations of dose established for members of emergency monitoring teams.

5.3.7   Evacuation of Persons Across Borders

The possibility exists that the most appropriate way of protecting the public of the States involved in an emergency may be the evacuation of affected persons across the borders. The provision of facilities such as food, reception centres, transport, decontamination facilities, medical aid and identification passes should be considered.

5.3.8   Consistency in Emergency Planning Zones

The extent of Emergency Planning Zones should be consistent and agreed among the involved States.

17. CHINA-UNITED STATES, AGREEMENT FOR COOPERATION CONCERNING PEACEFUL USES OF NUCLEAR ENERGY
23 July 1985, Washington D.C.

Editorial Note

This Agreement between China and the United States is an example of a general treaty governing the transfer of information, technology, material, facilities and components relating to the peaceful uses of nuclear energy. Article 9, which obliges the Parties to consult so as to identify the international environmental implications arising from activities under the Agreement, also requires them to cooperate in protecting the international environment from, *inter alia*, radioactive contamination arising from the peaceful nuclear cooperation envisaged.

Date of signature:	23 July 1985
Entry into force:	30 December 1985
Authentic languages:	Chinese and English
Text reprinted from:	24 *ILM* 1394 (1985)

Text

CHINA-UNITED STATES, AGREEMENT FOR COOPERATION CONCERNING PEACEFUL USES OF NUCLEAR ENERGY

The Government of the United States of America and the Government of the People's Republic of China,

DESIRING to establish extensive cooperation in the peaceful uses of nuclear energy on the basis of mutual respect for sovereignty, non-interference in each other's internal affairs, equality and mutual benefit,

NOTING that such cooperation is one between two nuclear weapon states,

AFFIRMING their support of the objectives of the statute of the International Atomic Energy Agency (IAEA),

AFFIRMING their intention to carry out such cooperation on a stable, reliable and predictable basis,

MINDFUL that peaceful nuclear activities must be undertaken with a view to protecting the international environment from radioactive, chemical and thermal contamination,

HAVE AGREED as follows:

Article 1
Definitions
For the purposes of this agreement:

(1) "parties" means the Government of the United States of America and the Government of the People's Republic of China;

(2) "authorized person" means any individual or any entity under the jurisdiction of either party and authorized by that party to receive, possess, use, or transfer material, facilities or components;

(3) "person" means any individual or any entity subject to the jurisdiction of either party but does not include the parties to this agreement;

(4) "peaceful purposes" include the use of information, technology, material, facilities and components in such fields as research, power generation, medicine, agriculture and industry but do not include use in, research specifically on or development of any nuclear explosive device, or any military purpose;

(5) "material" means source material, special nuclear material or byproduct material, radioisotopes other than byproduct material, moderator material, or any other such substance so designated by agreement of the parties;

(6) "source material" means (i) uranium, thorium, or any other material so designated by agreement of the parties, or (ii) ores containing one or more of the foregoing materials, in such concentration as the parties may agree from time to time;

(7) "special nuclear material" means (i) plutonium, uranium 233, or uranium enriched in the isotope 235, or (ii) any other material so designated by agreement of the parties;

(8) "byproduct material" means any radioactive material (except special nuclear material) yielded in or made radioactive by exposure to the radiation incident to the process of producing or utilizing special nuclear material;

(9) "moderator material" means heavy water, or graphite or beryllium of a purity suitable for use in a reactor to slow down high velocity neutrons and increase the likelihood of further fission, or any other such material so designated by agreement of the parties;

(10) "high enriched uranium" means uranium enriched to twenty percent or greater in the isotope 235;

(11) "low enriched uranium" means uranium enriched to less than twenty percent in the isotope 235;

(12) "facility" means any reactor, other than one designed or used primarily for the formation of plutonium or uranium 233, or any other item so designated by agreement of the parties;

(13) "reactor" is defined in Annex I,[ii] which may be modified by mutual consent of the parties;

(14) "sensitive nuclear facility" means any plant designed or used primarily for uranium enrichment, reprocessing of nuclear fuel, heavy water production or fabrication of nuclear fuel containing plutonium;

(15) "component" means a component part of a facility or other item, so designated by agreement of the parties;

(16) "major critical component" means any part or group of parts essential to the operation of a sensitive nuclear facility;

(17) "sensitive nuclear technology" means any information (including information incorporated in a facility or an important component) which is not in the public domain and which is important to the design, construction, fabrication, operation or maintenance of any sensitive nuclear facility, or such other information so designated by agreement of the parties.

Article 2
Scope of cooperation

1. The parties shall cooperate in the use of nuclear energy for peaceful purposes in accordance with the provisions of this agreement. Each party shall implement this agreement in accordance with its respective applicable treaties, national laws, regulations and license requirements concerning the use of nuclear energy for peaceful purposes. The parties recognize, with respect to the observance of this agreement, the principle of international law that provides that a party may not invoke the provisions of its internal law as justification for its failure to perform a treaty.

2. Transfers of information, technology, material, facilities and components under this agreement may be undertaken directly between the parties or through authorized persons. Such cooperation shall be subject to this agreement and to such additional terms and conditions as may be agreed by the parties.

3. Material, facilities and components will be regarded as having been transferred pursuant to this agreement only upon receipt of confirmation by the supplier party, from the appropriate Government authority of the recipient party, that such material, facilities or components will be subject to this agreement and that the proposed recipient of such material, facilities or components, if other than the recipient party, is an authorized person.

4. Any transfer of sensitive nuclear technology, sensitive nuclear facilities, or major critical components will, subject to the principles of this agreement, require additional provisions as an amendment to this agreement.

[¹ Annex I is not reproduced here.]

Article 3
Transfer of information and technology
Information and technology concerning the use of nuclear energy for peaceful purposes may be transferred. Transfers of such information and technology shall be that which the parties are permitted to transfer and may be accomplished through various means, including reports, data banks, computer programs, conferences, visits and assignments of persons to facilities. Fields which may be covered include, but shall not be limited to, the following:

(1)   research, development, experiment, design, construction, operation, maintenance and use and retirement of reactors and nuclear fuel fabrication technology;

(2)   the use of material in physical and biological research, medicine, agriculture and industry;

(3)   nuclear fuel cycle research, development and industrial application to meet civil nuclear needs, including multilateral approaches to guaranteeing nuclear fuel supply and appropriate techniques for management of nuclear wastes;

(4)   health, safety, environment, and research and development related to the foregoing;

(5)   assessing the role nuclear power may play in international energy plans;

(6)   codes, regulations and standards for the nuclear energy industry; and

(7)   such other fields as may be agreed by the parties.

Article 4
Transfer of material, facilities and components
1.   Material, facilities and components may be transferred pursuant to this agreement for applications consistent with this agreement. Any special nuclear material to be transferred under this agreement shall be low enriched uranium except as provided in paragraph 4 of this article.

2.   Low enriched uranium may be transferred for use as fuel in reactors and reactor experiments, for conversion or fabrication, or for such other purposes as may be agreed by the parties.

3.   The quantity of special nuclear material transferred under this agreement shall be the quantity which the parties agree is necessary for any of the following purposes: the loading of reactors or use in reactor experiments, the efficient and continuous operation of such reactors or conduct of such reactor experiments, and the accomplishment of such other purposes as may be agreed by the parties.

4. Small quantities of special nuclear material may be transferred for use as samples, standards, detectors, targets, radiation sources and for such other purposes as the parties may agree.

Article 5
Retransfers, storage, reprocessing, enrichment, alteration, and no use for military purposes
1. Material, facilities, components or special nuclear material transferred pursuant to this agreement and any special nuclear material produced through the use of such material or facilities may be retransferred by the recipient party, except that any such material, facility, components or special nuclear material shall not be retransferred to unauthorized persons or, unless the parties agree, beyond its territory.
2. Neither party has any plans to enrich to twenty percent or greater, reprocess, or alter in form or content material transferred pursuant to this agreement or material used in or produced through the use of any material or facility so transferred. Neither party has any plans to change locations for storage of plutonium, uranium 233 (except as contained in irradiated fuel elements), or high enriched uranium transferred pursuant to this agreement or used in or produced through the use of any material or facility so transferred. In the event that a party would like at some future time to undertake such activities, the parties will promptly hold consultations to agree on a mutually acceptable arrangement. The parties undertake the obligation to consider such activities favorably, and agree to provide pertinent information on the plans during the consultations. Inasmuch as any such activities will be solely for peaceful purposes and will be in accordance with the provisions of this agreement, the parties will consult immediately and will seek agreement within six months on long-term arrangements for such activities. In the spirit of cooperation the parties agree not to act within that period of time. If such an arrangement is not agreed upon within that period of time, the parties will promptly consult for the purpose of agreeing on measures which they consider to be consistent with the provisions of the agreement in order to undertake such activities on an interim basis. The parties agree to refrain from actions which either party believes would prejudge the long-term arrangements for undertaking such activities or adversely affect cooperation under this agreement. The parties agree that the consultations referred to above will be carried out promptly and mutual agreement reached in a manner to avoid hampering, delay or undue interference in their respective nuclear programs. Neither party will seek to gain commercial advantage. Nothing in this article shall be used by either party to inhibit the legitimate development and

exploitation of nuclear energy for peaceful purposes in accordance with this agreement.

3. Material, facilities or components transferred pursuant to this agreement and material used in or produced through the use of any material, facility or components so transferred shall not be used for any nuclear explosive device, for research specifically on or development of any nuclear explosive device, or for any military purpose.

Article 6
Physical security

1. Each party shall maintain adequate physical security with respect to any material, facility or components transferred pursuant to this agreement and with respect to any special nuclear material used in or produced through the use of any material or facility so transferred.

2. The parties agree to the levels for the application of physical security set forth in Annex II,[2] which levels may be modified by mutual consent of the parties. The parties shall maintain adequate physical security measures in accordance with such levels. These measures, as minimum protection measures, shall be comparable to the recommendations set forth in IAEA document INFCIRC/225/Revision 1 entitled ''The Physical Protection of Nuclear Material'', or in any revision of that document agreed to by the parties.

3. The parties shall consult at the request of either party regarding the adequacy of physical security measures maintained pursuant to this article.

4. Each party shall identify those agencies or authorities responsible for ensuring that levels of physical security are adequately met and having responsibility for coordinating response and recovery operations in the event of unauthorized use or handling of material subject to this article. Each party shall also designate points of contact within its national authorities to cooperate on matters of out-of-country transportation and other physical security matters of mutual concern.

Article 7
Cessation of cooperation

1. Each party shall endeavor to avoid taking any actions that affect cooperation under this agreement. If either party at any time following entry into force of this agreement does not comply with the provisions of this agreement, the parties shall promptly hold consultations on the problem, it being understood that the other party shall have the rights to cease further cooperation under this agreement.

[² Annex II is not reproduced here.]

2. If either party decides to cease further cooperation under this agreement, the parties shall make appropriate arrangements as may be required.

Article 8
Consultations
1. The parties shall consult at the request of either party regarding the implementation of this agreement, the development of further cooperation in the field of peaceful uses of nuclear energy, and other matters of mutual concern.

2. The parties recognize that this cooperation in the peaceful uses of nuclear energy is between two nuclear-weapon states and that bilateral safeguards are not required. In order to exchange experience, strengthen technical cooperation between the parties, ensure that the provisions of this agreement are effectively carried out, and enhance a stable, reliable, and predictable nuclear cooperation relationship, in connection with transfers of material, facilities and components under this agreement the parties will use diplomatic channels to establish mutually acceptable arrangements for exchanges of information and visits to material, facilities and components subject to this agreement.

3. The parties shall exchange views and information on the establishment and operation of their respective national accounting and control systems for source and special nuclear material subject to this agreement.

Article 9
Environmental protection
The parties shall consult, with regard to activities under this agreement, to identify the international environmental implications arising from such activities and shall cooperate in protecting the international environment from radioactive, chemical or thermal contamination arising from peaceful nuclear cooperation under this agreement and in related matters of health and safety.

Article 10
Entry into force and duration
1. This agreement shall enter into force on the date of mutual notifications of the completion of legal procedures by the parties and shall remain in force for a period of thirty years. This term may be extended by agreement of the parties in accordance with their respective applicable procedures.

2. Notwithstanding the suspension, termination or expiration of this agreement or any cooperation hereunder for any reason, the provisions of articles 5, 6, 7 and 8 shall continue in effect so long as any material, facility or

components subject to these articles remain in the territory of the party concerned or any material, facility or components subject to these articles remain subject to that party's right to exercise jurisdiction or to direct disposition elsewhere.

IN WITNESS WHEREOF, the undersigned, being duly authorized, have signed this agreement.

DONE at Washington this 23rd day of July 1985, in English and Chinese, both equally authentic.

Select Bibliography

Gorove, "Controls over Atoms-for-Peace: US Bilateral Agreements with other Nations", 4 *Colum. J Transnat'l Law* 181 (1966).

Pelzer, "The Nature and Scope of International Co-operation in Connection with the Peaceful Uses of Nuclear Energy and its Limits—an Assessment", 27 *NLB* 34 (1981).

A large number of similar agreements have been concluded. They include:

(1) Thailand-USA, Agreement for Co-operation Concerning Civil Uses of Atomic Energy, 13 March 1956;
reprinted in: TIAS 3522;
also in: 7 *UST* 416;
amended: 27 March 1957, 11 June 1960, 31 May 1962, 8 June 1964;
Amending Agreements reprinted respectively in: TIAS 3842, 8 *UST* 832; *TIAS* 4533, 11 *UST* 1874; *TIAS* 5122, 13 *UST* 1776; *TIAS* 5765.

(2) India-USA, Agreement for Co-operation Concerning Civil Uses of Nuclear Energy, 8 August 1963;
amended by: Exchange of Notes, 30 November 1982;
reprinted in: TIAS 5446.

(3) Finland-UK, Collaboration Agreement on the Peaceful Uses of Nuclear Energy, 24 May 1968;
noted in: 7 *NLB* 36 (1971).

(4) Philippines-USA, Co-operation Agreement on the Civil Uses of Atomic Energy, 19 July 1968;
noted in: 6 *NLB* 38 (1970).

(5) Finland-Sweden, Collaboration Agreement on the Peaceful Uses of Nuclear Energy, 15 October 1968;
noted in: 7 *NLB* 36 (1971).

(6) Finland-USSR, Collaboration Agreement on the Peaceful Uses of Nuclear Energy, 14 May 1969;
noted in: 7 *NLB* 36 (1971).

(7) Finland-USA, Agreement for Co-operation Concerning Civil Uses of Atomic Energy, 8 April 1970;
noted in: 7 *NLB* 36 (1971).

(8) France-Switzerland, Co-operation Agreement for the Use of Atomic Energy, 14 May 1970;
noted in: 9 *NLB* 35 (1972).

(9) FRG-India, Co-operation Agreement on the Peaceful Uses of Nuclear Energy, 5 October 1971;
noted in: 11 *NLB* 36 (1973).

(10) Belgium-Romania, Co-operation Agreement in the Nuclear Field, 29 January 1974;
reprinted in: Belgian Gazette of 13 July 1977.

(11) Argentina-India, Agreement on Co-operation in the Peaceful Uses of Nuclear Energy, 28 May 1974;
noted in: 31 *NLB* 28 (1983).

(12) Austria-USA, Co-operation Agreement Concerning Civil Uses of Atomic Energy, 14 June 1974;
reprinted in: TIAS 7912.

(13) Brazil-FRG, Agreement Concerning Co-operation in the Field of Peaceful Uses of Nuclear Energy, 27 June 1975;
reprinted in: 16 *NLB* 43 (1975).

(14) France-Iraq, Agreement on Co-operation on the Peaceful Uses of Nuclear Energy, 18 November 1975;
reprinted in: Journal officiel de la République française of 18 June 1976 by Decree No. 76-524 of 14 June 1976;
also in: Rüster *et al., International Protection of the Environment,* Vol. XXVII, p. 214 (1982).

(15) FRG-Iran, Agreement on Co-operation in the Peaceful Uses of Nuclear Energy, 4 July 1976;
reprinted in: Bundesgesetzblatt 1978, II, p. 284.

(16) Argentina-Chile, Agreement on Co-operation on the Peaceful Uses of Nuclear Energy, 3 November 1976;
noted in: 32 *NLB* 28 (1983).

(17) Brazil-FRG, Agreement on Exchange of Technical Information and Co-operation on Nuclear Safety, 10 March 1978;
reprinted in: Bundesgesetzblatt 1978, II, p. 950.

(18) Belgium-USA, Agreement on Exchange of Technical Information and Co-operation in Reactor Safety Research, 6 June 1978;
noted in: 23 *NLB* 50 (1979).

(19) FRG-Spain, Agreement for Co-operation in the Field of the Peaceful Uses of Nuclear Energy, 5 December 1978;
reprinted in: Bundesgesetzblatt 1979, II, p. 133.

(20) FRG-UK, Agreement on Exchange of Information on Measures For the Safety of Nuclear Installations, 4 April 1979;
reprinted in: Bundesgesetzblatt 1979, II, p. 434.

(21) Brazil-Iraq, Agreement for Co-operation in the Peaceful Uses of Nuclear Energy, 5 January 1980;
noted in: 29 *NLB* 36 (1982).

(22) Argentina-Brazil, Co-operation Agreement for the Development and Application of Nuclear Energy for Peaceful Purposes, 17 May 1980;
reprinted in: 27 *NLB* 30 (1981).

(23) France-Portugal, Agreement on Scientific and Technical Co-operation in the Peaceful Uses of Nuclear Energy, 27 November 1980;
noted in: 30 *NLB* 37 (1982).

(24) Brazil-Colombia, Agreement on Co-operation in the Peaceful Uses of Nuclear Energy, 12 March 1981;
reprinted in: Brazilian Official Gazette of 31 March 1986.

(25) France-Egypt, Agreement on Co-operation in the Peaceful Uses of Nuclear Energy, 27 March 1981;
reprinted in: Journal officiel de la République française of 26 May 1982 by Decree No. 82-430 of 19 May 1982.

(26) FRG-USA, Agreement on Exchange of Technical Information and Co-operation in Nuclear Safety, 6 July 1981;
reprinted in: Bundesgesetzblatt 1981, II, p. 657.

(27) France-Republic of Korea, Agreement on Co-operation in the Peaceful Uses of Nuclear Energy, 4 August 1981;
reprinted in: Journal officiel de la République française of 2 June 1982.

(28) Argentina-FRG, Agreement on the Exchange of Technical Information and Co-operation in the Field of Nuclear Installations, 8 October 1981;
reprinted in: Bundesgesetzblatt 1981, II, p. 958.

(29) Egypt-FRG, Agreement on Co-operation in the Peaceful Uses of Nuclear Energy, 26 October 1981;
reprinted in: Bundesgesetzblatt 1982, II, p. 567.

(30) Japan-Australia, Revised Agreement on Co-operation in the Peaceful Uses of Nuclear Energy, 5 March 1982;
noted in: 30 *NLB* 36 (1982).

(31) China-FRG, Agreement on Co-operation in the Field of Peaceful Uses of Nuclear Energy, 9 May 1984;
reprinted in: Bundesgesetzblatt 1984, II, p. 554.

(32) Brazil-China, Memorandum of Understanding for Co-operation concerning Peaceful Uses of Nuclear Energy, 29 May 1984;
reprinted in: 24 *ILM* 1392 (1985).

(33) Egypt-Switzerland, Agreement on Co-operation in the Peaceful Uses of Nuclear Energy, 13 November 1984;
noted in: 35 *NLB* 54 (1985).

(34) Argentina-China, Agreement for Co-operation in the Peaceful Uses of Nuclear Energy, 15 April 1985;
noted in: 38 *NLB* 51 (1986).

(35) Japan-China, Agreement on Co-operation in the Peaceful Uses of Nuclear Energy, 31 July 1985;
noted in: 36 *NLB* 41 (1985).

(36) FRG-Republic of Korea, Agreement on Co-operation in the Peaceful Uses of Nuclear Energy, 11 April 1986;
reprinted in: Bundesgesetzblatt 1986, II, p. 726.

18. GROUP OF SEVEN, STATEMENT ON THE IMPLICATIONS OF THE CHERNOBYL NUCLEAR ACCIDENT
5 May 1986

Editorial Note

On 5 May 1986, at the Tokyo Economic Summit, the Group of Seven major industrial nations, consisting of Canada, France, Italy, Japan, the Federal Republic of Germany, the United Kingdom and the United States, made the following statement concerning the Chernobyl accident.

Text reprinted from: 25 *ILM* 1005 (1986)

Text

GROUP OF SEVEN, STATEMENT ON THE IMPLICATIONS OF THE CHERNOBYL NUCLEAR ACCIDENT

1.   We, the Heads of State or Government of seven major industrial nations and the Representatives of the European Community, have discussed the implications of the accident at the Chernobyl nuclear power station. We express our deep sympathy for those affected. We remain ready to extend assistance, in particular medical and technical, as and when requested.

2.   Nuclear power is and, properly managed, will continue to be an increasingly widely used source of energy. For each country the maintenance of safety and security is an international responsibility, and each country engaged in nuclear power generation bears full responsibility for the safety of the design, manufacture, operation and maintenance of its installations. Each of our countries meets exacting standards. Each country, furthermore, is responsible for prompt provision of detailed and complete information on nuclear emergencies and accidents, in particular those with potential transboundary consequences. Each of our countries accepts that responsibility, and we urge the Government of the Soviet Union, which did not do so in the case of Chernobyl, to provide urgently such information, as our and other countries have requested.

3.   We note with satisfaction the Soviet Union's willingness to undertake discussions this week with the Director-General of the International Atomic

Energy Agency (IAEA). We expect that these discussions will lead to the Soviet Union's participation in the desired post-accident analysis.

4. We welcome and encourage the work of the IAEA in seeking to improve international cooperation on the safety of nuclear installations, the handling of nuclear accidents and their consequences, and the provision of mutual emergency assistance. Moving forward from the relevant IAEA guidelines, we urge the early elaboration of an international convention committing the parties to report and exchange information in the event of nuclear emergencies or accidents. This should be done with the least possible delay.

19. IAEA, STATEMENT SUMMARIZING DECISIONS TAKEN AT THE SPECIAL SESSION OF THE BOARD OF GOVERNORS CONCERNING THE CHERNOBYL NUCLEAR ACCIDENT
22 May 1986

Editorial Note

Reproduced below is a statement by the IAEA following a Special Session of the Board of Governors convened in May 1986 to discuss the Chernobyl accident.

The statement stresses the need to learn from the Chernobyl accident and, in particular, to improve on existing arrangements for co-operation in nuclear safety.

Text reprinted from: 25 *ILM* 1009 (1986)

Text

IAEA, STATEMENT SUMMARIZING DECISIONS TAKEN AT THE SPECIAL SESSION OF THE BOARD OF GOVERNORS CONCERNING THE CHERNOBYL NUCLEAR ACCIDENT

Vienna, 22 May 1986—The Chairman of the IAEA Board of Governors, H.E. Artati Sudirdjo, from Indonesia, today issued the following statement, which summarizes the decisions taken at the special session of the Board which concluded on 21 May.

1.   The Board has considered the recent reactor accident at the Chernobyl Nuclear Power Station and other accidents in the past, and noted the evident need for greater co-operation in nuclear safety.

2.   The Board expressed its deepest sympathy with all those who have suffered as a result of the nuclear accident at Chernobyl.

3.   The Board recalled the Communiqué of 9 May 1986, issued in Moscow at the end of the Director General's visit to the USSR, which announced that information on the Chernobyl accident would be discussed at a meeting of nuclear safety experts so that IAEA Member States might learn from this accident and further improve nuclear power safety.

4.   The Board also noted recent statements by a number of world political leaders on the need to broaden international co-operation in the field of nuclear

safety, including a system of prompt notification and supply of information in the event of nuclear emergencies, within the framework of the IAEA.

5.   The Board recognizes that the highest standards of safety have to be maintained so that the utilization of nuclear energy will continue to be an important source of energy for meeting the needs of mankind.

6.   The Board reviewed suggestions in a Secretariat paper circulated on 16 May 1986 concerning the expansion of current Agency activities in the field of nuclear safety, and also considered further comments on this matter by the Director General.

7.   The Board took note of the information provided by the USSR on the course of events, the consequences of the accident and measures being taken for their alleviation, and welcomed the readiness of the USSR to provide comprehensive further information in the near future.

8.   The Board commended the Director General for the prompt and vigorous efforts of the Secretariat in responding to the accident at Chernobyl, and requested him to continue the Agency's active efforts in nuclear safety and to co-operate with other international organizations.

9.   Taking into account the various proposals and suggestions made by Board members, including a draft resolution, the Board has decided to request the Director General to present to the June Board of Governors meetings his detailed suggestions on the implementation of the following programme:

   A. To convene, within three months, a post-accident review meeting with widely representative participation of experts. The meeting results should be transmitted to the Board before its September meetings, with recommendations for further Agency action.

   B. To establish representative groups of government experts to draft, on an urgent basis, international agreements, as follows:

   (i) one would commit its parties to provide early notification and comprehensive information about nuclear accidents with possible transboundary effects, and take into account current Agency guidelines in document INFCIRC/321.

   (ii) the other would commit its parties to co-ordinate emergency response and assistance in the event of a nuclear accident which could involve transboundary radiological release, and would take into account guidelines in document INFCIRC/310.

   The groups would endeavour to produce drafts of instruments as early as possible and report to the Board.

All Board members confirmed that, even before entry into force of these agreements, their responsible authorities would provide prompt notification and information in the event of a nuclear accident with potential transboundary effects and urged all Member States to do likewise.

C. To establish an expert working group to consider, over a longer period, additional measures to improve co-operation in the field of nuclear safety, including ways and means to further refine nuclear safety standards.

D. To convene, under IAEA auspices, at an early date a conference of governmental representatives on the full range of nuclear safety issues, including nuclear safety policy, and to consider recommendations including any made by the expert groups referred to in sub-paragraphs 9.B(i) and (ii) and those on which the Secretariat is now focusing.

10.   The Director General is also requested to prepare proposals for expanded IAEA nuclear safety activities as outlined above and, taking into account the proposals of Members of the Board, to submit an analysis of associated costs and priorities for consideration at the regular June 1986 meetings of the Board, which will then establish budgetary limits.

Select Bibliography

IAEA, ''Report by Board of Governors on Measures to Strengthen International Co-operation in Nuclear Safety and Radiological Protection'', *IAEA Doc.* GC(SPL.1)/2, 24 September 1986 (incl. Annexes 1-5).

20. USSR, PROPOSED PROGRAMME FOR ESTABLISHING AN INTERNATIONAL REGIME FOR THE SAFE DEVELOPMENT OF NUCLEAR ENERGY
25 September 1986

Editorial Note

The proposal by the USSR to establish a comprehensive international regime for the peaceful uses of nuclear energy is a significant development. Of particular note is the recognition within the proposal of the importance of the question of liability to the establishment of such a regime, and the suggestion that a possible multilateral instrument to deal with this issue might be drawn up.

The framework proposed includes the early notification of accidents or breakdowns; the provision of assistance in emergencies; the further development of safety guidelines by the IAEA (including siting, design and construction); and the collection, processing and exchange of information on all aspects of nuclear energy.

Text reprinted from: *IAEA Doc.* GC(SPL.1)/8

Text

USSR, PROPOSED PROGRAMME FOR ESTABLISHING AN INTERNATIONAL REGIME FOR THE SAFE DEVELOPMENT OF NUCLEAR ENERGY

Proposals by the USSR

The use of nuclear energy is a reality of today. Yet nuclear power became part of the life of mankind not through creative endeavour, but through the death of hundreds of thousands of people. The sinister shadow of the tragedy of Hiroshima and Nagasaki lies between the development by Enrico Fermi of the first facility and the first industrial atomic power station designed by Igor Kurchatov.

The nuclear arsenals have now increased to such an extent that they threaten to exterminate our very life on Earth. The time has come to realize that the preservation of human civilization is a matter of concern to all States, for nuclear war will inevitably affect each and every one. While there is still time, it is imperative to put an end to the suicidal build-up of nuclear arms, to abandon the policy of catastrophic confrontation and embark upon the process of genuine disarmament.

In putting forward its programme for eliminating nuclear arms and other weapons of mass destruction throughout the world, the Soviet Union has been guided by an awareness of the reality of the danger threatening mankind. The close of the twentieth century should be marked by the complete elimination of nuclear weapons under conditions of peace and genuine and equal security for all States and peoples. The security of the peoples on our planet is inconceivable without an end to material preparations for nuclear war. The Soviet Union is convinced that the cessation of nuclear-weapon tests can become a turning point in efforts to achieve this goal. That is why the USSR announced, and has since repeatedly extended, a unilateral moratorium on all nuclear explosions.

However, even the peaceful uses of the atom are fraught with considerable hazard. This is evidenced by the effects of accidents at nuclear installations. That is why the USSR has proposed that all countries should work together with a view to minimizing any risk of a nuclear accident in the world and to ensuring the safe development of nuclear energy.

These two tasks— ensuring the safety of the peaceful uses of nuclear energy and ridding our planet of nuclear weapons—call for broad international co-operation and joint efforts by all States, first and foremost nuclear States, by international organizations and by public bodies interested in establishing a comprehensive and reliable system of international security. This applies equally to both the community of nations and each individual State.

At present there are about 370 nuclear power reactors operating in the world. By the year 2000 nuclear power is expected to account for more than 20% of the world's total energy production. In some countries nuclear power stations already generate more than 50% of the electric energy produced. More than 30 years of experience in operating nuclear power plants have convincingly proved their viability, economic efficiency and ecological safety.

In recent years the geography of nuclear power production has considerably expanded. Nuclear power plants and research reactors are being built and operated in the developing countries of Asia, Latin America and Africa.

The time has also come to speed up the exploitation of controlled thermonuclear fusion, potentially an inexhaustible source of energy. Following the initiative by the Soviet Union, and with the participation of scientists from a number of West European countries as well as from the United States and Japan, an international fusion reactor pilot project, known as INTOR, has been under way in Vienna since 1978. Further development of international co-operation in nuclear fusion meets the interests of the overwhelming majority of countries of the world who, given the current situation, are vitally interested in obtaining new sources of energy. And what is of special importance, this trend has nothing to do with any military use. Equally significant is the fact that thermonuclear energy will have only a very slight effect on the environment compared with other sources of energy. Today we are already in a position to state that building such a reactor is feasible and that it may take only a relatively short time to do so.

Peaceful uses of the atom will make it possible to meet ever increasing needs of mankind in energy for industry, agriculture and scientific research.

At present there is no other equivalent alternative in the field of energy resources. At the same time, one cannot fail to see that in the process of developing nuclear energy mankind faces the danger that this formidable force may get out of control.

More than 150 accidents with resultant radioactive leakage have been recorded at nuclear power plants throughout the world. Some of those accidents in the United States, Federal Republic of Germany and Great Britain, and finally in Chernobyl, have been very serious and have led to grave consequences causing economic and psychological damage. Events of this kind can affect neighbouring States as well. They show how small, in fact, is the world we live in, how great is the interdependence of States. The realities of the nuclear and space ages make it imperative for the peoples to see themselves as members of one family on planet Earth.

The conclusion that the Soviet Union has come to, following the Chernobyl accident, is clear and unambiguous: the nuclear power industry should develop under conditions ensuring maximum safety for people and the environment. The accident has shown that wide-ranging international co-operation and joint efforts are necessary to guarantee nuclear safety in the broad sense of the word.

Convinced of the necessity to tackle, without delay and in a practical manner, the task of ensuring the safe development of nuclear energy, the Soviet Union wishes to propose to the international community of States a programme of action for establishing an international regime for the safe development of nuclear energy on the basis of close co-operation between all States. This programme envisages the creation of a material, scientific and technological base for the safe development of nuclear energy, supplemented with international regulations and agreements.

First: it is necessary to set up, in the immediate future, a system of early notification of nuclear accidents or breakdowns at nuclear power plants with concomitant radioactive discharges that may involve the risk of a transboundary release. The objective of such a system would be to minimize the consequences of such accidents for other countries and to take timely measures to protect the health and safety of the population, as well as property and the environment.

The draft international convention on early notification of a nuclear accident, worked out at the IAEA meeting, could lay the basis for such a system. The Soviet Union is prepared to become party to that convention. It would strictly comply with all its provisions, including those that envisage notification of all nuclear accidents, particularly, nuclear weapons- and nuclear test-related accidents, and it calls upon all other States to do likewise.

The establishment of an international data bank on radiation background levels in some agreed geographical areas could be an important component of that system, thereby supplementing the convention. Those data could be used to assess the effects of a possible transboundary release in the event of a nuclear accident. Data could be collected by national centres and subsequently transmitted to a single international centre or centres. A significant role in this context could be played by the World Meteorological Organization.

In view of the fact that the scope of the protective measures is determined by the concentration of radioactive substances in the environment, there is a need to agree upon common international standards for accident-induced concentrations of radionuclides and levels of radioactive contamination of the affected area. Such internationally agreed standards and norms could be used both for the adequate application of protective measures by all States as well as for the justification of claims for damages in connection with a transboundary release of radioactivity.

Second: Since many States are not able to cope with a major accident on their own, it is proposed to set up a well co-ordinated mechanism for providing assistance in emergencies and accidents as a component of the international regime for the safe development of nuclear energy.

The draft convention on assistance in the event of a nuclear accident or radiological emergency worked out at the special IAEA meeting of government experts could be an important part of that regime.

The drafting of international recommendations on methodological principles for eliminating the consequences of nuclear accidents and for emergency planning could be a part of the mechanism for assistance to States in eliminating the consequences of accidents.

Third: Another component of the international regime for the safe development of nuclear energy could be agreement that all States in their nuclear activities should be guided by the recommendations formulated by the IAEA on the safety of nuclear installations. Those recommendations could cover, in particular, such questions as the siting of a facility, its design, construction, exploitation and decommissioning, and the treatment of the radioactive waste.

A first step in that direction could be the reaching of an agreement between States exporting nuclear installations and nuclear fuel to observe IAEA recommendations on the safety of nuclear power plants in their exports.

To render practical assistance, the IAEA might send, at regular intervals and at their request, groups of competent experts on nuclear safety to States party to the agreement.

Fourth: An essential element in the system of accident-prevention measures is the collection, processing and exchange of information on nuclear plant accidents, their causes, their development and their consequences.

The IAEA workshop on enhancing nuclear energy safety, held in late August, was of great importance for strengthening international co-operation in this field. The objective and detailed information provided by the Soviet Union concerning the causes, evolution and consequences of the Chernobyl accident, as well as an exchange of information about accidents and clean-up operations in other countries, make it possible to draw up major guidelines for international co-operation in technical arrangements to ensure the safe development of nuclear energy.

The Agency's system for nuclear power plant incident reporting is a good basis for establishing a data bank on nuclear accidents to be used by all nuclear energy countries. It is desirable that this system be further expanded and developed.

Fifth: Joint elaboration of a project or projects related to new generation reactor systems based both on thermal and fast neutrons could be an important element in focusing the efforts of countries aimed at ensuring nuclear plant safety. Those projects could incorporate the most up-to-date safety technology when dealing with problems such as reducing the sensitivity of a reactor system to operator error, or, in other words, taking into account the "human factor", reducing the possibility of a meltdown, and monitoring hydrogen formation.

In organizational terms, such a project or projects for fail-safe reactors or energy centres could be implemented within the IAEA in exactly the same way as the international thermonuclear reactor project. What is more, the relevant Agency working groups could contribute to those activities.

Sixth: As is known, the deliberate destruction of nuclear power plants, research reactors and other similar facilities could trigger a release of radioactive materials and cause radioactive contamination of the terrain.

All this shows that, in terms of its effects, the destruction of peaceful nuclear plants even with conventional weapons would, in fact, be tantamount to a nuclear attack, i.e. to actions that the United Nations has already described as the gravest crime against humanity.

The Soviet Union proposes that a reliable system of measures to prevent attacks against nuclear installations should be developed. It is essential to work out a relevant international convention under which all States would undertake not to attack nuclear power facilities.

An equally sound set of measures should be devised with regard to nuclear terrorism. The instances that have occurred of deliberate damage to nuclear industrial plants as well as cases of the theft of highly concentrated fissionable materials cannot but cause concern.

The radiation hazard and high toxicity of nuclear materials make it imperative to ensure reliable protection of them against criminal designs. It is conceivable that such materials, if seized, might be used to fabricate some sort of elementary nuclear explosive device for the purposes of sabotage and terrorism, blackmail and extortion. There is urgent need to develop a reliable set of measures to prevent any form of nuclear terrorism. We are ready to work towards reaching a separate, independent agreement on this issue and addressing this matter as part of the overall efforts to combat international terrorism.

Seventh: Steps must be taken to ensure that the Convention on Physical Protection of Nuclear Materials enters into force as soon as possible. The Soviet Union has signed and ratified the Convention. We call upon other States to promptly follow suit so that it can become operational as a factor promoting nuclear safety.

Eighth: The question of liability for nuclear damage occupies an important place in activities relating to the international regulation of various aspects of nuclear power safety. Attempts have already been made to draw up international legal instruments governing those matters, but the issue of the material, moral and political damage caused by nuclear accidents has not yet been sufficiently studied; this has resulted in sporadic attempts to make use of nuclear accidents for creating tension and mistrust in relations between States.

It is essential, in the event of a nuclear accident, for States to provide free medical assistance, housing and other material support for the population concerned. A possible multilateral international legal instrument could envisage the liability of States for international damage in terms of the transboundary effects of nuclear accidents, as well as for material, moral and political damage caused by unwarranted action taken under the pretext of protection against the consequences of nuclear accidents (the spreading of untrue information, introduction of unjustified restrictive measures, etc.).

Ninth: A reliable regime for the safe development of nuclear energy will require efforts not only on the part of the States themselves, but also of international organizations and institutions that could serve as focal points in the implementation of nuclear safety measures. The IAEA should take the lead in this field. It is essential to enhance the role and potential of this unique international organization, to broaden the scope of its activity, and to make greater use of its experience in studying various aspects of the nuclear safety problem.

Specialized United Nations agencies, such as the World Health Organization, United Nations Environment Programme, UNESCO and various others, could make a substantial contribution to the regime for the safe development of nuclear energy. We believe that the UN Committee on the Effects of Atomic Radiation should be more active in making the regime efficient.

Joint co-ordinated research and exchange of views on various matters related to the development of nuclear energy should involve the active participation of international organizations; these matters should include the following:

—Development of methods related to accident prevention and clean-up operations;

—Analysis of accident causes and evolution of emergency situations, including a probability analysis;

—Development of robots, machinery and equipment to be used in clean-up operations;

—Development of effective decontamination methods, machinery and equipment as well as reliable means for protecting people against radiation;

—Development of medicines, equipment and techniques for treatment of radiation sickness;

—Development of methods for training personnel servicing nuclear power plants.

Today, mankind faces an historic choice: either to allow itself to slide down the path of the arms race towards the abyss of a nuclear holocaust, or to bring its thinking and its actions into line with the realities of the nuclear and space ages.

The continuing arms race, above all the nuclear arms race, poses a direct threat to the existence of mankind. Guided by the philosophy of shaping a secure world, the Soviet Union advocates a broad constructive programme of action aimed at ending the arms race and at disarmament.

A regime for the safe development of nuclear energy would make a tangible contribution to ensuring universal security. Such a regime, meeting the interests of all mankind, can and must be established by the joint efforts of all States.

The Soviet Union calls upon all States and international organizations concerned to co-operate in this important endeavour, vital for the further development of human civilization.

21. VIENNA CONVENTION ON EARLY NOTIFICATION OF A NUCLEAR ACCIDENT
26 September 1986

Editorial Note

Immediately after the Chernobyl accident, the IAEA organized a series of meetings to consider nuclear safety issues. On 21 May 1986 the Board of Governors proposed that a group of governmental experts convene to draft two international agreements, one on Early Notification of a Nuclear Accident and the other on Assistance in the Case of a Nuclear Accident or Radiological Emergency (see below at No. 22). Experts from 62 Member States and representatives of 10 international organizations met at the IAEA's headquarters in Vienna from 21 July to 15 August 1986; they had before them two working drafts which had been prepared a few weeks earlier by the IAEA's Secretariat. At its final plenary session on 15 August 1986, a mere 4 weeks after the commencement of negotiations, the group of governmental experts adopted by consensus texts of the two draft Conventions. The texts were presented to the IAEA Board of Governors for consideration and on 22 September 1986 the Board decided to commend them to Member States and to transmit them to the first special session of the IAEA General Conference which was to meet in Vienna between 24 and 26 September 1986. The two Conventions were opened for signature on 26 September 1986 after being adopted by consensus by the General Conference.

The essence of the Convention on Early Notification is found in Article 2 which provides that in the event of a nuclear accident within the scope of the Convention (see Article 1), "States which are or may be physically affected" and the IAEA must be notified "forthwith" and provided with the information listed in Article 5. Each State Party must make available "continuously" a contact responsible for issuing and receiving the relevant notification and information (Article 7). Notification and information may be given directly or through the IAEA which under Article 4 must perform certain additional functions. Provision is made in Article 6 for consultations "with a view to minimizing the radiological consequences" in the affected State. In the event of a dispute concerning the interpretation or application of the Convention, Article 11 imposes a duty to consult. If the dispute is not settled within one year from the request for consultation, it can be submitted to arbitration or referred to the ICJ; but when signing, ratifying, accepting, approving or acceding to the Convention, a State may declare that it does not consider itself bound by either or both of these dispute settlement procedures.

The greatest difficulty during the negotiations of the Group of Experts concerned the scope of application of the Convention. Most States were in favour of "full-scope coverage" to include accidents caused by nuclear weapons and their testing. This was strongly opposed by some of the nuclear weapons States. A compromise was finally reached after delegates from the nuclear weapons States gave assurances as to their preparedness to give notification of all accidents, including those associated with nuclear weapons. The result was the inclusion in the Convention of Article 3. During the special session of the IAEA General Conference the five nuclear weapons States made statements of voluntary application of the Early Notification Convention to accidents not covered by the Convention. These statements are reproduced below.

Date of signature:	26 September 1986
Entry into force:	27 October 1986
Depositary:	Director General of the IAEA
Authentic languages:	Arabic, Chinese, English, French, Russian and Spanish
Text reprinted from:	*IAEA Doc.* GC(SPL.1)/2, Annex II
Also published in:	25 *ILM* 1370 (1986)

Text

VIENNA CONVENTION ON EARLY NOTIFICATION OF A NUCLEAR ACCIDENT

THE STATES PARTIES TO THIS CONVENTION,

AWARE that nuclear activities are being carried out in a number of States,

NOTING that comprehensive measures have been and are being taken to ensure a high level of safety in nuclear activities, aimed at preventing nuclear accidents and minimizing the consequences of any such accident, should it occur,

DESIRING to strengthen further international co-operation in the safe development and use of nuclear energy,

CONVINCED of the need for States to provide relevant information about nuclear accidents as early as possible in order that transboundary radiological consequences can be minimized,

NOTING the usefulness of bilateral and multilateral arrangements on information exchange in this area,

HAVE AGREED as follows:

Article 1
Scope of application
1.   This Convention shall apply in the event of any accident involving facilities or activities of a State Party or of persons or legal entities under its jurisdiction or control, referred to in paragraph 2 below, from which a release of radioactive material occurs or is likely to occur and has resulted or may result in an international transboundary release that could be of radiological safety significance for another State.

2. The facilities and activities referred to in paragraph 1 are the following:
(a) any nuclear reactor wherever located;
(b) any nuclear fuel cycle facility;
(c) any radioactive waste management facility;
(d) the transport and storage of nuclear fuels or radioactive wastes;
(e) the manufacture, use, storage, disposal and transport of radioisotopes for agricultural, industrial, medical and related scientific and research purposes; and
(f) the use of radioisotopes for power generation in space objects.

Article 2
Notification and information
   In the event of an accident specified in article 1 (hereinafter referred to as a "nuclear accident"), the State Party referred to in that article shall:
(a) forthwith notify, directly or through the International Atomic Energy Agency (hereinafter referred to as the "Agency"), those States which are or may be physically affected as specified in article 1 and the Agency of the nuclear accident, its nature, the time of its occurrence and its exact location where appropriate; and
(b) promptly provide the States referred to in sub-paragraph (a), directly or through the Agency, and the Agency with such available information relevant to minimizing the radiological consequences in those States, as specified in article 5.

Article 3
Other nuclear accidents
   With a view to minimizing the radiological consequences, States Parties may notify in the event of nuclear accidents other than those specified in article 1.

Article 4
Functions of the Agency
   The Agency shall:
(a) forthwith inform States Parties, Member States, other States which are or may be physically affected as specified in article 1 and relevant international intergovernmental organizations (hereinafter referred to as "international organizations") of a notification received pursuant to sub-paragraph (a) of article 2; and
(b) promptly provide any State Party, Member State or relevant international organization, upon request, with the information received pursuant to sub-paragraph (b) of article 2.

Article 5
Information to be provided
1. The information to be provided pursuant to sub-paragraph (b) of article 2 shall comprise the following data as then available to the notifying State Party:
> (a) the time, exact location where appropriate, and the nature of the nuclear accident;
> (b) the facility or activity involved;
> (c) the assumed or established cause and the foreseeable development of the nuclear accident relevant to the transboundary release of the radioactive materials;
> (d) the general characteristics of the radioactive release, including, as far as is practicable and appropriate, the nature, probable physical and chemical form and the quantity, composition and effective height of the radioactive release;
> (e) information on current and forecast meteorological and hydrological conditions, necessary for forecasting the transboundary release of the radioactive materials;
> (f) the results of environmental monitoring relevant to the transboundary release of the radioactive materials;
> (g) the off-site protective measures taken or planned;
> (h) the predicted behaviour over time of the radioactive release.

2. Such information shall be supplemented at appropriate intervals by further relevant information on the development of the emergency situation, including its foreseeable or actual termination.

3. Information received pursuant to sub-paragraph (b) of article 2 may be used without restriction, except when such information is provided in confidence by the notifying State Party.

Article 6
Consultations
A State Party providing information pursuant to sub-paragraph (b) of article 2 shall, as far as is reasonably practicable, respond promptly to a request for further information or consultations sought by an affected State Party with a view to minimizing the radiological consequences in that State.

Article 7
Competent authorities and points of contact
1. Each State Party shall make known to the Agency and to other States Parties, directly or through the Agency, its competent authorities and point of contact responsible for issuing and receiving the notification and information

referred to in article 2. Such points of contact and a focal point within the Agency shall be available continuously.

2.   Each State Party shall promptly inform the Agency of any changes that may occur in the information referred to in paragraph 1.

3.   The Agency shall maintain an up-to-date list of such national authorities and points of contact as well as points of contact of relevant international organizations and shall provide it to States Parties and Member States and to relevant international organizations.

Article 8
Assistance to States Parties
   The Agency shall, in accordance with its Statute and upon a request of a State Party which does not have nuclear activities itself and borders on a State having an active nuclear programme but not Party, conduct investigations into the feasibility and establishment of an appropriate radiation monitoring system in order to facilitate the achievement of the objectives of this Convention.

Article 9
Bilateral and multilateral arrangements
   In furtherance of their mutual interests, States Parties may consider, where deemed appropriate, the conclusion of bilateral or multilateral arrangements relating to the subject matter of this Convention.

Article 10
Relationship to other international agreements
   This Convention shall not affect the reciprocal rights and obligations of States Parties under existing international agreements which relate to the matters covered by this Convention, or under future international agreements concluded in accordance with the object and purpose of this Convention.

Article 11
Settlement of disputes
   1.   In the event of a dispute between States Parties, or between a State Party and the Agency, concerning the interpretation or application of this Convention, the parties to the dispute shall consult with a view to the settlement of the dispute by negotiation or by any other peaceful means of settling disputes acceptable to them.

   2.   If a dispute of this character between States Parties cannot be settled within one year from the request for consultation pursuant to paragraph 1, it shall, at the request of any party to such dispute, be submitted to arbitration or referred to the International Court of Justice for decision. Where a dispute

is submitted to arbitration, if, within six months from the date of the request, the parties to the dispute are unable to agree on the organization of the arbitration, a party may request the President of the International Court of Justice or the Secretary-General of the United Nations to appoint one or more arbitrators. In cases of conflicting requests by the parties to the dispute, the request to the Secretary-General of the United Nations shall have priority.

3. When signing, ratifying, accepting, approving or acceding to this Convention, a State may declare that it does not consider itself bound by either or both of the dispute settlement procedures provided for in paragraph 2. The other States Parties shall not be bound by a dispute settlement procedure provided for in paragraph 2 with respect to a State Party for which such a declaration is in force.

4. A State Party which has made a declaration in accordance with paragraph 3 may at any time withdraw it by notification to the depositary.

Article 12
Entry into force
1. This Convention shall be open for signature by all States and Namibia, represented by the United Nations Council for Namibia, at the Headquarters of the International Atomic Energy Agency in Vienna and at the Headquarters of the United Nations in New York, from 26 September 1986 and 6 October 1986 respectively, until its entry into force or for twelve months, whichever period is longer.

2. A State and Namibia, represented by the United Nations Council for Namibia, may express its consent to be bound by this Convention either by signature, or by deposit of an instrument of ratification, acceptance or approval following signature made subject of ratification, acceptance or approval, or by deposit of an instrument of accession. The instruments of ratification, acceptance, approval or accession shall be deposited with the depositary.

3. This Convention shall enter into force thirty days after consent to be bound has been expressed by three States.

4. For each State expressing consent to be bound by this Convention after its entry into force, this Convention shall enter into force for that State thirty days after the date of expression of consent.

5. (a) This Convention shall be open for accession, as provided for in this article, by international organizations and regional integration organizations constituted by sovereign States, which have competence in respect of the negotiation, conclusion and application of international agreements in matters covered by this Convention.

(b) In matters within their competence such organizations shall, on their own behalf, exercise the rights and fulfil the obligations which this Convention attributes to States Parties.

(c) When depositing its instrument of accession, such an organization shall communicate to the depositary a declaration indicating the extent of its competence in respect of matters covered by this Convention.

(d) Such an organization shall not hold any vote additional to those of its Member States.

Article 13
Provisional application

A State may, upon signature or at any later date before this Convention enters into force for it, declare that it will apply this Convention provisionally.

Article 14
Amendments

1. A State Party may propose amendments to this Convention. The proposed amendment shall be submitted to the depositary who shall circulate it immediately to all other States Parties.

2. If a majority of the States Parties request the depositary to convene a conference to consider the proposed amendments, the depositary shall invite all States Parties to attend such a conference to begin not sooner than thirty days after the invitations are issued. Any amendment adopted at the conference by a two-thirds majority of all States Parties shall be laid down in a protocol which is open to signature in Vienna and New York by all States Parties.

3. The protocol shall enter into force thirty days after consent to be bound has been expressed by three States. For each State expressing consent to be bound by the protocol after its entry into force, the protocol shall enter into force for that State thirty days after the date of expression of consent.

Article 15
Denunciation

1. A State Party may denounce this Convention by written notification to the depositary.

2. Denunciation shall take effect one year following the date on which the notification is received by the depositary.

Article 16
Depositary

1. The Director General of the Agency shall be the depositary of this Convention.

2.   The Director General of the Agency shall promptly notify States Parties and all other States of:

(a) each signature of this Convention or any protocol of amendment;

(b) each deposit of an instrument of ratification, acceptance, approval or accession concerning this Convention or any protocol of amendment;

(c) any declaration or withdrawal thereof in accordance with article 11;

(d) any declaration of provisional application of this Convention in accordance with article 13;

(e) the entry into force of this Convention and of any amendment thereto; and

(f) any denunciation made under article 15.

Article 17
Authentic texts and certified copies

The original of this Convention, of which the Arabic, Chinese, English, French, Russian and Spanish texts are equally authentic, shall be deposited with the Director General of the International Atomic Energy Agency who shall send certified copies to States Parties and all other States.

IN WITNESS WHEREOF the undersigned, being duly authorized, have signed this Convention, open for signature as provided for in paragraph 1 of article 12.

ADOPTED by the General Conference of the International Atomic Energy Agency meeting in special session at Vienna on the twenty-sixth day of September one thousand nine hundred and eighty-six.

Signatories and Parties

State	Date of Signature	Date of Ratification or Accession (A)
Afghanistan	26 September 1986	
Australia	26 September 1986	
Austria	26 September 1986	
Belgium	26 September 1986	
Brazil	26 September 1986	
Bulgaria	26 September 1986	
Byelorussian SSR	26 September 1986	26 January 1987
Canada	26 September 1986	
Chile	26 September 1986	
China	26 September 1986	

State	Date of Signature	Date of Ratification or Accession (A)
Costa Rica	26 September 1986	
Cuba	26 September 1986	Signature, 26 September 1986
Czechoslovakia	26 September 1986	Signature, 26 September 1986
Denmark	26 September 1986	
Egypt	26 September 1986	
Finland	26 September 1986	Deposit of approval, 11 December 1986
France	26 September 1986	
German Democratic Republic	26 September 1986	29 April 1987
Germany, Federal Republic	26 September 1986	
Greece	26 September 1986	
Guatemala	26 September 1986	
Holy See	26 September 1986	
Hungary	26 September 1986	10 March 1987
Iceland	26 September 1986	
India	29 September 1986	
Indonesia	26 September 1986	
Iran	26 September 1986	
Ireland	26 September 1986	
Israel	26 September 1986	
Italy	26 September 1986	
Ivory Coast	26 September 1986	
Japan	6 March 1987	Acceptance, 9 June 1987
Jordan	2 October 1986	
Korea, Democratic People's Republic	29 September 1986	
Lebanon	26 September 1986	
Liechtenstein	26 September 1986	
Luxembourg	29 September 1986	
Mali	2 October 1986	
Mexico	26 September 1986	
Monaco	26 September 1986	
Mongolia	8 January 1987	11 June 1987
Morocco	26 September 1986	
Netherlands	26 September 1986	
New Zealand		11 March 1987 (A)
Niger	26 September 1986	
Nigeria	21 January 1987	

State	Date of Signature	Date of Ratification or Accession (A)
Norway	26 September 1986	Signature, 26 September 1986
Panama	26 September 1986	
Paraguay	2 October 1986	
Poland	26 September 1986	
Portugal	26 September 1986	
Senegal	15 June 1987	
Sierra Leone	25 March 1987	
South Africa	10 August 1987	10 August 1987
Spain	26 September 1986	
Sudan	26 September 1986	
Sweden	26 September 1986	27 February 1987
Switzerland	26 September 1986	
Syrian Arab Republic	2 July 1987	
Tunisia	24 February 1987	
Turkey	26 September 1986	
Ukrainian SSR	26 September 1986	26 January 1987
USSR	26 September 1986	23 December 1986
United Kingdom	26 September 1986	
USA	26 September 1986	
Yugoslavia	27 May 1987	
Zaire	30 September 1986	
Zimbabwe	26 September 1986	

STATEMENTS OF VOLUNTARY APPLICATION OF EARLY NOTIFICATION CONVENTION TO ACCIDENTS NOT COVERED BY THE CONVENTION

Text reprinted from: 25 *ILM* 1394 (1986)

China
    "Now, I would like to announce that I will sign the two Conventions on behalf of the Government of the People's Republic of China and declare that China will notify on a voluntary basis nuclear accidents other than those specified in Article I of the Convention on Early Notification of a Nuclear Accident which might produce transboundary radiological effects. This shows China's sincerity of committing itself to international cooperation in nuclear safety."

France

"France will of course sign these texts. Furthermore, the Government of the French Republic declares that independent of the commitments to which it will subscribe in becoming a party to the Convention on Early Notification of a Nuclear Accident, and in accordance with the option offered by Article 3 of the Convention, France intends to furnish the appropriate information concerning nuclear accidents capable of producing beyond its borders significant consequences in the area of radiological safety and which are not covered by Article 1 of this Convention. The French Government will provide information on all nuclear accidents, under the conditions established in the declaration of its representative to the Group of Experts, done August 15, 1986 and recorded in the minutes."[translation]

Union of Soviet Socialist Republics

"We declare that the USSR is ready to sign these conventions immediately. The Soviet Union is ready to notify of all nuclear accidents which could entail the danger of transboundary transfer of radioactive release."

United Kingdom

"We are ready to sign the Conventions that are before us. Ratification will be needed in the normal way, but in the meantime we shall apply both Conventions as from today. The British Government will also voluntarily inform the IAEA and any states affected of any other serious accident involving the United Kingdom's military facilities or equipment, so that the nuclear industry in both the military and energy sectors will carry out their responsibility to provide the information needed by others."

United States

"On behalf of the United States, I am prepared to sign this Convention, subject to ratification, at this Special Session. I would also like to make the following statements that reaffirm current U.S. policy. Pending ratification by the United States of the Convention on Early Notification of a Nuclear Accident, the United States will, in the event of a nuclear accident that would be covered by Article I of the Convention, voluntarily notify states that are, or may be, physically affected and the Agency, and will voluntarily provide them available information relevant to minimizing the radiological consequences. The United States will also voluntarily provide notification with respect to any other nuclear accident which has or may have transboundary effects of radiological safety significance."

CONVENTION ON EARLY NOTIFICATION
OF A NUCLEAR ACCIDENT

CONVENTION ON ASSISTANCE IN THE CASE OF A NUCLEAR
ACCIDENT OR RADIOLOGICAL EMERGENCY

Reservations/Declarations

Part I: Reservations/Declarations made upon or following signature
Part II: Reservations/Declarations made upon or following deposit of instrument expressing consent to be bound[1]

Part I

Afghanistan   [26 September 1986][2]

" . . . the Government of the Democratic Republic of Afghanistan reserves its right to make whatever declaration it deems appropriate at the time of deposit of its instrument of ratification."
(Original in English)

Australia   [26 September 1986][2]

"Australia will make any declarations as provided for by the Conventions only upon ratification."
"Attention is also drawn to the statement by the Leader of the Australian delegation to the first Special Session of the General Conference, in particular the sections of the statement which refer to the relationship between the conventions and customary international law."
(Original in English)

---

[1] Reservations and Declarations provided by the Secretariat of the IAEA. Both the Reservations and Declarations made in Part I and those made in Part II have been included because even where a State having made a Reservation or Declaration in Part I subsequently makes a Reservation or Declaration in Part II, the latter does not necessarily override the former. This is because in a number of cases States have accepted the provisional application of the Convention pending its formal entry into force for that State.
[2] Date of deposit of reservations/declarations.

Bulgaria   [26 September 1986] [2]

''From the time of signature and until the conventions come into force for the People's Republic of Bulgaria, the latter will apply both conventions provisionally.''

''The People's Republic of Bulgaria does not consider itself bound by the dispute settlement procedures provided for in article 11, paragraph 2 of the Convention on Early Notification of a Nuclear Accident and in article 13, paragraph 2 of the Convention on Assistance in the Case of a Nuclear Accident or Radiological Emergency.''

(Original in Russian; translation by the Secretariat)

Byelorussian Soviet Socialist
Republic   [26 September 1986] [2]

''The Byelorussian SSR also declares that it accepts provisionally the obligations under the conventions in question from the time of their signature and until their ratification. The Byelorussian SSR will not consider itself bound by the provisions of article 11, paragraph 2 of the Convention on Early Notification of a Nuclear Accident and article 13, paragraph 2 of the Convention on Assistance in the Case of a Nuclear Accident or Radiological Emergency, which envisage the possibility of submitting a dispute between States Parties to arbitration or referring it to the International Court of Justice at the request of any party, and states that for submission of any international dispute to arbitration or referral to the International Court of Justice the agreement of all parties in each individual case is necessary.''

(Original in Russian; translation by the Secretariat)

Canada   [26 September 1986] [2]

The following identical communication was received in respect of both Conventions:
'' . . . the Government of Canada reserves its right to make whatever declarations it deems appropriate at the time of deposit of its instrument of ratification.''

(Original in English)

China   [26 September 1986] [2]

''The Government of the People's Republic of China has decided to sign the

Convention on Early Notification of a Nuclear Accident and hereby states the following:

1.   China does not consider itself bound by either of the dispute settlement procedures provided for in article 11, paragraph 2, of the Convention.

2.   In view of the urgency of the question of nuclear safety, China accepts article 13, the provisionally applicable clause of the Convention before the Convention's entry into force for China.''

''The Government of the People's Republic of China has decided to sign the Convention on Assistance in the Case of a Nuclear Accident or Radiological Emergency and hereby states the following:

1.   In cases of gross negligence by the individuals who caused the death, injury, loss or damage, article 10, paragraph 2, of the Convention shall not apply to China.

2.   China does not consider itself bound by either of the dispute settlement procedures provided for in article 13, paragraph 2, of the Convention.

3.   In view of the urgency of the question of nuclear safety, China accepts article 15, the provisionally applicable clause of the Convention before the Convention's entry into force for China.''

(Original in Chinese and English; supplied by the Government)

Cuba   [26 September 1986] [2]

''With regard to the settlement of disputes as described in article 11 of the Convention on Early Notification of a Nuclear Accident, the Government of Cuba does not consider itself bound by the procedure for referring disputes to the International Court of Justice nor by any decision which the International Court of Justice takes in application of this Convention and which affects Cuba.''

''With regard to the settlement of disputes as described in article 13 of the Convention on Assistance in the Case of a Nuclear Accident or Radiological Emergency, the Government of Cuba does not consider itself bound by the procedure for referring disputes to the International Court of Justice nor by any decision which the International Court of Justice takes in application of this Convention and which affects Cuba.''

(Original in Spanish; translation by the Secretariat)

Czechoslovakia   [26 September 1986] [2]

''The Czechoslovak Socialist Republic does not consider itself bound by the

procedures of settling disputes provided for in article 11, item 2, of the Convention on Early Notification of a Nuclear Accident and in Article 13, item 2, of the Convention on Assistance in the Case of a Nuclear Accident or Radiological Emergency.''
(Original in English)

*Democratic People's Republic
of Korea*   [29 September 1986] [2]

''1.   The Democratic People's Republic of Korea does not consider itself bound by either of the dispute settlement procedures provided for in article 11, paragraph 2 of the Convention on Early Notification of a Nuclear Accident and in article 13, paragraph 2 of the Convention on Assistance in the Case of a Nuclear Accident or Radiological Emergency.
2.   In view of the urgency of the question of nuclear safety the Democratic People's Republic of Korea will apply both conventions provisionally.''
(Original in English)

France   [26 September 1986] [2]

1. Convention on Assistance in the Case of a Nuclear Accident or Radiological Emergency
Article 8. *Privileges, immunities and facilities*
   The Government of the French Republic declares, in accordance with paragraph 9 of article 8, that France does not consider itself bound by the provisions of paragraphs 2 and 3 of that article.
Article 10. *Claims and compensation*
   The Government of the French Republic declares, in accordance with paragraph 5 of article 10, that France does not consider itself bound by paragraph 2 of that article.
Article 13. *Settlement of disputes*
   The Government of the French Republic declares, in accordance with paragraph 3 of article 13, that France does not consider itself bound by the provisions of paragraph 2 of that article.

2. Convention on Early Notification of a Nuclear Accident
Article 11. *Settlement of disputes*
   The Government of the French Republic declares, in accordance with

paragraph 3 of article 11, that France does not consider itself bound by the provisions of paragraph 2 of that article.
(Original in French; translation by the Secretariat)

German Democratic Republic [26 September 1986] [2]

"1. The German Democratic Republic will apply, in accordance with article 13, the Convention on Early Notification of a Nuclear Accident provisionally.
In doing so it does not consider itself bound by the dispute settlement procedure provided for in paragraph 2 of article 11.
2. The German Democratic Republic nominates in accordance with article 7 of the Convention on Early Notification of a Nuclear Accident the National Board for Atomic Safety and Radiation Protection of the German Democratic Republic as competent authority and point of contact."

"1. The German Democratic Republic will apply, in accordance with article 15, the Convention on Assistance in the Case of a Nuclear Accident or Radiological Emergency provisionally. In doing so it does not consider itself bound by the dispute settlement procedure provided for in paragraph 2 of article 13.
2. The German Democratic Republic nominates in accordance with article 4 of the Convention on Assistance in the Case of a Nuclear Accident or Radiological Emergency the National Board for Atomic Safety and Radiation Protection of the German Democratic Republic as competent authority and point of contact."
(Original in English and German; supplied by the Government)

Germany, Federal Republic of [26 September 1986] [2]

The Convention on Early Notification of a Nuclear Accident
"1. With reference to article 13 of the aforementioned Convention, the Federal Republic of Germany will as of today, in accordance with the law applicable in the Federal Republic of Germany, apply the Convention provisionally.
2. The Federal Republic of Germany is of the view that in the case of a nuclear accident information about the effects of the accident should also be

exchanged between neighbouring States affected by the accident and expresses its wish that also other countries would act accordingly.''

The Convention on Assistance in the Case of a Nuclear Accident or Radiological Emergency
'' . . . with reference to article 15 of the aforementioned Convention, that the Federal Republic of Germany will as of today, in accordance with the law applicable in the Federal Republic of Germany, apply the Convention provisionally.''
(Original in English and German; supplied by the Government)

Greece   [26 September 1986][2]

The Convention on Early Notification of a Nuclear Accident
The Convention on Assistance in the Case of a Nuclear Accident or Radiological Emergency
''According to their respective articles 13 and 15, the above two conventions will be provisionally applied in Greece within the framework of the existing internal legislation.''
(Original in English)

Hungary   [26 September 1986][2]

The Convention on Early Notification of a Nuclear Accident
''The Hungarian People's Republic does not consider itself bound by the dispute settlement procedures provided for in paragraph 2 of article 11 of the Convention since, in its opinion, the jurisdiction of any arbitral tribunal or of the International Court of Justice can be founded only on the voluntary prior acceptance of such jurisdiction by all the Parties concerned.''

The Convention on Assistance in the Case of a Nuclear Accident or Radiological Emergency
''The Hungarian People's Republic does not consider itself bound by the dispute settlement procedures provided for in article 13, paragraph 2, of the Convention since, in its opinion, the jurisdiction of any arbitral tribunal or of the International Court of Justice can be founded only on the voluntary prior acceptance of such jurisdiction by all the Parties concerned.''
(Original in English and Hungarian; supplied by the Government)

India   [29 September 1986] [2]

"While signing the two conventions that were approved by the special session last week, I would like to express the disappointment of my Government that the Convention on Early Notification of a Nuclear Accident does not cover all kinds of accidents. It should have been a full-scope convention covering accidents from whatever source—civil or military, including accidents emanating from nuclear weapons or nuclear weapons tests, since the transboundary effects of radiological safety significance from any source would be equally damaging. Nevertheless, we have decided to sign both conventions, subject to ratification, in view of the solemn assurance that has been given by the five nuclear-weapon States to the effect that they undertake to notify all accidents. This is in keeping with our policy of according to public declarations of State policy equal validity with other international commitments.

While ratifying these conventions, it is our intention to indicate our reservations with respect to certain articles of the two conventions, as already provided for in them."
(Original in English)

Indonesia   [26 September 1986] [2]

"The Permanent Mission has further the honour to inform the Secretariat that the Government of Indonesia wishes to make the following reservations:
(i) article 13 on Settlement of Disputes of the Convention on Assistance in the Case of a Nuclear Accident or Radiological Emergency; and
(ii) article 11 on Settlement of Disputes of the Convention on Early Notification of a Nuclear Accident."
(Original in English)

Ireland   [26 September 1986] [2]

"Ireland hereby declares that in accordance with article 8, paragraph 9 of the Convention on Assistance in the Case of a Nuclear Accident or Radiological Emergency, it does not consider itself bound by the provisions of paragraphs 2 and 3 of article 8 thereof."
"Ireland hereby declares that in accordance with article 10, paragraph 5 of the Convention on Assistance in the Case of a Nuclear Accident or

Radiological Emergency, it does not consider itself bound by the provisions of paragraph 2 of article 10 thereof.''
(Original in English)

Italy   [26 September 1986][2]

''The Italian Government, upon signature of the Convention on Early Notification of a Nuclear Accident, declares that the clauses of article 1 are not satisfactory, in so far as they impose on a contracting party the obligation to notify only accidents from which derives the release of radioactive materials which might transcend or has transcended an international boundary, or could have other consequences outside its jurisdiction or control.

The Italian Government considers that every accident should be notified, also those which have consequences limited to the territory of the State concerned.''
(Original in English)

Mongolia   [8 January 1987][2]

The following identical reservation was made in respect of both Conventions:
''The Mongolian People's Republic states that it does not consider itself bound by the provisions of paragraph 2 of article 11 of the Convention on Early Notification of a Nuclear Accident and the provisions of paragraph 2 of article 13 of the Convention on Assistance in the Case of a Nuclear Accident or Radiological Emergency concerning the procedure of the settlement of disputes arising from the interpretation or application of the Conventions. In its opinion, for submission of any dispute of such nature to arbitration or the International Court of Justice, the consent of all the parties to the dispute is necessary.''
(Original in English and Russian)

Netherlands   [26 September 1986][2]

'' . . . declares today on the occasion of the signing of the Convention on Early Notification of a Nuclear Accident, and in accordance with article 13 of that Convention, that his Government, anticipating the entry into force of the Convention for the Kingdom of the Netherlands, will apply its provisions provisionally. This provisional application will come into effect thirty days from today, or, in case the Convention will not be in force for at least one other State at that time, on the date on which the Convention will have become applicable to one other State either by means of entry into force or by means of a declaration of provisional application.''

" . . . declares today on the occasion of the signing of the Convention on Assistance in the Case of a Nuclear Accident or Radiological Emergency, and in accordance with article 15 of that Convention, that his Government, anticipating the entry into force of the Convention for the Kingdom of the Netherlands, will apply its provisions provisionally. This provisional application will come into effect thirty days from today, or, in case the Convention will not be in force for at least one other State at that time, on the date on which the Convention will have become applicable to one other State either by means of entry into force or by means of a declaration of provisional application. The provisions of article 10, second paragraph, are being excluded from this provisional application.''

(Original in English)

Norway   [26 September 1986][2]

The Convention on Assistance in the Case of a Nuclear Accident or Radiological Emergency

"In conformity with article 8, paragraph 9 of the Convention, Norway does not consider herself bound by article 8, paragraph 2(a) as far as immunity from civil proceedings are concerned and by article 8, paragraph 2(b) as far as exemption from taxation, duties or other charges for personnel of the assisting party is concerned.''

(Original in English)

Poland   [26 September 1986][2]

"The Government of the Polish People's Republic declares that it will provisionally apply the Convention on Early Notification of a Nuclear Accident adopted at the Special Session of the General Conference of the International Atomic Energy Agency in Vienna on 26 September 1986, with the exception of article 11, paragraph 2, over the period between its entry into force and ratification.''

"The Government of the Polish People's Republic declares that it will provisionally apply the Convention on Assistance in the Case of a Nuclear

Accident or Radiological Emergency adopted in Vienna on 26 September 1986 with the exception of article 13, paragraph 2, over the period between its entry into force and ratification.''
(Original in English)

Turkey   [26 September 1986]²

'' . . . declarations or reservations will be made, if any, on article 11 of the Convention on Early Notification of a Nuclear Accident and on articles 8, 9 and 13 of the Convention on Assistance in the Case of a Nuclear Accident or Radiological Emergency during the course of the submission of the instrument of ratification to the depository.''
(Original in English)

Ukrainian Soviet Socialist
Republic   [26 September 1986]²

''The Ukrainian SSR also declares that it accepts provisionally the obligations under the Conventions in question from the time of their signature and until their ratification. The Ukrainian SSR will not consider itself bound by the provisions of article 11, paragraph 2 of the Convention on Early Notification of a Nuclear Accident and article 13, paragraph 2 of the Convention on Assistance in the Case of a Nuclear Accident or Radiological Emergency, which envisage the possibility of submitting a dispute between States Parties to arbitration or referring it to the International Court of Justice at the request of any party, and states that for the submission of any international dispute to arbitration or referral to the International Court of Justice the agreement of all parties in each individual case is necessary.''
(Original in Russian; translation by the Secretariat)

Union of Soviet Socialist
Republics   [26 September 1986]²

''From the time of signature and until the conventions come into force for the USSR, the latter will apply both conventions provisionally.''
''The USSR will not consider itself bound by the provisions of article 11, paragraph 2 of the Convention on Early Notification of a Nuclear Accident and article 13, paragraph 2 of the Convention on Assistance in the Case of a

Nuclear Accident or Radiological Emergency, which envisage the possibility of submitting a dispute between States Parties to arbitration or referring it to the International Court of Justice at the request of any party, and states that for the submission of any international dispute to arbitration or referral to the International Court of Justice the agreement of all parties in each individual case is necessary.''
(Original in Russian; translation by the Secretariat)

United Kingdom of Great Britain
and Northern Ireland   [26 September 1986][2]

The Convention on Early Notification of a Nuclear Accident
"The United Kingdom will apply this Convention provisionally from today's date to the extent permitted by its existing laws, regulations and administrative arrangements.

The United Kingdom Resident Representative affirms that, having regard to article 3 of the Convention, and as stated by the United Kingdom Secretary of State for Energy in his address to the Special Session of the General Conference on 24 September, the United Kingdom would in practice notify the IAEA and affected States in the event of an accident to military facilities or equipment which, although not of the type specified in article 1 of the Convention, had or might have the consequence specified in that article.''

The Convention on Assistance in the Case of a Nuclear Accident or Radiological Emergency
"The United Kingdom will apply this Convention provisionally from today's date to the extent permitted by its existing laws, regulations and administrative arrangements.''
(Original in English)

United States of America   [26 September 1986][2]

The Convention on Early Notification of a Nuclear Accident
"As provided for in paragraph 3 of article 11, the United States declares that it does not consider itself bound by either of the dispute settlement procedures provided for in paragraph 2 of that article.''

The Convention on Assistance in the Case of a Nuclear Accident or Radiological Emergency
"In accordance with paragraphs 3 and 4 of article 2 and paragraph 2 of article

7, the United States declares that reimbursement of costs is among the terms of assistance it may provide unless the United States explicitly specifies otherwise or waives reimbursement.

With respect to any other State Party that has declared pursuant to paragraph 9 of article 8 that it does not consider itself bound in whole or in part by paragraph 2 or 3, the United States declares pursuant to paragraph 9 that in its treaty relations with that State the United States does not consider itself bound by paragraphs 2 and 3 to the same extent provided in the declaration of that other State Party.

With respect to any other State Party that has declared pursuant to paragraph 5 of article 10 that it does not consider itself bound in whole or in part by paragraph 2 or that it will not apply paragraph 2 in whole or in part in cases of gross negligence, the United States declares pursuant to paragraph 5 that in its treaty relations with that State the United States does not consider itself bound by paragraph 2 to the same extent as provided in the declaration of that other State Party.

As provided for in paragraph 3 of article 13, the United States declares that it does not consider itself bound by either of the dispute settlement procedures provided for in paragraph 2 of that article.''
(Original in English)

Part II

Byelorussian Soviet Socialist
Republic   [26 January 1987] [2]

The following identical reservation was received in respect of both Conventions:
''The Byelorussian SSR will not consider itself bound by the provisions of Article 11, paragraph 2 of the Convention on Early Notification of a Nuclear Accident and Article 13, paragraph 2 of the Convention on Assistance in the Case of a Nuclear Accident or Radiological Emergency, which envisage the possibility of submitting a dispute between States Parties to arbitration or referring it to the International Court of Justice at the request of any party and states that, for submission of any international dispute to arbitration or referral to the International Court of Justice, the agreement of all parties in each individual case is necessary.''
(Original in Russian)

German Democratic Republic   [29 April 1987][2]

The Convention on Early Notification of a Nuclear Accident
''The German Democratic Republic does not consider itself bound by the dispute settlement procedure provided for in Paragraph 2 of Article 11.''

The Convention on Assistance in the Case of a Nuclear Accident or Radiological Emergency
''The German Democratic Republic does not consider itself bound by the dispute settlement procedure provided for in Paragraph 2 of Article 13.''
(Original in German; English translation supplied by the Government)

Hungary   [10 March 1987][2]

The Convention on Early Notification of a Nuclear Accident
''The Hungarian People's Republic does not consider itself bound by the dispute settlement procedures provided for in paragraph 2 of article 11 of the Convention since, in its opinion, the jurisdiction of any arbitral tribunal or of the International Court of Justice can be founded only on the voluntary prior acceptance of such jurisdiction by all the Parties concerned.''

The Convention on Assistance in the Case of a Nuclear Accident or Radiological Emergency
''The Hungarian People's Republic does not consider itself bound by the dispute settlement procedures provided for in article 13, paragraph 2, of the Convention since, in its opinion, the jurisdiction of any arbitral tribunal or of the International Court of Justice can be founded only on the voluntary prior acceptance of such jurisdiction by all the Parties concerned.''
(Original in English and Hungarian; supplied by the Government)

Japan   [9 June 1987][2]

The Convention on Assistance in the Case of a Nuclear Accident or Radiological Emergency
''The Government of Japan declares that it does not consider itself bound by Paragraph 2(b) of Article 8 with respect to the income tax, local inhabitant taxes and the enterprise tax as well as any identical or substantially similar taxes

on personnel acting on behalf of an assisting party and that it will afford to the said personnel exemption from these taxes to the extent provided for in a convention for the avoidance of double taxation between Japan and the State of which the personnel is a resident.''
(Original in English and Japanese)

Mongolia   [11 June 1987][2]

The Convention on Early Notification of a Nuclear Accident
''The Mongolian People's Republic states that it does not consider itself bound by the provisions of Article 11, paragraph 2 of the Convention on Early Notification of a Nuclear Accident, concerning the procedure of the settlement of disputes arising from the interpretation or application of the Convention. In its opinion, for submission of any dispute of such nature to arbitration or the International Court of Justice the consent of all the parties to the dispute is necessary.''

The Convention on Assistance in the Case of a Nuclear Accident or Radiological Emergency
''The Mongolian People's Republic states that it does not consider itself bound by the provisions of Article 13, paragraph 2 of the Convention on Assistance in the Case of a Nuclear Accident or Radiological Emergency, concerning the procedure of the settlement of disputes arising from the interpretation or application of the Convention. In its opinion, for submission of any dispute of such nature to arbitration or the International Court of Justice the consent of all the parties to the dispute is necessary.''
(Original in Mongolian; English translation supplied by the Government)

New Zealand   [11 March 1987][2]

The Convention on Assistance in the Case of a Nuclear Accident or Radiological Emergency
''In accordance with Article 8 (9) of that Convention I declare on behalf of the Government of New Zealand that New Zealand does not consider itself bound by the provisions of Article 8 (2) (a) and Article 8 (3) (b) of the Convention.''
(Original in English)

Ukrainian Soviet Socialist
Republic [26 January 1987][2]

The following identical reservation was received in respect of both Conventions:
"The Ukrainian SSR will not consider itself bound by the provisions of Article 11, paragraph 2 of the Convention on Early Notification of a Nuclear Accident and Article 13, paragraph 2 of the Convention on Assistance in the Case of a Nuclear Accident or Radiological Emergency, which envisage the possibility of submitting a dispute between States Parties to arbitration or referring it to the International Court of Justice at the request of any party, and states that for submission of any international dispute to arbitration or referral to the International Court of Justice the agreement of all parties in each individual case is necessary."
(Original in Russian)

Union of Soviet Socialist
Republics [23 December 1986][2]

The following identical reservation was received in respect of both Conventions:
"The USSR will not consider itself bound by the provisions of Article 11, paragraph 2 of the Convention on Early Notification of a Nuclear Accident and Article 13, paragraph 2 of the Convention on Assistance in the Case of a Nuclear Accident or Radiological Emergency, which envisage the possibility of submitting a dispute between States Parties to arbitration or referring it to the International Court of Justice at the request of any party, and states that for submission of any international dispute to arbitration or referral to the International Court of Justice the agreement of all parties in each individual case is necessary."
(Original in Russian)

Select Bibliography

Adede, *The IAEA Notification and Assistance Conventions in Case of a Nuclear Accident* (1987).

IAEA, Report by Board of Governors on Measures to Strengthen International Co-operation in Nuclear Safety and Radiological Protection, *IAEA Doc.* GC(SPL.I)/2, 24 September 1986 (includes summary record of the final plenary session of group of governmental experts convened to draft international agreements on early notification and assistance).

22. VIENNA CONVENTION ON ASSISTANCE IN THE CASE OF A NUCLEAR ACCIDENT OR RADIOLOGICAL EMERGENCY
26 September 1986

Editorial Note

The Convention on Assistance was negotiated at the same time and within the same framework as the Convention on Notification. In the event of a nuclear accident or radiological emergency, a State Party may request assistance from any other State Party and from the IAEA (Article 2(1)). The Convention does not require any State to provide assistance. There is a general obligation on States to cooperate among themselves and with the IAEA to facilitate prompt assistance, and this can be accomplished through bilateral or multilateral arrangements (Article 1). If a specific request for assistance is made, the State to which such request is directed "shall promptly decide and notify the requesting State . . . whether it is in a position to render the assistance requested, and the scope and forms of the assistance that might be rendered" (Article 2(3)). In addition, States must identify and notify the IAEA of the type and terms (especially financial) of assistance which could be made available (Article 2(4)).

The Convention contains several provisions which are specifically designed to make it easier for a State to give assistance. Article 7 deals with the reimbursement of costs; under Article 8, certain privileges and immunities are afforded to personnel of the assisting State, and equipment and property brought into the territory of the requesting State is immune from seizure, attachment or requisition; by Article 10, the assisting State and persons acting on its behalf are granted protection against legal proceedings brought against them in respect of death or injury to persons, or damage to property or the environment caused within the territory of the requesting State. A State may, however, when signing, ratifying, accepting or acceding to the Convention, declare that it does not consider itself bound by certain of these provisions in Articles 8 and 10. The Convention also contains a dispute settlement procedure identical to that found in the Convention on Notification.

The IAEA plays an important role in the Convention. If a request for assistance is made, it must provide "appropriate resources allocated for this purpose", transmit promptly the request to other States and international organizations and, if so requested by the requesting State, co-ordinate the available assistance at the international level (Article 2(6)). In addition, under Article 5, the IAEA collects and disseminates information and provides various types of assistance to States Parties and Member States.

Date of signature: 26 September 1986
Entry into force: 26 February 1987

Depositary: Director General of the IAEA
Authentic languages: Arabic, Chinese, English, French,
                               Russian and Spanish
Text reprinted from: *IAEA Doc.* GC(SPL.1)/2, Annex III
Also published in: 25 *ILM* 1377 (1986)

Text

VIENNA CONVENTION ON ASSISTANCE IN THE CASE OF A NUCLEAR ACCIDENT OR RADIOLOGICAL EMERGENCY

THE STATES PARTIES TO THIS CONVENTION,

AWARE that nuclear activities are being carried out in a number of States,

NOTING that comprehensive measures have been and are being taken to ensure a high level of safety in nuclear activities, aimed at preventing nuclear accidents and minimizing the consequences of any such accident, should it occur,

DESIRING to strengthen further international co-operation in the safe development and use of nuclear energy,

CONVINCED of the need for an international framework which will facilitate the prompt provision of assistance in the event of a nuclear accident or radiological emergency to mitigate its consequences,

NOTING the usefulness of bilateral and multilateral arrangements on mutual assistance in this area,

NOTING the activities of the International Atomic Energy Agency in developing guidelines for mutual emergency assistance arrangements in connection with a nuclear accident or radiological emergency,

HAVE AGREED as follows:

Article 1
General provisions
1.   The States Parties shall cooperate between themselves and with the International Atomic Energy Agency (hereinafter referred to as the ''Agency'') in accordance with the provisions of this Convention to facilitate prompt assistance in the event of a nuclear accident or radiological emergency to minimize its consequences and to protect life, property and the environment from the effects of radioactive releases.
2.   To facilitate such cooperation States Parties may agree on bilateral or multilateral arrangements or, where appropriate, a combination of these, for

preventing or minimizing injury and damage which may result in the event of a nuclear accident or radiological emergency.

3. The States Parties request the Agency, acting within the framework of its Statute, to use its best endeavours in accordance with the provisions of this Convention to promote, facilitate and support the cooperation between States Parties provided for in this Convention.

Article 2
Provision of assistance
1. If a State Party needs assistance in the event of a nuclear accident or radiological emergency, whether or not such accident or emergency originates within its territory, jurisdiction or control, it may call for such assistance from any other State Party, directly or through the Agency, and from the Agency, or, where appropriate, from other international intergovernmental organizations (hereinafter referred to as "international organizations").

2. A State Party requesting assistance shall specify the scope and type of assistance required and, where practicable, provide the assisting party with such information as may be necessary for that party to determine the extent to which it is able to meet the request. In the event that it is not practicable for the requesting State Party to specify the scope and type of assistance required, the requesting State Party and the assisting party shall, in consultation, decide upon the scope and type of assistance required.

3. Each State Party to which a request for such assistance is directed shall promptly decide and notify the requesting State Party, directly or through the Agency, whether it is in a position to render the assistance requested, and the scope and terms of the assistance that might be rendered.

4. States Parties shall, within the limits of their capabilities, identify and notify the Agency of experts, equipment and materials which could be made available for the provision of assistance to other States Parties in the event of a nuclear accident or radiological emergency as well as the terms, especially financial, under which such assistance could be provided.

5. Any State Party may request assistance relating to medical treatment or temporary relocation into the territory of another State Party of people involved in a nuclear accident or radiological emergency.

6. The Agency shall respond, in accordance with its Statute and as provided for in this Convention, to a requesting State Party's or a Member State's request for assistance in the event of a nuclear accident or radiological emergency by:

(a) making available appropriate resources allocated for this purpose;

(b) transmitting promptly the request to other States and international organizations which, according to the Agency's information, may possess the necessary resources; and

(c) if so requested by the requesting State, co-ordinating the assistance at the international level which may thus become available.

Article 3
Direction and control of assistance
Unless otherwise agreed:

(a) the overall direction, control, co-ordination and supervision of the assistance shall be the responsibility within its territory of the requesting State. The assisting party should, where the assistance involves personnel, designate in consultation with the requesting State, the person who should be in charge of and retain immediate operational supervision over the personnel and the equipment provided by it. The designated person should exercise such supervision in cooperation with the appropriate authorities of the requesting State;

(b) the requesting State shall provide, to the extent of its capabilities, local facilities and services for the proper and effective administration of the assistance. It shall also ensure the protection of personnel, equipment and materials brought into its territory by or on behalf of the assisting party for such purpose;

(c) ownership of equipment and materials provided by either party during the periods of assistance shall be unaffected, and their return shall be ensured;

(d) a State Party providing assistance in response to a request under paragraph 5 of article 2 shall co-ordinate that assistance within its territory.

Article 4
Competent authorities and points of contact

1.   Each State Party shall make known to the Agency and to other States Parties, directly or through the Agency, its competent authorities and point of contact authorized to make and receive requests for and to accept offers of assistance. Such points of contact and a focal point within the Agency shall be available continuously.

2.   Each State Party shall promptly inform the Agency of any changes that may occur in the information referred to in paragraph 1.

3.   The Agency shall regularly and expeditiously provide to States Parties, Member States and relevant international organizations the information referred to in paragraphs 1 and 2.

Article 5
Functions of the Agency
The States Parties request the Agency, in accordance with paragraph 3 of article 1 and without prejudice to other provisions of this Convention, to:
(a) collect and disseminate to States Parties and Member States information concerning:
    (i) experts, equipment and materials which could be made available in the event of nuclear accidents or radiological emergencies;
    (ii) methodologies, techniques and available results of research relating to response to nuclear accidents or radiological emergencies;
(b) assist a State Party or Member State when requested in any of the following or other appropriate matters:
    (i) preparing both emergency plans in the case of nuclear accidents and radiological emergencies and the appropriate legislation;
    (ii) developing appropriate training programmes for personnel to deal with nuclear accidents and radiological emergencies;
    (iii) transmitting requests for assistance and relevant information in the event of a nuclear accident or radiological emergency;
    (iv) developing appropriate radiation monitoring programmes, procedures and standards;
    (v) conducting investigations into the feasibility of establishing appropriate radiation monitoring systems;
(c) make available to a State Party or a Member State requesting assistance in the event of a nuclear accident or radiological emergency appropriate resources allocated for the purpose of conducting an initial assessment of the accident or emergency;
(d) offer its good offices to the States Parties and Member States in the event of a nuclear accident or radiological emergency;
(e) establish and maintain liaison with relevant international organizations for the purposes of obtaining and exchanging relevant information and data, and make a list of such organizations available to States Parties, Member States and the aforementioned organizations.

Article 6
Confidentiality and public statements
1. The requesting State and the assisting party shall protect the confidentiality of any confidential information that becomes available to either of them in connection with the assistance in the event of a nuclear accident or

radiological emergency. Such information shall be used exclusively for the purpose of the assistance agreed upon.

2. The assisting party shall make every effort to coordinate with the requesting State before releasing information to the public on the assistance provided in connection with a nuclear accident or radiological emergency.

Article 7
Reimbursement of costs

1. An assisting party may offer assistance without costs to the requesting State. When considering whether to offer assistance on such a basis, the assisting party shall take into account:

(a) the nature of the nuclear accident or radiological emergency;
(b) the place of origin of the nuclear accident or radiological emergency;
(c) the needs of developing countries;
(d) the particular needs of countries without nuclear facilities; and
(e) any other relevant factors.

2. When assistance is provided wholly or partly on a reimbursement basis, the requesting State shall reimburse the assisting party for the costs incurred for the services rendered by persons or organizations acting on its behalf, and for all expenses in connection with the assistance to the extent that such expenses are not directly defrayed by the requesting State. Unless otherwise agreed, reimbursement shall be provided promptly after the assisting party has presented its request for reimbursement to the requesting State, and in respect of costs other than local costs, shall be freely transferable.

3. Notwithstanding paragraph 2, the assisting party may at any time waive, or agree to the postponement of, the reimbursement in whole or in part. In considering such waiver or postponement, assisting parties shall give due consideration to the needs of developing countries.

Article 8
Privileges, immunities and facilities

1. The requesting State shall afford to personnel of the assisting party and personnel acting on its behalf the necessary privileges, immunities and facilities for the performance of their assistance functions.

2. The requesting State shall afford the following privileges and immunities to personnel of the assisting party or personnel acting on its behalf who have been duly notified to and accepted by the requesting State:

(a) immunity from arrest, detention and legal process, including criminal, civil and administrative jurisdiction, of the requesting State, in respect of acts or omissions in the performance of their duties; and

(b) exemption from taxation, duties or other charges, except those which are normally incorporated in the price of goods or paid for services rendered, in respect of the performance of their assistance functions.

3. The requesting State shall:

(a) afford the assisting party exemption from taxation, duties or other charges on the equipment and property brought into the territory of the requesting State by the assisting party for the purpose of the assistance; and

(b) provide immunity from seizure, attachment or requisition of such equipment and property.

4. The requesting State shall ensure the return of such equipment and property. If requested by the assisting party, the requesting State shall arrange, to the extent it is able to do so, for the necessary decontamination of recoverable equipment involved in the assistance before its return.

5. The requesting State shall facilitate the entry into, stay in and departure from its national territory of personnel notified pursuant to paragraph 2 and of equipment and property involved in the assistance.

6. Nothing in this article shall require the requesting State to provide its nationals or permanent residents with the privileges and immunities provided for in the foregoing paragraphs.

7. Without prejudice to the privileges and immunities, all beneficiaries enjoying such privileges and immunities under this article have a duty to respect the laws and regulations of the requesting State. They shall also have the duty not to interfere in the domestic affairs of the requesting State.

8. Nothing in this article shall prejudice rights and obligations with respect to privileges and immunities afforded pursuant to other international agreements or the rules of customary international law.

9. When signing, ratifying, accepting, approving or acceding to this Convention, a State may declare that it does not consider itself bound in whole or in part by paragraphs 2 and 3.

10. A State Party which has made a declaration in accordance with paragraph 9 may at any time withdraw it by notification to the depositary.

Article 9
Transit of personnel, equipment and property
Each State Party shall, at the request of the requesting State or the assisting party, seek to facilitate the transit through its territory of duly notified personnel, equipment and property involved in the assistance to and from the requesting State.

Article 10

Claims and compensation

1. The States Parties shall closely cooperate in order to facilitate the settlement of legal proceedings and claims under this article.

2. Unless otherwise agreed, a requesting State shall in respect of death or of injury to persons, damage to or loss of property, or damage to the environment caused within its territory or other area under its jurisdiction or control in the course of providing the assistance requested:

(a) not bring any legal proceedings against the assisting party or persons or other legal entities acting on its behalf;

(b) assume responsibility for dealing with legal proceedings and claims brought by third parties against the assisting party or against persons or other legal entities acting on its behalf;

(c) hold the assisting party or persons or other legal entities acting on its behalf harmless in respect of legal proceedings referred to in sub-paragraph (b); and

(d) compensate the assisting party or persons or other legal entities acting on its behalf for:

(i) death of or injury to personnel of the assisting party or persons acting on its behalf;

(ii) loss of or damage to non-consumable equipment or materials related to the assistance; except in cases of wilful misconduct by the individuals who caused the death, injury, loss or damage.

3. This article shall not prevent compensation or indemnity available under any applicable international agreement or national law of any State.

4. Nothing in this article shall require the requesting State to apply paragraph 2 in whole or in part to its nationals or permanent residents.

5. When signing, ratifying, accepting, approving or acceding to this Convention, a State may declare:

(a) that it does not consider itself bound in whole or in part by paragraph 2;

(b) that it will not apply paragraph 2 in whole or in part in cases of gross negligence by the individuals who caused the death, injury, loss or damage.

6. A State Party which has made a declaration in accordance with paragraph 5 may at any time withdraw it by notification to the depositary.

Article 11

Termination of assistance

The requesting State or the assisting party may at any time, after appropriate consultations and by notification in writing, request the termination of assistance received or provided under this Convention. Once such a request has been made the parties involved shall consult with each other to make arrangements for the proper conclusion of the assistance.

Article 12
Relationship to other international agreements
This Convention shall not affect the reciprocal rights and obligations of States Parties under existing international agreements which relate to the matters covered by this Convention, or under future international agreements concluded in accordance with the object and purpose of this Convention.

Article 13
Settlement of disputes
1. In the event of a dispute between States Parties, or between a State Party and the Agency, concerning the interpretation or application of this Convention, the parties to the dispute shall consult with a view to the settlement of the dispute by negotiation or by any other peaceful means of settling disputes acceptable to them.
2. If a dispute of this character between States Parties cannot be settled within one year from the request for consultation pursuant to paragraph 1, it shall, at the request of any party to such dispute, be submitted to arbitration or referred to the International Court of Justice for decision. Where a dispute is submitted to arbitration, if, within six months from the date of the request, the parties to the dispute are unable to agree on the organization of the arbitration, a party may request the President of the International Court of Justice or the Secretary-General of the United Nations to appoint one or more arbitrators. In cases of conflicting requests by the parties to the dispute, the request to the Secretary-General of the United Nations shall have priority.
3. When signing, ratifying, accepting, approving or acceding to this Convention, a State may declare that it does not consider itself bound by either or both of the dispute settlement procedures provided for in paragraph 2. The other States Parties shall not be bound by a dispute settlement procedure provided for in paragraph 2 with respect to a State Party for which such a declaration is in force.
4. A State Party which has made a declaration in accordance with paragraph 3 may at any time withdraw it by notification to the depositary.

Article 14
Entry into force
1. This Convention shall be open for signature by all States and Namibia, represented by the United Nations Council for Namibia, at the Headquarters

of the International Atomic Energy Agency in Vienna and at the Headquarters of the United Nations in New York, from 26 September 1986 and 6 October 1986 respectively, until its entry into force or for twelve months, whichever period is longer.

2.   A State and Namibia, represented by the United Nations Council for Namibia, may express its consent to be bound by this Convention either by signature, or by deposit of an instrument of ratification, acceptance or approval following signature made subject to ratification, acceptance or approval, or by deposit of an instrument of accession. The instruments of ratification, acceptance, approval or accession shall be deposited with the depositary.

3.   This Convention shall enter into force thirty days after consent to be bound has been expressed by three States.

4.   For each State expressing consent to be bound by this Convention after its entry into force, this Convention shall enter into force for that State thirty days after the date of expression of consent.

5.   (a) This Convention shall be open for accession, as provided for in this article, by international organizations and regional integration organizations constituted by sovereign States, which have competence in respect of the negotiation, conclusion and application of international agreements in matters covered by this Convention.

   (b) In matters within their competence such organizations shall, on their own behalf, exercise the rights and fulfil the obligations which this Convention attributes to States Parties.

   (c) When depositing its instrument of accession, such an organization shall communicate to the depositary a declaration indicating the extent of its competence in respect of matters covered by this Convention.

   (d) Such an organization shall not hold any vote additional to those of its Member States.

Article 15
Provisional application
   A State may, upon signature or at any later date before this Convention enters into force for it, declare that it will apply this Convention provisionally.

Article 16
Amendments
1.   A State Party may propose amendments to this Convention. The proposed amendment shall be submitted to the depositary who shall circulate it immediately to all other States Parties.

2.   If a majority of the States Parties request the depositary to convene a

conference to consider the proposed amendments, the depositary shall invite all States Parties to attend such a conference to begin not sooner than thirty days after the invitations are issued. Any amendment adopted at the conference by a two-thirds majority of all States Parties shall be laid down in a protocol which is open to signature in Vienna and New York by all States Parties.

3.   The protocol shall enter into force thirty days after consent to be bound has been expressed by three States. For each State expressing consent to be bound by the protocol after its entry into force, the protocol shall enter into force for that State thirty days after the date of expression of consent.

Article 17
Denunciation
1.   A State Party may denounce this Convention by written notification to the depositary.
2.   Denunciation shall take effect one year following the date on which the notification is received by the depositary.

Article 18
Depositary
1.   The Director General of the Agency shall be the depositary of this Convention.
2.   The Director General of the Agency shall promptly notify States Parties and all other States of:
  (a) each signature of this Convention or any protocol of amendment;
  (b) each deposit of an instrument of ratification, acceptance, approval or accession concerning this Convention or any protocol of amendment;
  (c) any declaration or withdrawal thereof in accordance with articles 8, 10 and 13;
  (d) any declaration of provisional application of this Convention in accordance with article 15;
  (e) the entry into force of this Convention and of any amendment thereto; and
  (f) any denunciation made under article 17.

Article 19
Authentic tests and certified copies
The original of this Convention, of which the Arabic, Chinese, English, French, Russian and Spanish texts are equally authentic, shall be deposited with the Director General of the International Atomic Energy Agency who shall send certified copies to States Parties and all other States.

IN WITNESS WHEREOF the undersigned, being duly authorized, have signed this Convention, open for signature as provided in paragraph 1 of article 14.

ADOPTED by the General Conference of the International Atomic Energy Agency meeting in special session at Vienna on the twenty-sixth day of September one thousand nine hundred and eighty-six.

Signatories and Parties[1]

State	Date of Signature	Date of Ratification or Accession (A)
Afghanistan	26 September 1986	
Australia	26 September 1986	
Austria	26 September 1986	
Belgium	26 September 1986	
Brazil	26 September 1986	
Bulgaria	26 September 1986	
Byelorussian SSR	26 September 1986	26 January 1987
Canada	26 September 1986	
Chile	26 September 1986	
China	26 September 1986	
Costa Rica	26 September 1986	
Cuba	26 September 1986	
Czechoslovakia	26 September 1986	
Denmark	26 September 1986	
Egypt	26 September 1986	
Finland	26 September 1986	
France	26 September 1986	
German Democratic Republic	26 September 1986	29 April 1987
Germany, Federal Republic	26 September 1986	
Greece	26 September 1986	
Guatemala	26 September 1986	
Holy See	26 September 1986	
Hungary	26 September 1986	10 March 1987
Iceland	26 September 1986	
India	29 September 1986	
Indonesia	26 September 1986	
Iran	26 September 1986	

[1] Reservations and Declarations to this Convention are set out following the list of Signatories and Parties to the Notification Convention at No. 21 above, at pp. 246-60.

State	Date of Signature	Date of Ratification or Accession (A)
Ireland	26 September 1986	
Israel	26 September 1986	
Italy	26 September 1986	
Ivory Coast	26 September 1986	
Japan	6 March 1987	9 June 1987 (A)
Jordan	2 October 1986	
Korea, Democratic People's Republic	29 September 1986	
Lebanon	26 September 1986	
Liechtenstein	26 September 1986	
Mali	2 October 1986	
Mexico	26 September 1986	
Monaco	26 September 1986	
Mongolia	8 January 1987	11 June 1987
Morocco	26 September 1986	
Netherlands	26 September 1986	
New Zealand		11 March 1987 (A)
Niger	26 September 1986	
Nigeria	21 January 1987	
Norway	26 September 1986	Signature, 26 September 1986
Panama	26 September 1986	
Paraguay	2 October 1986	
Poland	26 September 1986	
Portugal	26 September 1986	
Senegal	15 June 1987	
Sierra Leone	25 March 1987	
South Africa	10 August 1987	10 August 1987
Spain	26 September 1986	
Sudan	26 September 1986	
Sweden	26 September 1986	
Switzerland	26 September 1986	
Syrian Arab Republic	2 July 1987	
Tunisia	24 February 1987	
Turkey	26 September 1986	
Ukrainian SSR	26 September 1986	26 January 1987
USSR	26 September 1986	23 December 1986
United Kingdom	26 September 1986	
USA	26 September 1986	
Zaire	30 September 1986	
Zimbabwe	26 September 1986	

23. INSTITUT DE DROIT INTERNATIONAL, RESOLUTION ON TRANSBOUNDARY AIR POLLUTION
20 September 1987

Editorial Note

In February 1984 the Bureau of the Institut de Droit International entrusted the 20th Commission of the Institut with the task of studying "La pollution de l'air à travers les frontières nationales". This followed the adoption by the Institut on 12 September 1979 of a Resolution on "The Pollution of Rivers and Lakes under International Law" (see 58 *Annuaire IDI*, II, p. 157 (1979)). Unlike the earlier Resolution of the ILA, this Resolution seeks to declare what international law should be: the Rapporteur, Mr do Nascimento e Silva, was clear to point out that it was not his aim to prepare a text *de lege lata* (62 *Annuaire IDI*, I, p. 250 (1987)).

The Resolution on Transboundary Air Pollution is of particular interest in that much of the work was carried out, and the final text drawn up, in the period immediately following the Chernobyl accident, which called for a "conscientious reappraisal of the rules of international law applicable to pollution of the atmosphere" (*id.* p. 160).

The Resolution calls for a regime of prevention (Articles 2-5), information (Articles 8 and 9(1)), assistance (Article 9(2)), responsibility (Article 6) and compensation (Article 7). It nevertheless differs from the ILA Resolution in a number of respects. The definition of pollution in Article 1 is widened to include natural pollution; States are under an obligation to be especially rigorous in the prevention of pollution where activities involve dangerous materials (Article 3(2)); the special dangers and difficulties of nuclear pollution (Article 10), the ozone layer (Article 11) and acid rain (Article 12) are recognized. Of particular note is the provision recognizing the need of developing States (Article 13).

Text reprinted from: Final document of the Cairo Session of the Institut de Droit International. To be published in 62 *Annuaire IDI*, II.

Text

INSTITUT DE DROIT INTERNATIONAL, RESOLUTION ON TRANSBOUNDARY AIR POLLUTION

THE INSTITUTE OF INTERNATIONAL LAW
RECALLING its Resolution of Athens in 1979 on the Pollution of Rivers and Lakes and International Law;

CONSIDERING that transboundary air pollution is assuming increasingly alarming proportions, over a broad field, for example acid rain and nuclear contamination;

DEEPLY CONCERNED by the effects of transboundary air pollution on the environment and on human health, on soil, agriculture and production, forests, life in lakes, rivers and the sea, and the ozone layer;

EQUALLY CONCERNED by irreparable damage to buildings, monuments and sites, many of which are part of the cultural and natural heritage of mankind;

RECALLING the obligation to respect the sovereignty of every State over its territory, as a result of which each State has the duty to prohibit and to prevent any use of its territory likely to cause injury in the territory of another State;

BEARING IN MIND the need to protect areas beyond the limits of national jurisdiction;

ADOPTS the following articles:

Article 1

1. For the purposes of this Resolution, "transboundary air pollution" means any physical, chemical or biological alteration in the composition or quality of the atmosphere which results directly or indirectly from human acts or omissions, and produces injurious or deleterious effects in the environment of other States or of areas beyond the limits of national jurisdiction.

2. In specific cases, the existence and characteristics of pollution shall, to the extent possible, be determined by reference to environmental norms established through agreements or by the competent international organizations and commissions.

Article 2

In the exercise of their sovereign right to exploit their resources pursuant to their own environmental policies, States shall be under a duty to take all appropriate and effective measures to ensure that their activities or those conducted within their jurisdiction or under their control cause no transboundary air pollution.

Article 3

1. For the purpose of fulfilling their obligation under Article 2, States shall take, and adapt to the circumstances, all appropriate and effective measures, in particular:

(a) to prevent any new forms of transboundary air pollution or any increase in the existing degree of pollution; and

(b) progressively to eliminate existing transboundary air pollution within the shortest possible time.

2. Such measures shall be especially rigorous in the case of activities which:
    (a) involve particularly dangerous materials; or
    (b) threaten areas or environments requiring special protection.

Article 4

In order to comply with the obligations set forth in Articles 2 and 3, States shall in particular use the following means:

(a) at the national level, enactment of all necessary laws and regulations, and adoption of efficient and adequate administrative and technical measures and judicial procedures for the enforcement of such laws and regulations;
(b) at the international level, regional or universal co-operation in good faith with other States concerned.

Article 5

States are under a duty to take all appropriate and effective measures to prevent any extension, through the export of polluted products or other polluted objects, of the harmful effects of a pollution of their atmosphere resulting from the activities of other States.

Article 6

States incur responsibility under international law for any breach of their international obligations with respect to transboundary air pollution.

Article 7

With a view to ensuring an effective system of prevention and of compensation for victims of transboundary air pollution, States should conclude international treaties and enact laws and regulations concerning, in particular:

(a) systems of strict liability and compensation funds;
(b) environmental norms, whether regional or universal, in particular quality and safety norms;
(c) the jurisdiction of courts, the applicable law and the enforcement of judgments.

Article 8

1. In carrying out their duty to co-operate, States shall:
    (a) regularly inform other States concerned of all appropriate data on air pollution in their territories, including its causes, its nature, whether man-made or natural, the damage resulting from it, and the preventive measures taken or proposed;

(b) notify other States concerned in due time of any activities envisaged in their own territories which may cause a significant threat of transboundary air pollution.

(c) consult with other States concerned on actual or potential problems of transboundary air pollution so as to reach, by methods of their own choice, solutions consistent with their interests and with the protection of the environment.

2.   States shall, where appropriate, conclude agreements in order to:

(a) co-ordinate or pool their scientific and technical research programmes to combat air pollution, whether man-made or natural;

(b) set up international or regional commissions with the widest terms of reference, providing where appropriate for the participation of local authorities, or strengthen the powers of co-ordination of existing institutions;

(c) establish co-ordinated or unified networks for permanent observation and control of air pollution, whether man-made or natural;

(d) attempt a harmonisation of environmental norms as well as of norms relating to the level of contamination of consumer goods.

3.   States shall also develop safeguards for persons who may be affected by transboundary air pollution, in relation both to prevention and compensation, by granting on a non-discriminatory basis the widest access to judicial and administrative procedures in the States in which such pollution originates.

Article 9

1.   In the event of an accident or activities causing a sudden increase in the level of air pollution, even if due to natural causes, which is capable of causing substantial harm in another State, the State of origin is under a duty:

(a) promptly to warn all affected or potentially affected States;

(b) to take all appropriate steps to reduce the effects of any such increase.

2.   In the event of a disaster involving air pollution in the territory of a State, other States and competent international organisations should, as a matter of urgency and with the consent of the State concerned, undertake humanitarian action to assist the victims.

Article 10

1.   Without prejudice to their other obligations relating to nuclear explosions, States shall prohibit, prevent and refrain from carrying out any nuclear explosion likely to cause transboundary air pollution of a radioactive nature.

2. In order to ensure compliance with applicable health and safety standards, States should open nuclear power plants on their territory to international inspection.

Article 11

States shall take all necessary measures to protect the ozone layer against adverse effects resulting or likely to result from human action, in order to protect life and the environment.

Article 12

States shall take all necessary measures to prevent the emission, in their territories, of fumes which, by reason of their quantity or chemical composition, are likely to contribute to the formation of acid rain.

Article 13

Developed States and competent international organisations should provide developing States with appropriate technical or other assistance, in order to assist them in fulfilling the obligations and in implementing the recommendations referred to in this Resolution.

Article 14

This Resolution is without prejudice to any obligation which a State may have to protect individuals from the effects of air pollution other than transboundary air pollution.

Select Bibliography

"Air Pollution across National Frontiers", 62 *Annuaire IDI,* I, pp. 159-294 (1987).

ANNEX

FEDERAL REPUBLIC OF GERMANY ATOMIC ENERGY ACT VII (10) 1985

Editorial Note

This Act replaces the 1976 Atomic Energy Act (see above at No. 1). Reproduced below is that section of the Act which deals with liability for nuclear damage and incorporates, *inter alia,* the Paris Convention into German law.

Section 38, in particular, came into play in the aftermath of the Chernobyl accident. This section provides that, if certain criteria are met, the German Government will pay compensation in respect of nuclear damage suffered in the territory of the Federal Republic of Germany by Germans. First, the damage must have been caused by a nuclear installation located outside the Federal Republic of Germany. Second, the victim must not be able to obtain compensation—or must only be able to obtain considerably less compensation than under German law—under the relevant foreign law.

As these criteria were clearly satisfied in the case of the Chernobyl accident, the German Government issued, pursuant to section 38, Guidelines dated 21 May 1986 which set forth the amounts of compensation that would be paid for various types of nuclear damage. In respect of certain other types of damage, the Guidelines provided for compensation on an *ex aequo et bono* basis. The purpose of the Guidelines was to speed up the compensation process by avoiding the need for individual assessments in each case.

Text reprinted from: 36 *NLB* (1985), Supplement, p. 3

Text

FEDERAL REPUBLIC OF GERMANY ATOMIC ENERGY ACT VII (10) 1985

Chapter IV
Liability

Section 25—Liability for installations
(1)   If damage is caused by a nuclear incident originating from a nuclear installation, the liability of the operator of the nuclear installation shall be governed by the provisions of this Act in addition to the provisions of the Paris

Convention. The Paris Convention shall be applicable within the Federal Republic of Germany irrespective of whether or not it is binding at international law, to the extent that its rules are not conditional on reciprocity brought about by the coming into force of the Convention.

(2) Where in the case of the carriage of nuclear substances, including storage incidental thereto, the carrier has assumed liability by contract in place of the operator of a nuclear installation situated within the area of application of this Act, such carrier shall be deemed the operator of a nuclear installation from the moment at which he assumes liability. The contract shall be in writing. Such assumption of liability shall be valid only if it has been authorised, upon application by the carrier, by the authority competent under Section 4, prior to the commencement of the carriage of nuclear substances or any storage incidental thereto. Such authorisation may be granted only if the carrier has been licensed as such, or has his main place of business within the area of application of this Act and the operator of the nuclear installation has declared his consent to the authority.

(3) The provisions of Article 9 of the Paris Convention concerning the exemption from liability for damage caused by nuclear incidents directly due to armed conflict, hostilities, civil war, insurrection, or a grave natural disaster of an exceptional character, shall not be applicable. If the damage is suffered in another state, the first sentence shall apply only to the extent that the other state, at the time of the nuclear incident, has compensation arrangements in relation to the Federal Republic of Germany which are equivalent in nature, extent and amount.

(4) The operator of a nuclear installation shall be liable without the territorial restrictions provided for in Article 2 of the Paris Convention.

(5) The operator of a nuclear installation shall not be liable under the Paris Convention if the damage has been caused by a nuclear incident involving nuclear substances specified in Annex 2 [1] to this Act.

Section 25a—Liability for nuclear ships

(1) The provisions of this Chapter shall apply to the liability of an operator of a nuclear ship with the following modifications:

1. The provisions of the Paris Convention shall be replaced by the corresponding provisions of the Brussels Convention on the Liability of Operators of Nuclear Ships (*BGBl* 1975 II page 977). The latter shall be applicable within the Federal Republic of Germany irrespective of whether or not it is binding at international law, to the extent that its rules are not

---

[1 Annex 2 is not reproduced here.]

conditional on reciprocity brought about by the coming into force of the Convention.

2. If the damage is suffered in another state, Section 31(1) shall be applicable as regards the amounts exceeding the maximum amounts of liability under the Brussels Convention on the Liability of Operators of Nuclear Ships, only to the extent that the legislation of that State provides, at the time of the nuclear incident, for a third party liability regime for operators of nuclear ships which is applicable in relation to the Federal Republic of Germany and is equivalent in nature, extent and amount. Sections 31(2), 36, 38(1) and 40 shall not apply.

3. Section 34 shall apply only to nuclear ships authorised to sail under the flag of the Federal Republic of Germany. If, within the area of application of this Act, a nuclear ship is built or equipped with a reactor for another state, or persons of another state, Section 34 shall apply until the nuclear ship is registered in the other state or acquires the right to sail under the flag of another state. Seventy-five per cent of the indemnification under Section 34 shall be borne by the *Bund* and the remainder by the *Land* competent for the licensing of the nuclear ship under Section 7.

4. In the case of nuclear ships which are not entitled to sail under the flag of the Federal Republic, this chapter shall apply only if the nuclear damage caused by the nuclear ship has been suffered within the area of application of this Act.

5. The courts of the state under whose flag the nuclear ship is entitled to sail shall have jurisdiction over actions for compensation; in the case referred to in No. 4, the court of the place within the area of application of this Act where the nuclear damage was suffered shall equally have jurisdiction.

(2) To the extent that international agreements on liability for nuclear ships contain mandatory provisions at variance with this Act, such provisions shall override the provisions of this Act.

Section 26—Liability in other cases

(1) Where, in cases other than those specified by the Paris Convention, taken with Section 25(1) to (4), loss of life, personal injury, or deterioration of health is caused to any person or damage is caused to property by the effects of any nuclear fission process or radiation from radioactive substances or the effects of an accelerator, the holder of the substances affected by the nuclear fission, of the radioactive substances or of the accelerator shall be liable to pay compensation for damage in accordance with Sections 27 to 30, 31(3), 32(1), (4) and (5) and Section 33. There shall be no liability to pay compensation if the damage was caused by an event which the holder and such persons as are acting for them in connection with such possession could not avoid, even by

taking every reasonable precaution, and which is due neither to a defective condition of the safety devices nor to any failure in their performance.

(2)   Sub-section (1) shall apply *mutatis mutandis* where damage of the kind specified in sub-section (1) was caused by the effects of nuclear fission.

(3)   Any person who has lost possession of the substances, without having transferred them to a person entitled to such possession in accordance with this Act or any regulation made thereunder, shall be liable as if he were the holder.

(4)   The provisions of sub-sections (1) to (3) shall not apply

1.   where the radioactive substances or the accelerators have been applied to the injured person by a physician or dentist, or under the supervision of a physician or dentist, in the course of medical treatment, and the substances, and accelerators used and the necessary measuring apparatus have complied with the current state of science and technology and the damage is not due to the fact that such substances, accelerators or measuring apparatus have not been properly maintained,

2.   where a legal relationship exists between the holder and the injured person under which the latter has accepted the risk associated with the substances.

(5)   The second sentence of sub-section (1) and sub-section (4) No. 2 shall not apply to the use of radioactive substances on human beings in the course of medical research. Where the holder of the radioactive substances disputes the causal link between the use of the radioactive substances and damage or injury which has occurred, he shall prove that, in the current state of medical science, there is no reasonable probability of such link existing.

(6)   A person who carries substances on behalf of a third party shall not be liable to pay compensation under sub-sections (1) to (3). So long as the consignee has not taken charge of the substances, the consignor shall remain liable under the aforementioned provisions, regardless of whether or not he is the holder of such substances.

(7)   Within the scope of application of the first sentence of sub-section (1), no legal provisions shall be affected pursuant to which the holder referred to in sub-section (1) and any person deemed the holder under sub-section (3), are liable to a greater extent than under the provisions of this Act or pursuant to which another person is liable for the damage.

Section 27—Contributory fault of the injured person
Where a fault of the injured person has contributed to the injury sustained, Article 254 of the Civil Code shall apply; in the event of damage to property, the fault of the person in actual control thereof, shall be deemed to be that of the injured person.

Section 28—Extent of compensation in case of death
(1)   On the event of death, compensation shall be provided for the costs of any attempted cure as well as for the pecuniary loss sustained by the deceased during his illness by reason of loss or reduction of his earning capacity, increase of his needs or handicap in regard to his career. In addition, the person liable shall refund funeral costs to the person required to bear such costs.
(2)   If, at the time of the injury, the deceased was, or might have been, under a legal obligation to provide maintenance for a third person who loses such maintenance as a result of the decease, the person liable shall pay compensation to such third person, to the extent of the maintenance for which the deceased would have been liable during his expected life. Such liability shall also exist where, at the time of the injury, the third person was conceived but not yet born.

Section 29—Extent of compensation in case of personal injury
(1)   In the event of personal injury or damage to health, compensation shall comprise the costs of medical treatment and the pecuniary loss sustained by the injured person by reason of temporary or permanent loss or reduction of his earning capacity, increase of his needs or handicap in regard to his career as a result of the injury.
(2)   In case of personal injury or damage to health, the injured person may claim adequate compensation also for pain and suffering, if the damage has been caused wilfully or by negligence. Such claims shall not be transferable or inheritable except if acknowledged by contract or subject to a pending action.

Section 30—Annuity
(1)   Compensation for any loss or reduction of earning capacity, any special needs or any handicap in regard to the career of the injured person, and any compensation due to a third person under Section 28(2) shall be provided by means of an annuity.
(2)   The provisions of Article 843(2) to (4) of the Civil Code shall apply as appropriate.
(3)   Where the court awarding an annuity has not required security from the defendant, the plaintiff shall nevertheless, be entitled to demand security, if the financial situation of the person liable has also significantly deteriorated; likewise, the plaintiff shall also be entitled to demand an increase in the amount of any security specified in the judgment.

Section 31—Liability ceiling
(1)   The liability of an operator of a nuclear installation under the Paris

Convention taken with Section 25(1), (2) and (4) shall be unlimited. In cases under Section 25(3) the liability of an operator shall be limited to the maximum amount of the State guarantee.

(2)   Where damage occurs in another State the liability of an operator of a nuclear installation shall be limited to

1.   300 million Special Drawing Rights (SDR) in regard to Contracting States of the Paris Convention, for which the Brussels Supplementary Convention as contained in the Protocol of 16th November 1982 has come into force,

2.   120 million SDR in regard to Contracting States of the Paris Convention, for which the Brussels Supplementary Convention as contained in the Supplementary Protocol of 28th January 1964 has come into force,

3.   15 million SDR in regard to other states.

The limitation of liability in the first sentence shall not apply where the state in which damage has occurred has, at the time of the nuclear incident, compensation arrangements in relation to the Federal Republic under sub-section (1) of equivalent nature, extent and amount.

(3)   The person liable under the Paris Convention taken with Section 25(1) to (4) or under Section 26, shall be liable in case of damage to property only up to the ordinary value of the damaged property, plus the cost of protection against radiation hazards originating therefrom. In case of liability under the Paris Convention taken with Section 25 (1) to (4) compensation for damage to the means of transport upon which the nuclear substances involved were at the time of the nuclear incident shall be paid only if such satisfaction of other claims in cases under sub-section (1) has been secured from the maximum amount of the state guarantee, and in cases under sub-section (2) from the maximum amount of liability.

Section 32—Limitation

(1)   Claims for compensation under this Chapter shall expire three years from the date on which the person entitled to compensation became aware or from the date on which he ought reasonably to have known of both the damage and the person liable, and in any case thirty years from the date of the event which caused the damage.

(2)   In cases specified under Article 8(b) of the Paris Convention, the thirty-year limitation period under sub-section (1) shall be replaced by a period of twenty years from the date of the theft, loss, jettison or abandonment.

(3)   Claims against the operator of a nuclear installation for death and personal injury under the Paris Convention brought before the court within ten years of the nuclear incident shall have priority over claims made after the expiry of that period.

(4)   Where negotiations concerning compensation are under way between the person liable to pay and the person entitled to compensation, the limitation period shall cease to run until such time as one or other of the parties withdraws from such negotiations.

(5)   In all other respects, the provision of the Civil Code relating to limitation periods shall apply.

Section 33—Several persons liable

(1)   If several persons are legally liable to pay compensation for damage caused by a nuclear incident or otherwise by the effects of nuclear fission, or radiation emitted by radioactive substances, or the effects of ionising radiation emitted by an accelerator, they shall be jointly and severally liable, save as otherwise provided in Article 5(d) of the Paris Convention.

(2)   In cases under sub-section (1) the amount of compensation due from each of the persons liable shall be apportioned between them according to the circumstances and the extent to which the damage was caused by one or the other, save as otherwise provided in Article 5(d) of the Paris Convention. However, the operator of a nuclear installation shall not be required to pay compensation exceeding the maximum amounts established pursuant to Section 31(1) and (2).

Section 34—Indemnification

(1)   Where the operator of a nuclear installation situated within the area of application of this Act is legally liable to pay compensation for damage caused by a nuclear incident under the provisions of the Paris Convention taken with Section 25(1) to (4), or under a foreign law applicable to the incident, the operator shall be indemnified against liability to pay compensation to the extent that such liability is not covered or cannot be met out of his financial security. The maximum amount of indemnification shall be twice the maximum financial security. The obligation to indemnify the operator shall be restricted to this maximum amount less the amount which is covered and can be met by the financial security.

(2)   If, after a nuclear incident has occurred, it is to be expected that indemnification will be necessary, the operator of the nuclear installation shall be required

1.   to give notification thereof without delay to the Federal Minister designated by the Federal Government and to the authorities of the *Länder* designated by their governments,

2.   to inform without delay the competent Federal Minister and the competent authorities of the *Länder* of any claims for compensation raised or of any inquiry instituted against him, as well as to provide on request all

information necessary to examine the circumstances of the case and their appreciation at law,

3. to comply, in the event of negotiations for the settlement of claims for compensation in or outside court, with the instructions of the competent authorities of the *Länder*,

4. to refrain from admitting or satisfying any claim for compensation without the consent of the competent authorities of the *Länder* except if such admission or satisfaction cannot reasonably be refused.

(3) In all other respects Sections 62 and 67 and the provisions of Title 6 of Chapter II of the Insurance Contracts Act, except for Section 152, shall apply *mutatis mutandis* to the obligation to indemnify.

Section 35—Apportionment

(1) Where legal liability to pay compensation for damage caused by an incident is expected to exceed the funds available, their apportionment and the procedure to be observed shall be governed by an Act or, pending its enactment, by regulation.

(2) The regulation referred to in sub-section (1) may only make such provision regarding apportionment of the funds available as compensation for damage as are required to avert hardship. Such regulation shall ensure that satisfaction of the claims of all insured persons will not be unduly prejudiced by the satisfaction of individual claims.

Section 36—Distribution of the indemnification between the Bund and the Länder

The *Bund* shall bear seventy-five per cent of indemnification under Section 34. The remainder shall be borne by the *Land* where the nuclear installation at the origin of the nuclear incident is situated.

Section 37—Recourse in the case of indemnification

If the operator of a nuclear installation has been indemnified under Section 34, recourse may be had against him to the extent that compensation has been paid, if

1. the operator has violated his obligations under Section 34(2) or (3); however, recourse shall be excluded to the extent that such violations have not influenced the evaluation of the damage nor the extent of the compensation paid,

2. the operator or, in the case of a corporate body, its legal representative has, in the performance of his functions, caused the damage wilfully or by gross negligence,

3. compensation has been paid because the extent and amount of the

financial security available have not corresponded to the determination by the competent authority.

Section 38—Compensation from the Bund

(1)   If a person having suffered nuclear damage within the area of application of this Act cannot obtain compensation under the law of another Contracting State to the Paris Convention applicable to the incident because

1.   the nuclear incident occurred in the territory of a non-Contracting State to the Paris Convention,

2.   the damage was caused by a nuclear incident directly due to armed conflict, hostilities, civil war, insurrection or a grave natural disaster of an exceptional character,

3.   the applicable law excludes liability for damage to the means of transport upon which the nuclear substances involved were at the time of the nuclear incident,

4.   the applicable law does not provide for the operator's liability for damage caused by ionizing radiation emitted by another source of radiation inside the nuclear installation,

5.   the applicable law provides for a shorter period of limitation or shorter time limit than this Act, or

6.   the total funds available for compensation fall short of the maximum amount of state indemnification,

the *Bund* shall pay compensation up to the maximum amount of state indemnification.

(2)   The *Bund* shall also pay compensation up to the maximum amount of state indemnification if the foreign law or provisions of an internal agreement applicable to damage suffered within the area of application of this Act provide for compensation for the injured person which in nature, extent and amount falls considerably short of the compensation which the injured person would have obtained had this Act applied.

(3)   Sub-sections (1) and (2) shall not apply to injured persons who are not German within the meaning of Article 116(1) of the Basic Law and who do not have their habitual residence within the area of application of this Act, unless their country of origin has, at the time of the nuclear incident, compensation arrangements in relation to the Federal Republic of Germany of equivalent nature, extent and amount.

(4)   Claims under sub-sections (1) and (2) shall be brought before the Federal Agency for Administration. They shall lapse three years from the date on which the decision on compensation rendered under foreign or international law becomes final.

Section 39—Exemptions of the Bund and the Länder from the obligation to indemnify
(1)   In the case of indemnification under Section 34, and compensation under Section 38, claims for compensation shall not be taken into account which have subsidiary rank under Section 15(1) and (2).
(2)   Compensation paid under Section 29(2) shall qualify for indemnification under Section 34 and compensation under Section 38 only if the payment of such compensation is necessary to avoid serious inequity because of the particular gravity of the injury.

Section 40—Actions against the operator of a nuclear installation situated in another Contracting State
(1)   If under the provisions of the Paris Convention, a court within the area of operation of this Act has jurisdiction over actions for compensation against the operator of a nuclear installation situated in another Contracting State to the Paris Convention, the liability of the operator shall be governed by the provisions of this Act.
(2)   Contrary to sub-section (1), the following shall be determined by the law of the Contracting State in which the nuclear installation is situated:
    1.   who is to be considered as operator,
    2.   whether the operator's liability extends to nuclear damage suffered in a non-Contracting State to the Paris Convention,
    3.   whether the operator's liability extends to nuclear damage caused by ionizing radiation emitted by another source of radiation inside a nuclear installation,
    4.   whether and to what extent the operator's liability extends to damage to the means of transport upon which the nuclear substances involved were at the time of the nuclear incident,
    5.   the ceiling on the operator's liability,
    6.   after what period claims against the operator will be statute-barred or extinguished,
    7.   to what extent nuclear damage will qualify for compensation in the cases set out in Article 9 of the Paris Convention.

MAP SECTION

Map 1
First observations of increased radiation levels following the Chernobyl accident, as reported to the IAEA. (Based on information taken from 28 *IAEA Bulletin,* No. 3, p. 19 (1986).)

Map 2
Areas covered by the main body of the radioactive cloud released from the Chernobyl nuclear power plant on various dates during the release. (Based on information taken from NRPB, *A Preliminary Assessment of the Chernobyl Reactor Accident on the Population of the European Community* (1987) (report prepared under contract to the Commission of the European Communities).)

Map 1

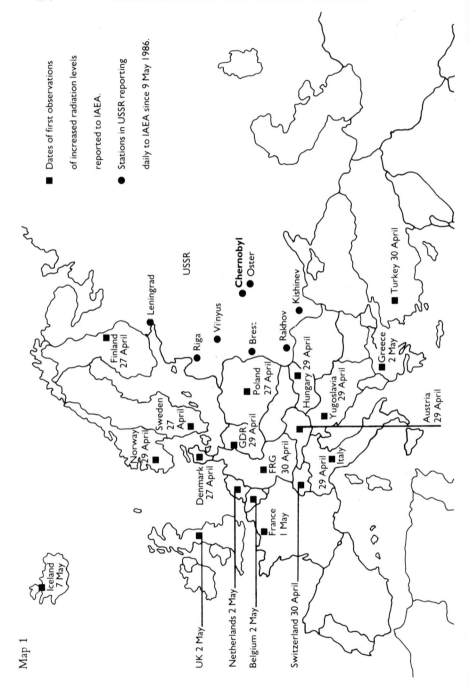

Dates of first observations of increased radiation levels reported to IAEA.

Stations in USSR reporting daily to IAEA since 9 May 1986.

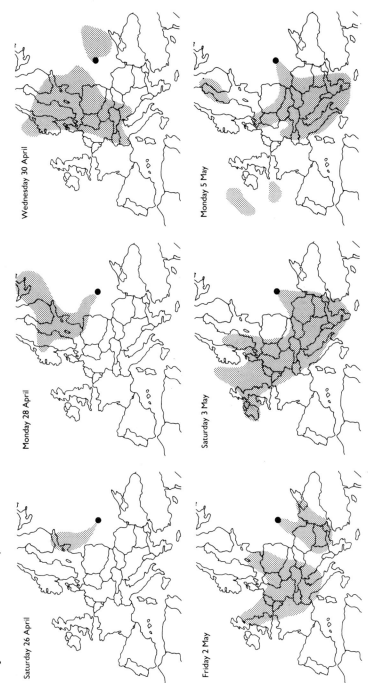

Map 2   Areas Covered by the Radioactive Cloud

Saturday 26 April

Monday 28 April

Wednesday 30 April

Friday 2 May

Saturday 3 May

Monday 5 May

SELECT GENERAL BIBLIOGRAPHY

Angerholzer, Laurich, Mahlati & Reiweger, "Transboundary Air Pollution", 20 *Jahrbuch der Diplomatischen Akademie* 63 (1984/85).

Arangio-Ruiz, "Some International Legal Problems of the Civil Uses of Nuclear Energy", 107 *RC* 499 (1962).

Barile, "Diritto Internazionale ed Energia Nucleare", 49 *Riv. dir. internaz.* 3 (1966).

Barnett, "United States and Canadian Approaches to Air Pollution Control and the Implications for the Control of Transboundary Air Pollution", 7 *Cornell Int'l LJ* 148 (1974).

Barros & Johnston, *The International Law of Pollution* (1974).

Billingsley, "Private Party Protection against Transnational Radiation Pollution through Compulsory Arbitration: a Proposal", 14 *Case W Res. J Int. L* 339 (1982).

Blix, "The Post-Chernobyl Outlook for Nuclear Power", 28 *IAEA Bulletin* 9 (1986).

Bothe (ed.), *Trends in Environmental Policy and Law* (1980).

Bourne, "Legal Aspects of Transfrontier Pollution: Canada-United States Experience", 28 *NIL Rev* 188 (1981).

Coggins, "Grizzly Bears don't Stop at Customs: a Preface to Transboundary Problems in Natural Resources Law", 32 *UKLR* 1 (1983).

Deprimoz, "International Co-operation in Providing Insurance Cover for Nuclear Damage to Third Parties and for Damage to Nuclear Installations", 32 *NLB* 33 (1983).

Dickstein, "National Environmental Hazards and International Law", 23 *ICLQ* 426 (1974).

Dupuy, P.-M., "Sur des Tendences Récentes dans le Droit International de l'Environnement", 20 *AFDI* 815 (1974).

Dupuy, P.-M., *La Responsabilité internationale des Etats pour les Dommages d'origine technologique et industrielle* (1977).

Dupuy, R.-J. (ed.), *The Future of the International Law of the Environment*, Hague Academy Workshop (1984).

Edwards, "International Legal Aspects of Safeguards and the Non-Proliferation of Nuclear Weapons", 33 *ICLQ* 1 (1984).

Eisenstein, "Economic Implications of European Transfrontier Pollution: National Prerogative and Attribution of Responsibility", 11 *Ga. J Int'l & Comp. L* 519 (1981).

Erler, *Die Rechtsentwicklung der internationalen Zusammenarbeit im Atombereich* (1962).

Flinterman, Kwiatkowska & Lammers (eds.), *Transboundary Air Pollution* (1986).

Glickman, "Keep Your Pollution to Yourself: Institutions for Regulating Transboundary Pollution and the United States-Mexico Approach", 25 *Virg. J Int'l L* 693 (1985).

Goldie, "International Principles of Responsibility for Pollution", 9 *Colum. J Transnat'l Law* 281 (1970).

Gross & Scott, "Comparative Environmental Legislation and Action", 29 *ICLQ* 619 (1980).

Handl, "Territorial Sovereignty and the Problem of Transnational Pollution", 69 *AJIL* 50 (1975).

Handl, "State Liability for Accidental Transnational Environmental Damage by Private Persons", 74 *AJIL* 525 (1980).

Hardy, "Nuclear Liability: the General Principles of Law and Further Proposals", 36 *BYIL* 223 (1960).

Hardy, "International Protection Against Nuclear Risks", 10 *ICLQ* 739 (1961).

Hargrove (ed.), *Law, Institutions, and the Global Environment* (1972).

Hassett, "Air Pollution: Possible International Legal and Organizational Responses", 5 *NYU J Int'l L & Pol* 1 (1972).

Herrero de la Fuente, "The Legal Force of Rules Relating to Nuclear Risks", 30 *NLB* 47 (1982).

Higgins, "Pollution: International Conventions, Federal and State Legislation", 53 *Tul. L Rev* 1328 (1979).

Hoffman, "State Responsibility in International Law and Transboundary Pollution Injuries", 25 *ICLQ* 509 (1976).

Keeny, *Nuclear Power: Issues and Choices* (1977).

Kelson, "State Responsibility and the Abnormally Dangerous Activity", 13 *Harv. Int'l LJ* 197 (1972).

Kiss, "La Protection de l'Environnement et les Organisations Européenes", 21 *AFDI* 895 (1973).

Kromarek, "Pollution Transfrontalière—Colloque de Sarrebruck", 9 *Env. Policy & Law* 88 (1982).

Lammers, *Pollution of International Watercourses* (1984).

Levin, *Protecting the Human Environment* (1977).

Macdonald, "International and Domestic Remedies for Transboundary Air Pollution Injury", 69 *Fordham L Rev* 404 (1980).

McFadden, "A Selected Bibliography on Hazardous Activities, Technology and the Law: Bhopal and Beyond", 19 *Int. Law.* 1459 (1985).

MacNeill, "Transfrontier Pollution. Some Problems in the '70's and '80's", 8 *Env. Policy & Law* 17 (1982).

Mastellone, "The External Relations of the EEC in the Field of Environmental Protection", 30 *ICLQ* 104 (1981).

OECD, *Problems in Transfrontier Pollution* (Scott and Bramson, eds.), Record of a Seminar on Economic and Legal Aspects of Transfrontier Pollution held at OECD (1972).

OECD, *Nuclear Legislation—Nuclear Third Party Liability* (1976).

OECD, *Legal Aspects of Transfrontier Pollution* (1977).

OECD, *Long-range Transport of Air Pollutants* (2nd ed.) (1979).

OECD, *Compensation for Pollution Damage* (1981).

OECD, *Nuclear Third Party Liability and Insurance*, Munich Symposium (1985).

OECD, *OECD and the Environment* (1986).

OECD, *Chernobyl and the Safety of Nuclear Reactors in OECD Countries* (1987).

Pelzer, "The Impact of the Chernobyl Accident on International Nuclear Energy Law", 25 *AV* 294 (1987).

Puget, *Aspects du Droit de l'Energie Atomique* (1965).
Rest, "Tschernobyl und die internationale Haftung", *Versicherungsrecht*, 1986, p. 609.
Rüster & Simma, *International Protection of the Environment* (1975).
Schachter, *Sharing the World's Resources* (1977).
Schneider, *World Public Order of the Environment: Towards an International Ecological Law and Organisation* (1979).
Smets, "A Propos d'un Eventuel Principe Pollueur-Payeur en Matière de Pollution Transfrontalière", 9 *Env. Policy & Law* 40 (1982).
Smith, "The United Nations and the Environment: Sometimes a Great Nation", 19 *Tex. Int'l LJ* 335 (1984).
Springer, "Towards a Meaningful Concept of Pollution in International Law", 26 *ICLQ* 531 (1977).
Staenberg, "Financial and Legal Implications of the Three Mile Island Accident", 24 *NLB* 65 (1979).
Stockholm International Peace Research Institute, *Nuclear Energy and Nuclear Weapon Proliferation* (1979).
Strohl, *La Coopération Internationale dans le Domaine de l'Énergie Nucléaire*, Société française pour le droit international, Colloque de Nancy, p. 122 (1982).
Strohl, "Tchernobyl et le Problème des Obligations internationales relatives aux Accident nucléaires", *Politique Etrangère* no. 4 / 1986, p. 1035.
Szasz, *The Law and Practice of the International Atomic Energy Agency* (1970).
Taubenfeld, "International Environmental Law: Air and Outer Space", 13 *Natural Resources J* 315 (1973).
Teclaff & Utton, *International Environmental Law* (1974).
United Nations, *Peaceful Uses of Atomic Energy: Proceedings of the International Conference in Geneva*, 16 vols. (1955).
United Nations, *Peaceful Uses of Atomic Energy: Proceedings of the Second International Conference on Atomic Energy*, 33 vols. (1958).
UNEP, "Report of the Group of Experts on Liability for Pollution and Other Environmental Damage and Compensation of such Damage", *UN Doc.* UNEP/WG.8/3 (1977).
Utton, "International Environmental Law and Consultation Mechanisms", 12 *Colum. J Transnat'l Law* 56 (1973).
Van Heijnsbergen, "The 'Pollution' Concept in International Law", 5 *Env. Policy & Law* 11 (1979).
Various authors, "International Regulation of Nuclear Energy", 16 *Colum. J Transnat'l Law* 386-469 (1977).
Wetstone & Rosencranz, "Transboundary Air Pollution: the Search for an International Response", 8 *Harv. Env. Law Review* 89 (1984).
Yates, "Unilateral and Multilateral Approaches to Environmental Problems", 21 *UTLJ* 182 (1971).
Zehetner, "Grenzüberschreitende Hilfe bei Störfallen und Unfällen", in Pelzer (ed.), *Friedliche Kernenenergienutzung und Staatsgrenzen in Mitteleuropa*, p. 118 (1987).

INDEX